Computational Models of Language Evolution

Editors: Luc Steels, Remi van Trijp

In this series:

1. Steels, Luc. The Talking Heads Experiment: Origins of words and meanings.

2. Vogt, Paul. How mobile robots can self-organize a vocabulary.

3. Bleys, Joris. Language strategies for the domain of colour.

4. van Trijp, Remi. The evolution of case grammar.

5. Spranger, Michael. The evolution of grounded spatial language.

ISSN: 2364-7809

Language strategies for the domain of colour

Joris Bleys

Joris Bleys. 2015. *Language strategies for the domain of colour* (Computational Models of Language Evolution 3). Berlin: Language Science Press.

This title can be downloaded at:
http://langsci-press.org/catalog/book/51
© 2015, Joris Bleys
Published under the Creative Commons Attribution 4.0 Licence (CC BY 4.0):
http://creativecommons.org/licenses/by/4.0/
ISBN: 978-3-946234-16-6 (Digital)
   978-3-946234-17-3 (Hardcover)
   978-3-944675-44-2 (Softcover)
ISSN: 2364-7809

Cover and concept of design: Ulrike Harbort
Typesetting: Joris Bleys, Felix Kopecky, Sebastian Nordhoff
Proofreading: Svetoslava Antonova-Baumann, Armin Buch, Rachele De Felice, Felix Kopecky, Daniela Schröder, Susanne Vejdemo
Fonts: Linux Libertine, Arimo, DejaVu Sans Mono
Typesetting software: X∃LATEX

Language Science Press
Habelschwerdter Allee 45
14195 Berlin, Germany
langsci-press.org

Storage and cataloguing done by FU Berlin

Language Science Press has no responsibility for the persistence or accuracy of URLs for external or third-party Internet websites referred to in this publication, and does not guarantee that any content on such websites is, or will remain, accurate or appropriate. Information regarding prices, travel timetables and other factual information given in this work are correct at the time of first publication but Language Science Press does not guarantee the accuracy of such information thereafter.

Contents

Preface — xi

Acknowledgements — xv

Abbreviations — xvii

I Introduction — 1

1 Language systems and language strategies — 3
- 1.1 Language strategies for colour — 4
  - 1.1.1 Basic colour strategy — 5
  - 1.1.2 Graded membership strategy — 6
  - 1.1.3 Compounding strategy — 6
  - 1.1.4 Basic modification strategy — 8
  - 1.1.5 Other strategies — 9
- 1.2 Modelling language strategies and linguistic interaction — 9
  - 1.2.1 Language games for colour — 10
  - 1.2.2 Background assumptions — 12
- 1.3 Self-organisation of language systems — 12
- 1.4 Modelling the self-organisation of language systems — 12
- 1.5 Evolution of language strategies — 13
- 1.6 Modelling evolution of language strategies — 14
- 1.7 Structure of this book — 15

2 Formalisms for language systems and language strategies — 17
- 2.1 Embodied cognitive semantics using IRL — 18
  - 2.1.1 Theoretical foundations — 18
  - 2.1.2 Semantic constraint network — 19
  - 2.1.3 Evaluation — 21
  - 2.1.4 Conceptualisation and chunking — 24
  - 2.1.5 Implementation of a primitive — 26

Contents

    2.2   Construction Grammar using FCG 27
          2.2.1   Theoretical foundations 27
          2.2.2   Language processing 28
          2.2.3   Coupled feature structures 28
          2.2.4   Application of a construction 29
          2.2.5   Structure building 30
          2.2.6   Linking through variable equalities 32
          2.2.7   Application of an example construction 33

II   Language strategies for colour   39

3   Basic colour strategy   43
    3.1   Related research 43
          3.1.1   Colour categories 43
          3.1.2   Models 44
    3.2   Semantic template 45
          3.2.1   Profiling 46
          3.2.2   Categorisation based on colour 46
          3.2.3   Selection based on activation 47
          3.2.4   Semantic constraint network 47
          3.2.5   Semantic primitives 48
    3.3   Syntactic templates 49
          3.3.1   Syntactic template 1.1: Semantic entities 50
          3.3.2   Syntactic template 1.2: Functional primitives 52
          3.3.3   Syntactic template 1.3: Contextual primitives 53
    3.4   Baseline experiment 54
          3.4.1   Measures of communicative success 54
          3.4.2   Results 55
    3.5   Conclusion 56

4   Graded membership strategy   57
    4.1   Related research 57
    4.2   Semantic template 58
          4.2.1   Profiling and categorisation based on colour 60
          4.2.2   Categorisation based on membership 60
          4.2.3   Selection based on activation 60
          4.2.4   Semantic constraint network 60
          4.2.5   Semantic primitives 61
          4.2.6   Alternative approaches to semantics 62

	4.3	Syntactic templates	63
		4.3.1 Syntactic template 1.1: Semantic entities	63
		4.3.2 Syntactic template 1.2: Functional primitives	65
		4.3.3 Syntactic template 2.1: Re-use of constructions	65
	4.4	Baseline experiment	66
	4.5	Conclusion	70

5 Category combination strategy — 71

- 5.1 Related research — 71
- 5.2 Semantic template — 73
  - 5.2.1 Profiling and first categorisation based on colour — 75
  - 5.2.2 Transformation of the set of colour categories — 75
  - 5.2.3 Second categorisation based on colour — 75
  - 5.2.4 Optional categorisation based on membership — 75
  - 5.2.5 Selection based on activation — 76
  - 5.2.6 Semantic constraint network — 76
  - 5.2.7 Semantic primitives — 76
  - 5.2.8 Alternative approaches to semantics — 78
- 5.3 Syntactic templates — 78
  - 5.3.1 Syntactic template 1.1: Semantic entities — 79
  - 5.3.2 Syntactic template 1.2: Functional primitives — 79
  - 5.3.3 Syntactic template 1.3: Contextual primitives — 79
  - 5.3.4 Syntactic template 2.2: Re-use of constructions — 81
- 5.4 Baseline experiment — 82
- 5.5 Conclusion — 85

6 Basic modification strategy — 87

- 6.1 Related research — 88
- 6.2 Semantic template — 88
  - 6.2.1 Profiling and first categorisation based on colour — 89
  - 6.2.2 Transformation of set of modifying categories — 90
  - 6.2.3 Second categorisation based on modifiers — 90
  - 6.2.4 Optional categorisation based on membership — 90
  - 6.2.5 Selection based on activation — 91
  - 6.2.6 Semantic constraint network — 91
  - 6.2.7 Semantic primitives — 92
- 6.3 Syntactic templates — 92
- 6.4 Baseline Experiment — 94
- 6.5 Conclusion — 96

Contents

III Self-organisation of language systems   99

7 Basic colour strategy   **103**
   7.1 Related models 103
   7.2 Adoption and alignment operators 104
        7.2.1 Acquisition experiment 104
        7.2.2 Measures 105
               7.2.2.1 Number of categories 105
               7.2.2.2 Interpretation variance 105
        7.2.3 Results 106
   7.3 Invention operator 108
        7.3.1 Formation experiment 109
        7.3.2 Results 110
               7.3.2.1 Brightness and hue strategy 110
               7.3.2.2 Brightness strategy 110
   7.4 Conclusion 113

8 Graded membership strategy   **115**
   8.1 Adoption and alignment operators 115
        8.1.1 Acquisition experiment 116
        8.1.2 Measures: Membership category variance 116
        8.1.3 Results 117
   8.2 Invention operator 118
        8.2.1 Formation experiment 119
        8.2.2 Measures: Number of membership categories 119
        8.2.3 Results 119
   8.3 Conclusion 121

9 Further experiments on basic colour systems   **123**
   9.1 Impact of environment on similarity to natural systems 123
        9.1.1 Data sets 124
        9.1.2 Extracting colour categories 125
        9.1.3 Comparison to human colour categories 127
        9.1.4 Conclusion 129
   9.2 Impact of language on universal trends 129
        9.2.1 Discrimination game 129
        9.2.2 Alignment within one population 130
        9.2.3 Alignment over different populations 130
        9.2.4 Conclusion 135

	9.3	Impact of embodiment on performance of operators	135
		9.3.1 Robotic setup and visual perception	136
		9.3.2 Perceptual deviation and structure in embodied data	139
		9.3.3 Discerning the impact of embodiment	141
		9.3.4 Resulting dynamics	142
		9.3.5 Comparison to human categories	144
		9.3.6 Conclusion	147
	9.4	General conclusion	147

IV Evolution and origins of language strategies — 149

10 Linguistic selection of language strategies — 153
10.1	Language strategies	154
10.2	Strategy selection	154
10.3	Experiment on linguistic selection	157
	10.3.1 Measures	157
	10.3.1.1 Strategy success	157
	10.3.1.2 Strategy usage	157
	10.3.1.3 Strategy coherence	157
	10.3.2 Results	158
10.4	Selective advantage	160
	10.4.1 Experiment	160
	10.4.2 Results	160
10.5	Conclusion	161

11 Origins of language strategies — 163
11.1	Generation of semantic templates	163
11.2	Repair strategies	165
	11.2.1 Construction of a syntactic category system	166
	11.2.1.1 Starting from scratch	166
	11.2.1.2 Substituting a primitive constraint	169
	11.2.1.3 Adding a primitive constraint	170
	11.2.2 Implementaton of repair strategies	171
	11.2.3 Repair strategy 1.1: Semantic entities	171
	11.2.4 Repair strategy 1.2: Functional primitives	173
	11.2.5 Repair strategy 1.3: Contextual primitives	174
	11.2.6 Re-use of syntactic categories	175
	11.2.7 Repair strategy 2.1: Re-use of constructions	176

Contents

	11.2.8	Experimental results	177
11.3	Conclusion		180

V Conclusion — 181

12 Discussion and conclusion — 183
- 12.1 Contributions ... 183
  - 12.1.1 Identification of language strategies ... 183
  - 12.1.2 Operationalisation of language strategies ... 184
  - 12.1.3 Self-organisation of language systems ... 185
  - 12.1.4 Evolution of language strategies ... 186
  - 12.1.5 Compositional semantics and language ... 186
- 12.2 Discussion ... 187
  - 12.2.1 Tractability ... 187
  - 12.2.2 Compositionality ... 187
  - 12.2.3 Flexiblity ... 188
  - 12.2.4 Generality ... 188
  - 12.2.5 Related models and approaches ... 189
    - 12.2.5.1 Models of colour naming ... 189
    - 12.2.5.2 Fuzzy sets ... 189
    - 12.2.5.3 Conceptual spaces ... 190
    - 12.2.5.4 Vantage theory ... 190
- 12.3 Possible applications ... 190
- 12.4 Future work ... 191

A Colour spaces and systems — 193
- A.1 CIE 1931 XYZ colour space ... 193
  - A.1.1 Illuminants and chromatic adaptation ... 194
  - A.1.2 Chromaticity diagrams and CIE xyY colour space ... 195
- A.2 CIE 1976 $L^*a^*b^*$ ... 196
- A.3 CIE 1976 $L^*u^*v^*$ ... 197
- A.4 Munsell colour system ... 198
  - A.4.1 Development ... 199
  - A.4.2 Conversion ... 200
- A.5 Natural Color System ... 201
- A.6 RGB ... 202
- A.7 YCbCr ... 202

References 205

Index 213
    Name index 213
    Subject index 216

Preface

Although languages around the world display an overwhelming variety in ways to describe colours, most of the research in the domain of colour has focussed on the use of single colour terms. This approach has allowed researchers in a wide range of fields to tackle interesting questions, such as the extent to which colour categories are innate or learned. In the field of artificial language evolution, the focus on single colour terms has enabled researchers to build computational models in which populations of linguistic agents can construct and coordinate their own colour category system so that they become successful in communication.

A few descriptive studies report on describing colours beyond the restriction of using a single colour term. The results of these studies seem conclusive: only a small minority (around 15%) of all colour samples would be described using a single colour term. Most samples are described using more elaborate expressions, for example by using modifiers or combinations of colour terms.

In this book, I show how the current models in artificial language evolution can be extended to allow for richer descriptions of colour samples. In order to do so, I deploy two powerful formalisms that have been developed to support this kind of experiments: Incremental Recruitment Language (IRL) to represent the semantics, or meaning, of linguistic utterances and Fluid Construction Grammar (FCG) to transform these meanings into linguistic utterances and back.

Four different language strategies are explored: the basic colour strategy ("blue"), the graded membership strategy ("greenish"), the category combination strategy ("blue-green") and the basic modification strategy ("dark blue"). Each of these strategies is realised in different languages around the world and some studies reported on the most prototypical colour samples that are associated with these expressions. For each strategy, I propose a semantic template which captures the general cognitive operations required to use that particular strategy and syntactic templates which represent general grammatical rules that can express semantic templates in language. I pursue a compositional approach, focussing on the re-use of semantic primitives and syntactic templates as much as possible. I show that more complicated language strategies can be conceived as minor extensions of the basic colour strategy and that only a few syntactic templates suffice

Preface

to express all these strategies. Once these strategies have been operationalised, I compare their naming behaviour to human data reported in the literature. The performance of the strategies can be compared in a baseline experiment in which simulated language users engage in linguistic interactions, the difficulty of which is carefully controlled.

The implementation of a language strategy can be completed by adding learning operators which allow an agent to pick up the language system of another agent and to extend the current language system whenever the communicative need arises. The performance of these operators is tested in an acquisition and a formation experiment. In an acquisition experiment, one agent knows a predefined language system and acts as a teacher. The goal of the learner agent is to acquire the predefined language system and to become as successful in communication as two agents which share perfect knowledge of the predefined language system. In a formation experiment, a population of agents need to invent and coordinate their own language system based on a particular language strategy. I present results for both the basic colour strategy and the graded membership strategy.

Once the implementation of a language strategy is completed, in-depth studies can be carried out. I show the results of three different studies using the basic colour strategy: (a) the positive impact of the statistical distribution of colours in the environment on the similarity between simulated and human basic colour systems (b) the coordinating role of language on simulated language systems and the positive impact of language on the similarity between simulated and human basic colour systems (c) the impact of embodiment on the performance of different learning operators. In embodied experiments, two robots perceive a shared environment through their vision systems. Although this introduces a certain level of noise as both robots perceive the world from a different perspective, the data contain a high level of structure as it is based on the colours of the objects presented to the robots. Overall, embodiment has a positive effect on the performance of the proposed learning operators.

In the history of a language, a competition between two strategies on how to express a particular domain might arise. In the domain of colour, this has been observed in a vast number of languages which shift from being brightness based to being hue based. The colour term *yellow* used to reflect the meaning 'to shine' in Old English but shifted to a hue sense in Middle English and could be used to refer to the colour of yolk or discoloured paper. I present a model in which a population of agents successfully aligns on which language strategy they use based on linguistic interactions. I show that this model is capable of reproducing the meaning shifts similar to those reported in literature.

Finally, I address some questions on the origins of new language strategies. New semantic templates can be generated through a combinatorial search process in which semantic primitives are combined to form complex semantic templates. I show that each of the proposed language strategies for the domain of colour can be the outcome of such a search process. The syntactic templates that have been introduced to express these templates in language can be incorporated in repair strategies which allow agents to invent, acquire and align their own set of grammatical rules. I demonstrate how these repair strategies allow a population of agents to form their own hierarchical language that includes some recursive rules. These recursive rules have the benefit of being able to express more complex meaning without the cost of alignment in the population.

Even though the examples in this book are limited to the domain of colour, the proposed templates can easily be extended to richer examples and deployed in other continuous domains. The proposed transformation processes could be used to name the colours of concepts that vary in colour, like for example the colours used to describe wine. Other possible domains include the spatial domain, in which spatial categories, such as near and far, also exhibit properties of graded membership which can be made explicit in language (eg. *very near*). The results reported in this book should hence not be thought of as final but rather as in interesting starting point for a whole line of research on the origins and evolution of natural languages.

Acknowledgements

Much of the research presented in this book could not have been completed without the use of systems and data that were developed by various members of the wonderful teams of both the Artificial Intelligence Laboratory at the Vrije Universiteit Brussel and the Sony CSL Laboratory in Paris.

I would like to thank Michael Spranger and Martin Loetzsch for their tremendous effort in recording data using the Sony humanoid robots. I am also much obliged to Joachim De Beule, Nicolas Neubauer, Pieter Wellens and Remi van Trijp for the development of FCG, and to Wouter Van den Broeck, Simon Pauw, Michael Spranger and Martin Loetzsch for the development of IRL. Some of the experiments on basic colour systems are also indebted to critical scientific input by Tony Belpaeme.

And, of course, it is hard to imagine any of this work to materialise without the continuous effort and scientific vision of Luc Steels, the director of both labs.

The research reported in this book has been financially supported by a doctoral grant of the Institute for the Promotion of Innovation through Science and Technology in Flanders (IWT-Vlaanderen).

Abbreviations

AI	Artificial Intelligence
CCD	Charge-coupled device
CIE	Commission Internationale de l'Eclairage
FCG	Fluid Construction Grammar
IRL	Incremental Recruitment Language
NCS	Natural Color System
PAL	Phase Alternating Line
RGB	Red, green and blue colour model
SC	Strategy coherence
SECAM	Séquentiel couleur à mémoire
SIS	Swedish Standards Institute
WCS	World Color Survey
YCBCR	YCbCr colour model

Part I

Introduction

1 Language systems and language strategies

Although languages around the world exhibit an overwhelming variety in the ways they describe colours, most of the research in the domain of colour has focussed on the use of single colour terms to describe colour. This approach has allowed psychologists to study the nature of categories and it is now widely accepted that colour categories are organised around a prototype which is the colour that represents a category best (Rosch 1973). The approach has also allowed to shed light on the ongoing nature-nurture debate in which the question is to what degree categories are innate and to what degree they are acquired during the development of a child (Berlin & Kay 1969).

In the field of artificial language evolution, researchers try to model the origins and evolution of artificial languages in a controlled environment. Within this field, the domain of colour has been intensively studied. The focus on using a single colour term to describe a colour sample has allowed researchers to formalise models of how a population of artificial language users can form and coordinate their own colour-related language system (Steels & Belpaeme 2005; Belpaeme & Bleys 2005b; 2007; Puglisi, Baronchelli & Loreto 2008; Baronchelli et al. 2010).

Only a few descriptive studies reported on the domain of colour beyond the restriction of using single terms. Some studies used an unconstrained naming procedure in which human subjects were asked to describe colour samples in any way they liked (Simpson & Tarrant 1991; Lin et al. 2001). The results of these studies seem conclusive: only a small minority (15% at most) of the colour samples would be described using a single colour term. The other samples would be described using a more elaborate expression in which modifiers or combinations of colour terms are used. The results of Lin et al. (2001) are shown in more detail in Table 1.

Previous artificial language evolution models in which the single term constraint has been lifted do exist, but all of these models deployed a rather simplified view on semantics such as conjunctive combinations of categories (Wellens, Loetzsch & Steels 2008) or predicate-argument expressions (Batali 2002; Smith,

1 Language systems and language strategies

Table 1.1: Results of an unconstrained colour naming experiment for British and Chinese broken down by linguistic category (after Lin et al. 2001). The basic category consists of all samples that were described using a single basic colour term, such as *red*. Modified basic corresponds to a basic modification of a single colour term, such as *dark red*. Compounding means combining two colour categories as in *bluish red*. Qualifier basic is any other combination of colour terms and modifiers (such as *dark bluish red*). Secondary means that the colour is described in more detail using another object, as in *blood red*. In idiosyncratic cases no clear classification could be made.

category	British (%)	Chinese (%)
basic	15.70	10.66
modifier-basic	23.20	17.36
compound	10.32	18.09
qualifier-basic	7.18	9.82
secondary	42.30	42.42
idiosyncratic	0.33	0.15
unnamed	0.96	1.49

Kirby & Brighton 2003; De Beule 2008). None of these models allow for semantics in continuous domains.

The main goal of this book is to study how the single term restriction can be lifted in the models of artificial language evolution for the continuous domain of colour by pushing both syntax and semantics to a higher level of complexity.

1.1 Language strategies for colour

Although the domain of colour might seem fairly restricted, it is fascinating to see how different languages around the world use different LANGUAGE STRATEGIES to express it. A language strategy is a particular approach to express one subarea of meaning. An example of such a strategy could be describing a colour using a single term which refers to a prototypical category. A LANGUAGE SYSTEM consists of specific choices in how a particular language strategy is realised in a language, like for example the exact location of the colour categories and which terms to use to refer to these prototypes.

1.1.1 Basic colour strategy

Currently, the most widely studied language strategy for colour is the one that uses a single term to describe a colour. Most studies restrict these terms even further to BASIC COLOUR TERMS which only refer to the domain of colour and which are non-compositional (Berlin & Kay 1969). The basic colour terms for English are: *white, black, red, green, yellow, blue, brown, grey, purple, pink* and *orange*, but exclude terms like *sea green* or *light brown*. These terms are generally believed to refer to colour categories. Each colour category has a FOCAL COLOUR which is the best example of a particular colour category. The focal colours to which these terms refer have been determined for a wide range of languages. These studies revealed universal tendencies as some colours are more likely to be named by basic colour terms than others (Regier, Kay & Cook 2005).

Even though the language systems based on this strategy seem to exhibit universal tendencies, they also show quite some variation. In Russian, the colours that are named by the term *blue* in English are named by two terms: *sinij* and *goluboj*, which could be translated as *dark blue* and *light blue* (Safuanova & Korzh 2007). Japanese and Mandarin colour systems do not make the distinction between green and blue, but use a single term that covers both regions (*ao* in Japanese and *qīng* in Mandarin). But the possible range of variation is even better illustrated in Berinmo, a language spoken in some villages near the Sepik River in Papua New Guinea, which uses only 5 basic colour terms: *mehi* which denotes red/orange/pink, *nol* which covers most of the blue and green area, *wor* which roughly corresponds to yellow/green/orange, *wap* corresponds to the light colours and *kel* to the dark colours but it also includes some purple (Roberson, Davies & Davidoff 2002). The geographic distribution of languages around the world based on the number of basic colour categories can be found in the World Atlas of Language Structures Online[1] and is reproduced in Figure 1.1 (Kay & Maffi 2008).

Other systems based on this strategy vary in which dimensions of the colour domain are relevant for the basic colour terms. The basic colour system of Hunanóo, a language spoken by the Mangyans in the Philippines, consists of four colour terms: *(ma)biru* ('blackness'), *(ma)lagti* ('whiteness'), *(ma)rara* ('redness') and *(ma)latuy* ('greenness'). In this system only the lightness and the red-green opponent channels are relevant to name colours whereas the yellow-blue opponent channel is ignored (Conklin 1995).

---

[1] Available online at http://wals.info/feature/133

1 Language systems and language strategies

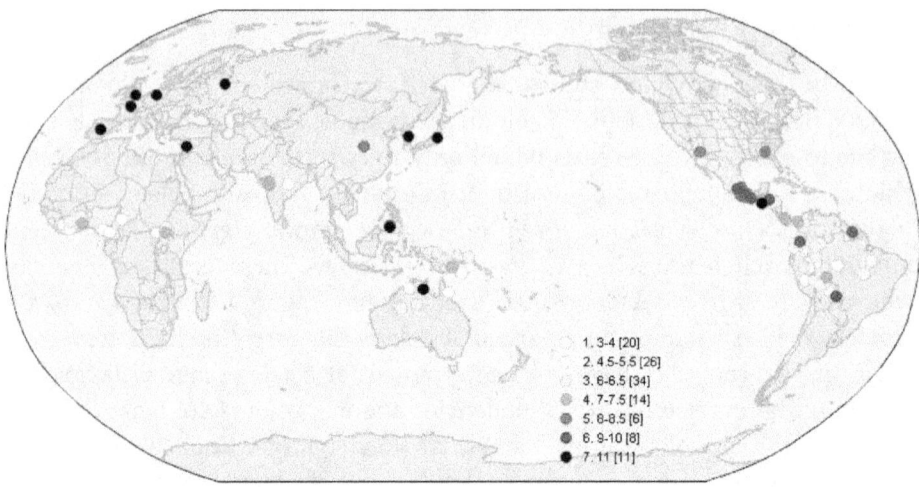

Figure 1.1: The number of basic colour terms in languages around the world (Kay & Maffi 2008).

1.1.2 Graded membership strategy

The fact that each colour category has a focal colour also implies that other colour samples are worse examples of a particular colour category. Some languages allow their users to mark how well a particular sample represents the prototype. In English this marking is optional and achieved through the adverb *very* and the modifying *-ish* suffix, for instance in the expression *greenish*. In other languages, such as Tarahumara, which is an indigenous language spoken in the North of Mexico, this marking is obligatory. This language has an elaborate system of modifiers that distinguishes three levels of membership: *-kame* which could be translated as 'very', *-name* which could be glossed as 'somewhat' and *-nanti* for the lowest degree of membership. An example of how this system is used for the Turahumara colour category for red: *sitá-* is shown in Figure 1.2 (Burgess, Kempton & MacLaury 1983).

1.1.3 Compounding strategy

Some languages also allow users to compound two colour categories into a new one. Especially to describe a colour sample that is not a good example of any of the basic colour categories, this might be a very productive strategy that increases expressivity. An example in English would be *blue-green*. This compound-

1.1 Language strategies for colour

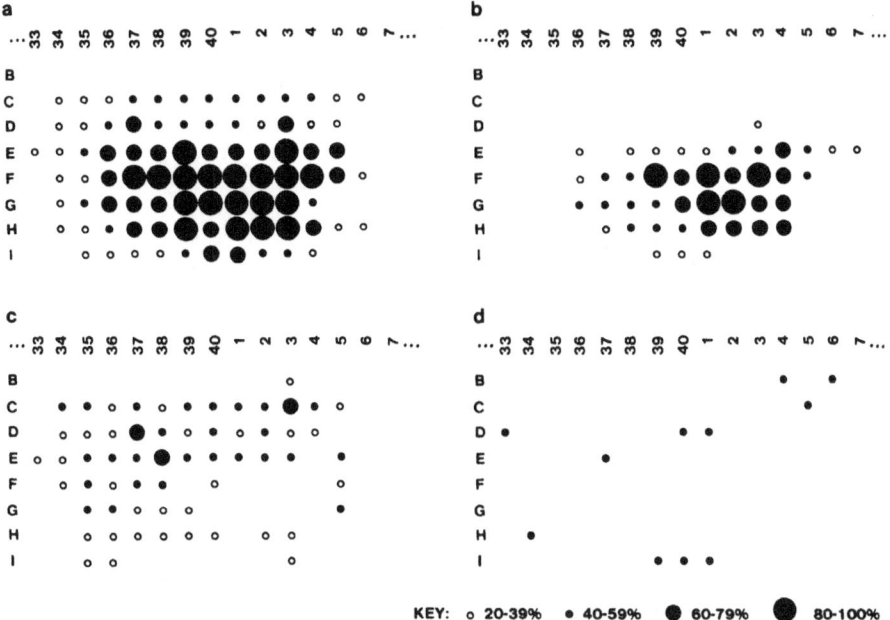

Figure 1.2: The use of modifiers to express graded membership in Tarahumara shown on an array of Munsell chips. The bigger the circle, the more it represents a particular colour expression. (a) aggregate of all expressions using the *sitá* root (b) *sitákame* (very red) (c) *sitáname* (somewhat red) (d) *sitánanti* (only slightly red). Note how each modifier specifies a region that is further removed from the prototypical colour of *sitá*. Figure from Burgess, Kempton & MacLaury (1983).

ing can also be modulated by additional markers, like for example the *-ish* marker as in *brownish-red* in English.

Safuanova & Korzh (2007) have collected data on the focal colours of compounds in Russian. One of their main findings is that in Russian the order in which colour terms are compounded has an influence on the resulting focal colour: the second term seems to be more important in the expression. This is illustrated in the upper left segment of Figure 1.3. The colours between *žëltyj* ('yellow') and *zelënyj* ('green') are for example named: *zelenovato-žëltyj* ('greenish-yellow'), *zelëno-žëltyj* ('green-yellow'), *žëlto-zelënyj* ('yellow-green') and *žëltovato-zelënyj* ('yellowish-green') where the suffix *-ato* acts as a modulator.

1 Language systems and language strategies

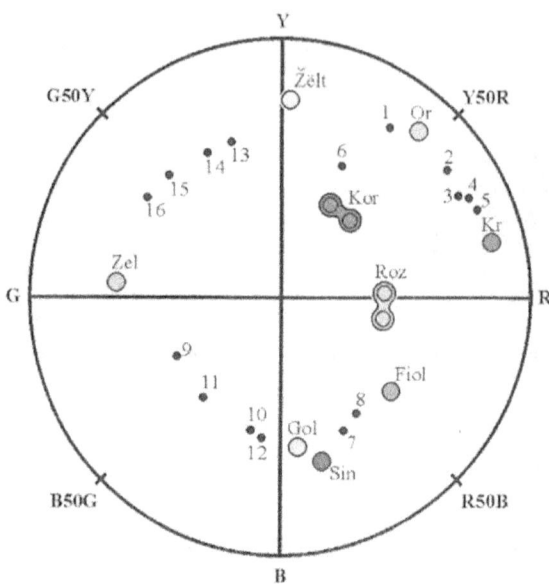

Figure 1.3: Compound chromatic terms projected on the hue plane of the NCS colour space. The second term in the compound clearly has a bigger impact on the resulting focal colour than the first one. The colours between *žëltyj* ('yellow') and *zelëno* ('green') are for example named: (13) *zelenovato-žëltyj* ('greenish-yellow'), (14) *zelëno-žëltyj* ('green-yellow'), (15) *žëlto-zelënyj* ('yellow-green') and (16) *žëltovato-zelënyj* ('yellowish-green'). Figure from Safuanova & Korzh (2007).

1.1.4 Basic modification strategy

Similarly, many language systems allow for the use of basic modifiers which modify some aspects of a colour category. In English for example, users can modify the brightness and the chromaticity of a colour category through the use of modifiers (*light* or *dark* for modifying the brightness and *bright* or *pale* for modifying the chromaticity). This strategy has been attested for a wide range of languages, including Vietnamese (Alvarado & Jameson 2002) and Chinese (Lin et al. 2001).

Although basic modifiers are quite commonly used, only a few papers report on the exact transformation that is implied by these modifiers. One exception is the study by Safuanova & Korzh (2007) of the Russian language, in which the authors determined the focal colours of the modified categories. An example of such an analysis in the Natural Color Sytem (see Appendix A.5) is shown in Figure 1.4. The modifiers *tëmno-* ('dark') and *svleto* ('light'), modify the focus of the basic category parallel to the blackness dimension (W-S). The modifiers *bledno-* ('pale') and *jarko-* ('bright') shift the chromaticity of the basic colour category (W-C or S-C) (Safuanova & Korzh 2007).

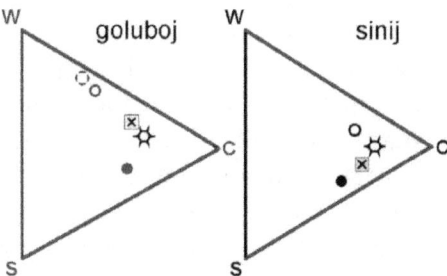

Figure 1.4: Location of modified basic colour foci in Russian projected into the NCS blackness-chromaticity triangle. *tëmno-* ('dark', solid circle), *jarko-* ('bright', sun), *svetlo-* ('light', open circle) and *bledno-* ('pale', dashed circle). Figure from Paramei (2005).

1.1.5 Other strategies

Another strategy that is often used to name colours, is suggesting colours by naming an object that is typical for that colour (like for example *lavender* or *salmon* in English). These object names can also be used in combination with basic colour terms (like *sky blue* or *cherry red*). Even though the abundant usage of these terms has been confirmed in unconstrained naming experiments, like for example in English and Chinese (Lin et al. 2001), the actual focal colours of these expressions have yet to be determined. The previous list of language strategies is not exhaustive, as other strategies to describe colours exist (for example using comparatives like in *most green*).

1.2 Modelling language strategies and linguistic interaction

Modelling a language strategy starts with the reverse engineering of the semantic and syntactic templates that allow language users to conceptualise and express a particular subarea of meaning in language. A language strategy also includes

1 Language systems and language strategies

the operationalisation of a series of learning operators, which will be discussed later.

In the BASIC COLOUR STRATEGY, the semantic template defines how to select the appropriate colour category to describe a colour sample, for example, the category that is most similar to that sample. The syntactic template could then define a lexicon in which categories are associated to terms. These templates can be used in both production and interpretation.

The performance of the semantic and syntactic templates can be evaluated in a BASELINE EXPERIMENT. In such an experiment, these templates are instantiated based on a natural language system that is provided by the experimenter. It allows to model a natural language system and to test its simulated performance in a benchmark using simulated language users, or agents.

In order to model the function of a language strategy, I will use the language game paradigm (Steels 1996a). In this paradigm, language users are modelled as AGENTS and a language community as a POPULATION OF AGENTS. These agents constantly engage in local interactions, or LANGUAGE GAMES in which they try to achieve COMMUNICATIVE GOALS, like for example drawing the attention of another agent to one of the objects in a shared environment or CONTEXT. Achieving these communicative goals is considered to be the function of a language strategy.

A language game typically involves two agents randomly drawn from the population. One is assigned the role of the speaker and the other the role of the hearer. The speaker selects a private communicative goal, for which it conceptualises a meaning. Using its current linguistic knowledge it produces an utterance to express this meaning. The hearer parses this utterance using its own current linguistic knowledge and interprets the resulting meaning in his own world model. This interpretation might lead to some actions which should allow the speaker to verify whether the intended communicative goal was reached. If this is not the case, the speaker reveals the communicative goal to the hearer. Both agents update their linguistic and conceptual knowledge in order to become more successful in future interactions. All the processes involved in one interaction are summarised in a SEMIOTIC CYCLE which is shown in Figure 1.5 (Steels 2003).

1.2.1 Language games for colour

The first language game in which colour could be expressed by the agents, was the Talking Heads experiment (Steels 1999). In this experiment contexts consisted of coloured geometrical figures on a whiteboard which were perceived by

1.2 Modelling language strategies and linguistic interaction

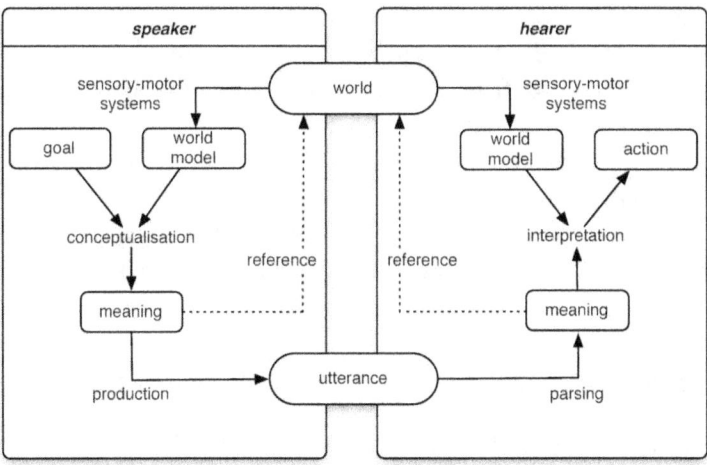

Figure 1.5: The semiotic cycle of a language game. The speaker selects a communicative goal using its own world model, conceptualises a meaning and renders an utterance for this meaning. The hearer parses this utterance into meaning which is interpreted using its own world model. This interpretation might lead to some action, upon which the speaker provides feedback (not shown in figure).

two pan-tilt cameras. Software agents could be embodied in these cameras. The communicative goal was to draw the attention of the other agent to one of these figures. The agents could describe several domains to achieve this goal, including the domain of colour. It soon became apparent that the domain of colour was rich and complex enough to be studied in isolation.

This observation led to the development of the COLOUR NAMING GAME (Steels & Belpaeme 2005; Belpaeme & Bleys 2005b; 2007; Puglisi, Baronchelli & Loreto 2008; Baronchelli et al. 2010) in which agents were restricted to use only the domain of colour to achieve the communicative goal. The use of information in other domains, for example spatial relations, was not allowed. The Colour Naming Game has been devised to study how a population of agents can form and align its own colour category systems. In these studies the contexts were based on the random selection of a number of colour samples from a large set of colour samples. A colour sample is an abstract representation that only contains colour information.

1 Language systems and language strategies

In the GROUNDED COLOUR NAMING GAME (see §9.3), embodied agents (robots) are placed in a closed office environment and the contexts consisted of toy-like objects that are placed in front of the agents. Although embodied agents could easily use different domains to describe the objects in front of them, they are only allowed to describe the colour information of these objects. In this language game, the utterances are still restricted to a single term.

I introduce the COLOUR DESCRIPTION GAME (see Chapters 4–6) in which the restriction of using a single colour term to describe the colour of an object is lifted.

1.2.2 Background assumptions

The language paradigm focusses on the functional and evolutionary aspect of languages, but this can only be achieved by making some assumptions. It is assumed that agents are capable of giving joint attention (Tomasello 1995), constructing world models, taking turns, being cooperative,[2] and so on. These assumptions are each interesting and far from trivial research topics by themselves. Although it is clear that these processes are prerequisites for studies in the language game paradigm, they are not in the main focus of this paradigm.

1.3 Self-organisation of language systems

A language system is not a static system, but rather a living system that is constantly evolving. In the self-organisation of language systems based on the basic colour strategy, language systems are expanded by the introduction of new colour categories. By studying a wide range of contemporary language systems for colour, some researchers have even proposed a universal evolutionary order by which colour categories are introduced to a language (Berlin & Kay 1969).

1.4 Modelling the self-organisation of language systems

In order to model the self-organisation of language systems, the implementation of a language strategy needs to be extended with a series of learning operators that specify:

1. how a language user can acquire a language system from other language users using ADOPTION OPERATORS

---

[2] Wang & Steels (2008) show that uncooperative agents can also bootstrap a language under certain conditions.

2. how language users can update their knowledge of the language system after a linguistic interaction using ALIGNMENT OPERATORS

3. how a language user can expand a language system using INVENTION OPERATORS

For the basic colour strategy, the adoption operator allows a user to adopt a new colour category and its associated colour term when a new unknown term is encountered. The invention operators allow users to introduce new colour terms that are associated to new colour categories to the language system. Finally, the alignment operator specifies that agents should update their colour categories to better represent the topic when the linguistic interaction was successful.

An ACQUISITION EXPERIMENT could be implemented in which the adoption and alignment operators of a language strategy are tested. Such an experiment involves two agents in which one needs to acquire a predefined language system from another agent. By comparing the performance of the agent that is acquiring the language system to the performance in the baseline experiment, the performance of the adoption and alignment operators can be evaluated.

The final step would be a FORMATION EXPERIMENT in which a population of agents needs to construct its own language system from scratch. Such an experiment checks the performance of the invention operators by comparing the performance of the population of agents in this experiment to the baseline performance.

Within the language game paradigm, a language system is considered to be a COMPLEX ADAPTIVE SYSTEM (Steels 2000a). It is shaped and reshaped by its users to suit their needs, even over the course of a single dialogue (Garrod & Doherty 1994), in order to become more successful in communication while minimising cognitive effort. No single user has a complete view of the language and no user can control the linguistic behaviour of the complete group. Instead, language is a self-organising system that emerges through local interactions or language games.

1.5 Evolution of language strategies

If one takes a historical perspective on language, one can also detect shifts in dominance from one language strategy to another. In the evolution of the basic colour terms in English an interesting meaning shift occurred: at their Indo-European root most colour terms had primarily a brightness meaning sense. Around the transition from Old to Middle English the hue meaning sense of all basic colour

1 Language systems and language strategies

terms became more dominant than the original brightness sense (Casson 1997). Both meaning senses could be thought of as different variations of the basic colour strategy.

This is illustrated in Figure 1.6 in which the history of the term *yellow* is shown. In Indo-European its syntactic form was *ghel* which was primarily used to refer to the shining (of yellow metals). In Old English the term *geolo* acquired a hue sense and could be used to refer to the colour of some silk cloth. In the transition to Middle English *yelou* the hue sense became the more dominant one and the term could also be used to refer to for example yolk and ripe corn, although it could still be used to refer to gold. The same is true for all other basic colour terms. Most interestingly, all colour terms that were introduced to English after this shift, like for example *orange*, never had a brightness sense but only a hue sense (Casson 1997). Similar meaning shifts have been reported in a wide range of languages (MacLaury 1992).

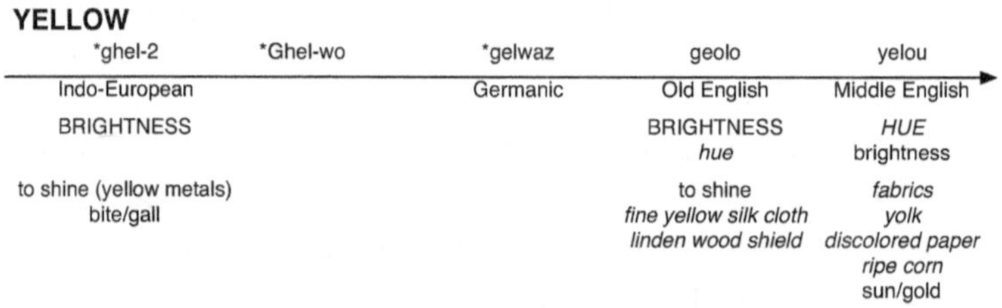

YELLOW				
*ghel-2	*Ghel-wo	*gelwaz	geolo	yelou
Indo-European		Germanic	Old English	Middle English
BRIGHTNESS			BRIGHTNESS	HUE
			hue	brightness
to shine (yellow metals)			to shine	fabrics
bite/gall			fine yellow silk cloth	yolk
			linden wood shield	discolored paper
				ripe corn
				sun/gold

Figure 1.6: The evolution of the term *yellow* in English. Like almost all other basic colour terms, its meaning shifted from brightness to hue around the transition from Old English to Middle English (Casson 1997).

1.6 Modelling evolution of language strategies

Given the observed evolution and selection at both the level of language strategies and the level of linguistic items that make up a particular language system, I explore the hypothesis that linguistic agents need explicit representations of language strategies which they use to keep track of how successful a particular strategy has been in communication. These explicit representations allow me to introduce an additional layer of selection at the level of language strategies.

1.7 Structure of this book

Chapter 2 will introduce the formalisms that will be used to model language strategies and language systems.

Part II of this book focusses on the reconstruction of the general semantic and syntactic structures that allow me to run baseline experiments for several of the language strategies identified in this chapter: the basic colour strategy, the graded membership strategy, the compounding strategy and the basic modification strategy.

In Part III, I will focus on the self-organisation of language systems that are based on one language strategy, namely the basic colour strategy, by introducing its adoption, alignment and invention operators. This will allow me to study the impact of embodiment on the performance of these operators. I will also show results of related experiments on language systems that are realisations of this strategy.

In Part IV, I will present a model that allows to study the evolution of language strategies based on linguistic selection. I will start by introducing two variants of the basic colour category and show an experiment that models the meaning shift as documented for the history of basic colour terms. I will also explore the origins of language strategies based on a combinatorial search process.

The concluding Part V will give an overview of the main results that have been achieved in this book and will outline some directions for future research.

2 Formalisms for language systems and language strategies

Modelling a language strategy encompasses defining semantic and syntactic templates and applying realised templates that make up a language system. Moreover, the language strategy needs to define adoption, alignment and invention operators. This imposes hard requirements on the formalisms that are needed to model a language strategy.

Standard first-order formalisms in logic that are commonly used in artificial language evolution research, such as predicate logic, are insufficient to represent the semantic templates of some of the strategies outlined in the previous chapter. For example, the meaning of a realisation of the graded membership strategy, such as *very red*, cannot be expressed using any first-order logical formalism in a satisfactory way as the the adverb *very* modifies the meaning of the adjective *red*.

The syntactic templates require a grammar formalism, as the word order seems to have an impact on the resulting focal colour that is intended. This is for example the case in the compounding strategy in Russian, where *zelëno-žëltyj* ('green-yellow') is different from *žëlto-zelënyj* ('yellow-green'). This difference implies that the lexical approach in which the lexicon captures a direct association between terms and colour category is no longer sufficient.

In this book, I have chosen to use Incremental Recruitment Language (IRL) to represent semantic templates and Fluid Construction Grammar (FCG) to represent syntactic templates. Both formalisms have been especially designed to support experiments in artificial language evolution (Loetzsch, Bleys & Wellens 2009).

This chapter provides a short introduction to both systems that introduces the design principles behind these formalisms and that should enable the reader to understand the models of language strategies that will be presented in future chapters. Readers can choose to skip this chapter and return to it when needed.

2 Formalisms for language systems and language strategies

2.1 Embodied cognitive semantics using IRL

2.1.1 Theoretical foundations

Although research on the emergence of communication systems with similar features as human natural language has shown important progress, the complexity of the meanings considered so far remains limited. Experiments either use simple categories (Steels & Belpaeme 2005; Belpaeme & Bleys 2005b), conjunctive combinations of categories (Wellens, Loetzsch & Steels 2008) or predicate-argument expressions (Batali 2002; Smith, Kirby & Brighton 2003; De Beule 2008). Natural languages are clearly capable of expressing second order semantics (Dowty, Wall & Peters 1981). For example, the adverb *very* in *very big* modifies the meaning of the adjective, it is not just a simple conjunction of the predicates *very* and *big*. Moreover the same predicate (e.g. *big*) can often be used in different ways, for example to further restrict the set of possible referents of a noun (as in *the big ball*), to state a property of an object (as in *the ball is big*), to reify the predicate itself and make a statement about it (as in *big says something about size*), to compare the elements of a set (as in *this ball is bigger than the others*), etc. The specific usage of a predicate in a particular utterance is clearly conveyed by the grammar, so any theory on the origins and evolution of grammar must address second order semantics.

The semantics of the utterances in this book are not represented in a standard logic, but in an alternative framework, Incremental Recruitment Language or IRL (Steels 2000b; Steels & Bleys 2005; Van den Broeck 2007; 2008). In this framework the meaning of a sentence is a SEMANTIC CONSTRAINT NETWORK that the speaker wants the hearer to evaluate in order to achieve the communicative goal selected by the speaker. This approach resonates with earlier work in AI on procedural semantics (Winograd 1972).

The IRL framework has been especially designed for experiments on artificial language evolution and therefore supports key features that have been proven successful in this field of research. It is *omni-directional*: not only can it be used for both conceptualisation and interpretation but also to complete partial semantic constraint networks. This feature does not only enable both speaker and hearer to use the same formalism, but it has also proven to be crucial when writing adoption, alignment and invention operators. The speaker can use it to diagnose potential problems in communication by interpreting its own utterance to detect potential ambiguities (Steels 2003). The hearer can try to reproduce a partially understood meaning together with the communicative goal, revealed by the speaker in a failed interaction, to infer which parts it misinterpreted or did not know yet. On a technical level, this strongly suggests a constraint-propagation language (Marriott & Stuckey 1998).

Another key feature of IRL is its *open-endedness* towards the cognitive operations it can represent. Previous research has deployed a wide range of such operations including discrimination trees (Steels 1996b), event feature detectors (Siskind 2001), nearest neighbour classification (Belpaeme & Bleys 2005b) and radial basis function networks (Steels & Belpaeme 2005). IRL aims to be an overarching formalism which can support any cognitive operation for which a tractable implementation on a computer exists. It can be used for rich semantics in which any of these operations can be combined and also for experiments in which the choice of the cognitive operation is not predetermined by the experimenter.

Finally, IRL is designed to support world models which are *grounded* in the sensory-motor system of the agent. These world models are non-symbolic and are based on the operation of their sensorimotor apparatus. Often (e.g. Batali 2002; Smith, Kirby & Brighton 2003; Wellens, Loetzsch & Steels 2008) it is assumed that there is a simple straightforward mapping of the non-symbolic world model onto a categorial situation model, which is a representation of the world in the form of facts in some variant of predicate calculus. But as different languages conceptualise the world in different ways, this mapping function is clearly non-trivial.

2.1.2 Semantic constraint network

The meaning of an utterance will be viewed as a SEMANTIC CONSTRAINT NETWORK, or SEMANTIC NETWORK for short. The basic nodes of these networks are PRIMITIVE CONSTRAINTS which reflect cognitive operations and which are provided by the experimenter. Each constraint has a number of arguments which can be bound to a certain variable. Variables are denoted using a question mark prefix. If a variable appears as an argument to more than one constraint, it means the value for this variable is constrained by more than one constraint. Some variables can be bound to a certain SEMANTIC ENTITY by means of a bind statement. Semantic entities are marked by square brackets.

An example network for an utterance like *the block* is shown in Figure 2.1 to identify the block within a hypothetical context. The EQUAL-TO-CONTEXT primitive (primitives will always be printed in small capitals) binds all entities in the context to ?s1. The FILTER-SET-PROTOTYPE primitive takes this entity-set as input, computes all entities that are similar to the prototype of a block (provided by the bind statement through ?p1) and binds the resulting set to ?s2. Finally, the SELECT-ELEMENT, of which the selector is specified as [unique], checks whether this set contains only one element and binds this element to ?t.

2 Formalisms for language systems and language strategies

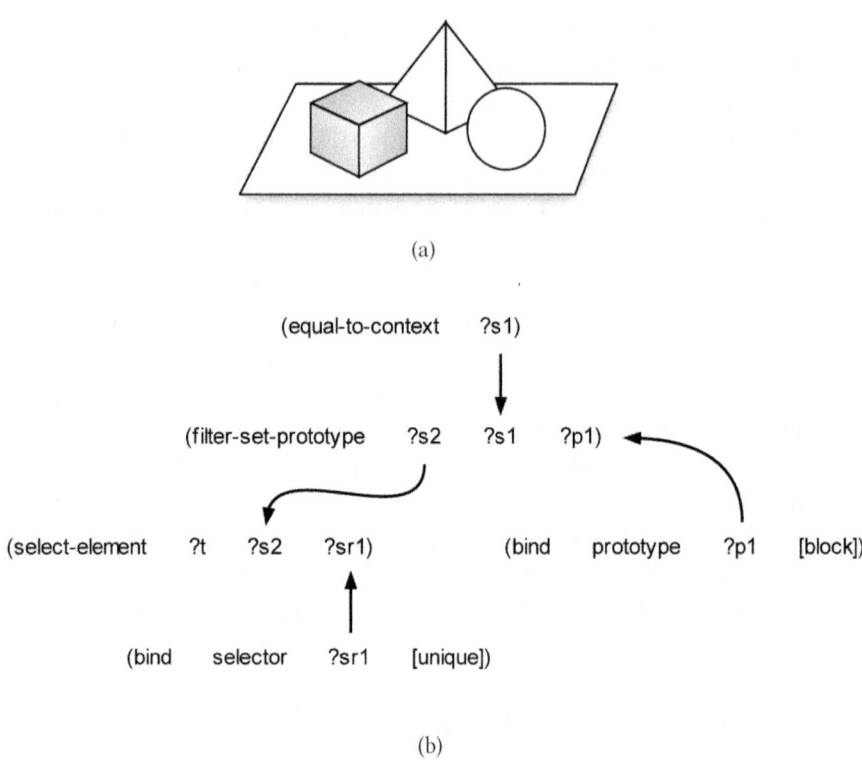

Figure 2.1: (a) a hypothetical context (b) an example of a semantic constraint network for *the block* to identify the topic within (a) (marked in grey for clarity)

The more complex the world (for example by adding a second block), the more complex the semantic constraint network will need to be in order to achieve this goal (for example extending the previous one with another filter operation based on size). An example of such a context and such a network is shown in Figure 2.2. This network could represent the meaning of an utterance like *the big block*. The entity-set of all blocks in ?s2 is now further filtered to contain only big blocks using the FILTER-SET-CATEGORY primitive, which binds the resulting set to ?s3 which is passed on to the SELECT-ELEMENT primitive. Note that the previous network in Figure 2.1(b) would fail in this context as the SELECT-ELEMENT primitive with a [unique] selector constrains the number of blocks in the context to be one at most.

2.1 Embodied cognitive semantics using IRL

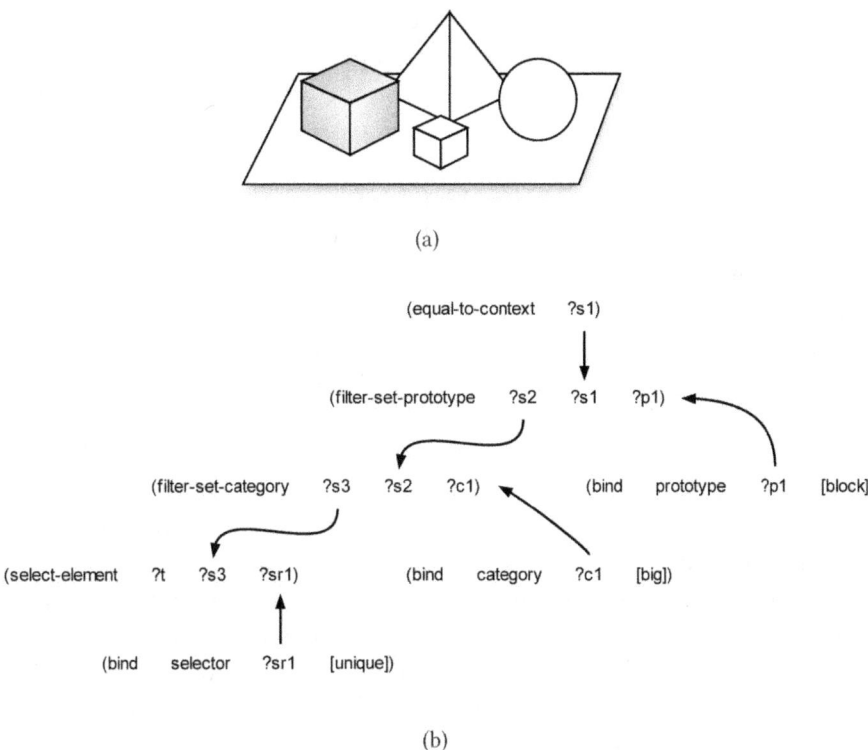

Figure 2.2: (a) a more complex hypothetical world (b) a more complex semantic constraint network to identify *the big block* (marked in grey for clarity)

2.1.3 Evaluation

The evaluation of a semantic constraint network involves cycling through the primitives of the network until each primitive has been successfully revised. The revision of a primitive has three possible outcomes: (1) validation with possible bindings for one or more of its arguments (2) rejection or (3) suspension. Whenever a primitive returns more than one possible solution, the evaluation tree which keeps tracks of possible bindings for each variable in the network, splits. This especially occurs during conceptualisation when the semantic entities of the primitive constraints are still unknown. Whenever a primitive rejects a particular set of bindings, that particular branch in the evaluation tree can not be explored any further. Whenever a primitive is not specified for a certain pattern of bound or open arguments, it is suspended and revised at a later moment.

2 Formalisms for language systems and language strategies

During conceptualisation, the topic is typically known but the semantic entities of the cognitive operators (like for example which prototype or which category to use) are not. During interpretation, the opposite is true: the semantic entities of the cognitive operators have been passed on in the utterance, but the topic has not. A typical network during interpretation is shown in Figure 2.2(b). The same network during conceptualisation is shown in Figure 2.3(a).

The evaluation process of this network is shown in Figure 2.3(b). The context consists of four objects: a big block (b-bk), a small block (s-bk), a ball (bl) and a pyramid (pd) and the goal is to identify the big block in this context, so we have a binding for $?t$. The only primitive that can be revised is EQUAL-TO-CONTEXT which can bind $?s1$ to the context: {b-bk, s-bk, bl, pd}. The next primitive that can be revised is FILTER-SET-PROTOTYPE and let us suppose it knows the prototypes for block and ball. This will cause a split in the evaluation tree: one in which $?p1$ is bound to [block] and $?s2$ is bound to {b-bk, s-bk} (node 2) and another branch in which $?p1$ is bound to [ball] and $?s2$ is bound to {bl} (node 3). The next primitive that can be revised is FILTER-SET-CATEGORY. Let us suppose this primitive is only defined when its second argument contains at least two entities. This will lead to a rejection of the branch of node 3 and to a further split of the branch of node 2: one in which $?c1$ is bound to [small] and $?s3$ is bound to {s-bk} (node 4) and another branch in which $?c1$ is bound to [big] and $?s4$ is bound to {b-bk} (node 5). The final primitive that needs to be revised is SELECT-ELEMENT, which checks whether $?s4$ contains only one entity that is equal to the big block. This leads to a rejection of the branch of node 4 but also to a successful evaluation of the branch of node 5 in which $?sr1$ is bound to [unique].

During acquisition of new semantic entities, the hearer will have been able to reconstruct the intended semantic constraint network for a large part. This network will be extended by the communicative goal that is revealed by the speaker and will be revised in order to acquire the semantic entity that fulfills the need in the current network.

An example of such a network is shown in Figure 2.4, which could have been parsed after hearing a sentence like *the wabado ball*. Due to the omni-directionality of IRL, the first two arguments of the FILTER-SET-CATEGORY primitive, $?s3$ and $?s2$ can be completely determined, which allows IRL to come up with either a category that is already known or with an entirely new category that would perform the correct filtering.

2.1 Embodied cognitive semantics using IRL

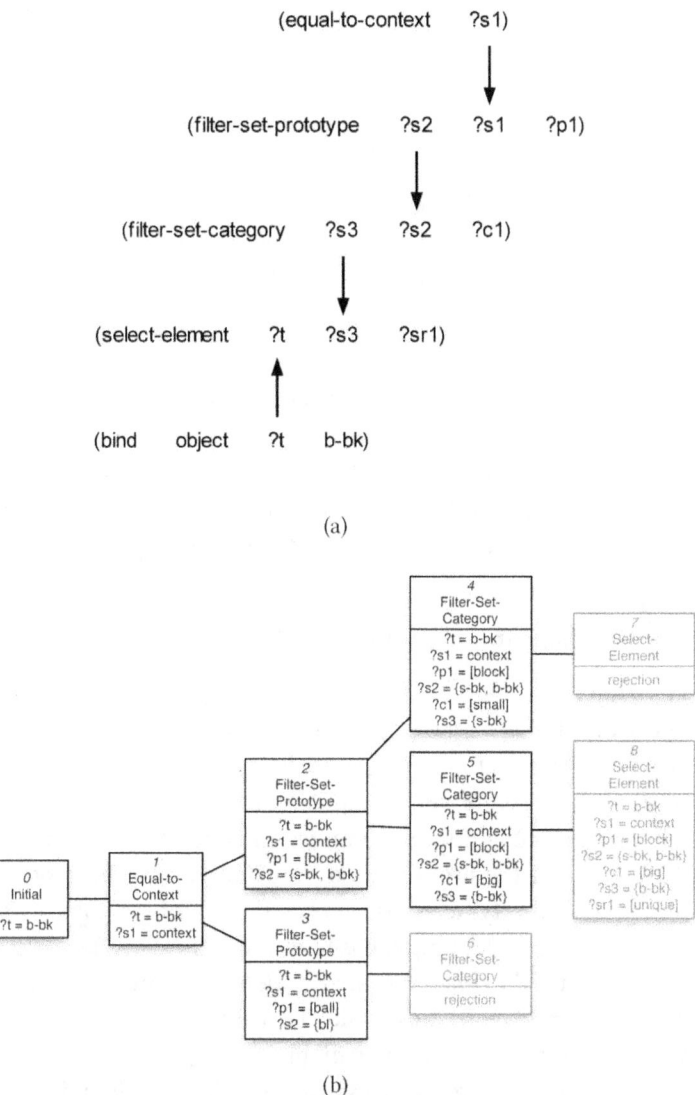

Figure 2.3: (b) The evaluation process of an example network (a) during conceptualisation in a context consisting of four objects: a big block (b-bk), a small block (s-bk), a ball (bl) and a pyramid (pd). The communicative goal is to identify the big block.

2 Formalisms for language systems and language strategies

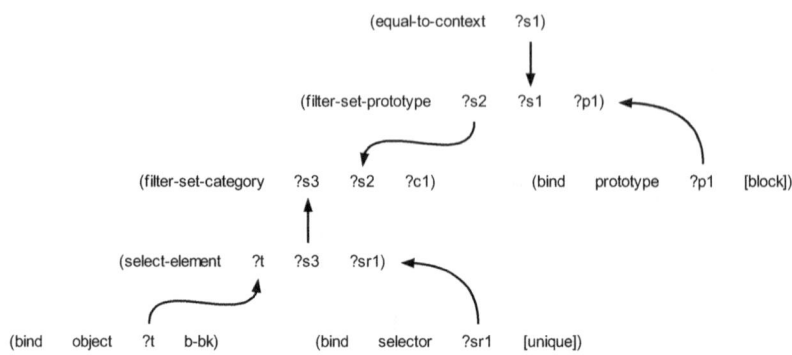

Figure 2.4: A partial network that could be reconstructed by combining information from parsing *the wabado ball* and the communicative goal revealed by the speaker. Due to the omni-directionality of IRL, the first two arguments of the FILTER-SET-CATEGORY primitive are sufficient to allow IRL to deduce a valid category for ?c1.

2.1.4 Conceptualisation and chunking

Conceptualisation can now be viewed as a search process in which a semantic constraint network that is suitable to achieve the communicative goal it selected (Steels & Bleys 2005) needs to be constructed. Agents start with a library of primitive constraints. These primitives are combined using heuristics to construct networks that become more and more complex. In general, these heuristics exploit the typical structure of the arguments of a primitive and the type information of these arguments. The typical structure is that the first argument is the target variable which can be computed based on the values of the other arguments. Type information is used to ensure that arguments that are linked are of compatible type. More elaborate heuristics, which for example avoid duplicate primitive constraints in one network, are also available.

An example of such a search process to identify a single object is shown in Figure 2.5 which starts from a library of four primitive constraints: EQUAL-TO-CONTEXT, FILTER-SET-PROTOTYPE, FILTER-SET-CATEGORY and SELECT-ELEMENT. The search process starts from a variable bound to the topic. This variable is considered to be an open variable for which a primitive with a compatible target argument needs to be found. Only one primitive in the library fulfils this requirement: SELECT-ELEMENT. This primitive again introduces an open variable

2.1 Embodied cognitive semantics using IRL

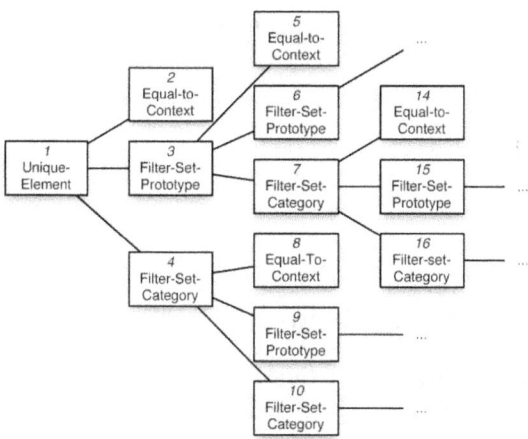

Figure 2.5: Example search tree during conceptualisation, starting from a library of four primitives: EQUAL-TO-CONTEXT, FILTER-SET-PROTOTYPE, FILTER-SET-CATEGORY and SELECT-ELEMENT. The number in each node of this tree reflects the order in which they are expanding, following a standard breadth-first heuristic. Node 5 corresponds to the network shown in Figure 2.1(b), node 14 to the one in Figure 2.2(b).

for its second argument which is of type entity-set. In the next expansion step of the search tree, three primitives are considered: EQUAL-TO-CONTEXT, FILTER-SET-PROTOTYPE and FILTER-SET-CATEGORY (nodes 2–4). Node 2 already contains a complete network and can be evaluated. If the context contains only one object this network succeeds and the conceptualisation process terminates. If this is not the case, nodes 3 and 4 will be further expanded as they again have an open variable of type entity-set. Both nodes can be expanded with the three primitive constraints that have a compatible target argument (nodes 5–10). If the topic can be identified using a single FILTER-SET-PROTOTYPE (node 5) or FILTER-SET-CATEGORY (node 8), conceptualisation has been completed. If not, the search process continues.

Earlier research on automatic programming in knowledge systems (see e.g. Barstow 1979) has shown that complex programs can only be derived fast enough if there is a set of powerful building blocks, and if the system progressively develops a library of rich subprograms and templates that are re-used or further extended, possibly aided by heuristics.

25

2 Formalisms for language systems and language strategies

We have followed a similar strategy that stores previous solutions (like nodes 2, 5, 8 and 14 in Figure 2.5) as a CHUNK which can later be re-used like any other primitive in the library. Some variables will be considered to be internal to the chunk but one variable will have the special state of target argument and the other external variables will become arguments to this chunk. Thanks to chunking, the search for a solution becomes progressively more efficient because more complex components are readily available.

2.1.5 Implementation of a primitive

Implementing a primitive involves the specification of its typed arguments and a set of revision specifications which specify how to deal with a particular pattern of open and bound arguments. In general, all open arguments will need to get bound simultaneously, but some patterns can be left unspecified so the primitive will get suspended until more slots are bound. An example of a semantic primitive is given below for FILTER-SET-PROTOTYPE.

2.1.5.1 *Semantic primitive* FILTER-SET-PROTOTYPE

description	Filters the entities in a source-set according to their similarity to a certain prototype. Constrains the filtered-set to contain all the elements from source-set that are similar to the prototype.
arguments	?filtered-set (of type entity-set)
	?source-set (of type entity-set)
	?prototype (of type prototype)
revision specs	?filtered-set ?source-set ?prototype: recomputes the filtering using the provided prototype and validates or rejects the bindings accordingly
	?filtered-set ?source-set: tries to find a stored prototype that could perform the correct filtering and binds it to ?prototype
	?source-set: computes the subsets of ?source-set that are similar to each stored prototype and returns pairwise bindings for ?prototype and ?filtered-set

2.2 Construction Grammar using FCG

2.2.1 Theoretical foundations

The main linguistic theory that we adopt is the one of Construction Grammar (Goldberg 1995; Goldberg 2003). This theory assumes that each unit of linguistic knowledge is a CONSTRUCTION which is specified both in the syntactic and the semantic domain. This contrasts sharply with a generative constituent structure grammar which focusses only on syntax, and in which semantics is supposed to be defined separately by translation rules (Chomsky 1957). Several variations of the theory of Contruction Grammar have been proposed, each focusing on a different linguistic aspect. Radical Construction Grammar argues that syntactical relations can not be studied autonomously and can only be understood in relation to the constructions they appear in (Croft 2001). Embodied Construction Grammar focusses on the semantic content of constructions, especially relating it to embodiment and sensorimotor experiences (Bergen & Chang 2005).

In this book I will use another variation of construction grammar as the main linguistic framework: Fluid Construction Grammar (FCG). FCG is a fully operational implementation of construction grammar. It is unification-based, similar to the widely used Head-Driven Phrase Structure Grammar (HPSG) frameworks (Pollard & Sag 1995). FCG is designed to support experiments in artificial language evolution and hence supports some unique features: reversibility and fluidity.

REVERSIBILITY refers to the idea that the same set of constructions can be used for both production and parsing. This feature does not only allow the agents to use the same formalism and set of constructions in both production and interpretation, but also has proven crucial to writing invention operators for grammar. Before uttering an utterance, a speaker can re-enter the utterance he is about to say and check whether potential ambiguities arise. This can be used as a trigger to add some additional grammar or syntax to the language (Steels & Wellens 2006).

Another feature that makes FCG suitable for experiments in artificial language evolution is its FLUIDITY, which states that agents will produce and parse as much information as possible, even if their linguistic knowledge is incomplete or conflicting. Incomplete knowledge might lead to the invention of a new construction in which the semantic information that could not be produced is associated with the syntactic information that could not be parsed. Conflicting knowledge might lead to multiple hypotheses about how to produce a certain meaning or how to parse a certain utterance.

2 Formalisms for language systems and language strategies

2.2.2 Language processing

During language processing, a LINGUISTIC STRUCTURE is being built up by applying a series of rules to it. The application process is organised as a search process in which each node consists of the linguistic structure so far and the children of each node are the result of applying a rule to the linguistic structure it contains. When more than one rule could apply or a rule could apply in more than one way, this results in a split in the application tree. This could for example occur when there are some homonyms or synonyms in the linguistic knowledge of the agent. Processing typically happens in a depth-first fashion and continues until no rule could be applied to the structure built up so far. An additional test might be provided to check whether this structure is satisfactory. Heuristics could be used to favour one branch over the other. An example of an application tree is shown in Figure 2.6.

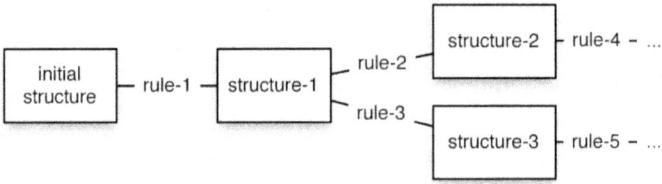

Figure 2.6: Typical language processing in FCG is organised as a search process. A linguistic structure is being built up by applying a series of rules to it. When two (conflicting) rules could apply to the same structure, this leads to a split in the application tree.

2.2.3 Coupled feature structures

The linguistic structure that is being built up is represented as COUPLED FEATURE STRUCTURES. Each coupled feature structure consists of two feature structures or POLES: one is defined in the semantic domain and the other in the syntactic domain. Each feature structure consists of a list of units, which are typically reflected in both poles. Each unit consists of a list of feature-value pairs which represent linguistic information. Special features, sem-subunits in the semantic pole and syn-subunits, allow to specify hierarchical relations between units to construct treelike relations between units.

2.2 Construction Grammar using FCG

FCG is open-ended to the features it can handle, but the features that are typically used are: meaning, referent and sem-cat in the semantic pole and form and syn-cat in the syntactic pole. The meaning feature refers to the conceptual meaning of a certain unit, which can be expressed in any formalism, including predicate logic or a semantic network in IRL. The referent is typically represented as a unique variable which is bound to the (physical) entity that a unit (including all its subunits) refers to. The form feature contains all possible form constraints, such as particular strings or word-order constraints between its subunits. The syn- and sem-cat are categories, either in the semantic or syntactic domain, that allow other rules to specify which units to select for.

An example of a simplified linguistic structure for an utterance like *le ballon* is shown in Figure 2.7 and its bracketed notation is shown below. The semantic pole is shown on the left and the syntactic pole on the right to show the structural similarity between both poles.

——————————— Example linguistic structure for "le ballon" ———————————
```
((top-unit                            ((top-unit
  (sem-subunits (det-np-unit)))         (syn-subunits (det-np-unit))
 (det-np-unit                          (det-np-unit
  (sem-subunits                         (syn-subunits
   (ballon-unit le-unit))                (ballon-unit le-unit))
  (referent x)                          (form ((meets le-unit ballon-unit)))
  (meaning ((grounded x)))              (syn-cat
  (sem-cat (object)))                    (determined-nounphrase)))
 (le-unit                              (le-unit
  (referent x)                          (form
  (meaning ((unique x)))                 ((string le-unit "le")))
  (sem-cat (selector)))                 (syn-cat (determiner)))
 (ballon-unit                          (ballon-unit
  (referent x)                          (form
  (meaning ((ball x)))                   ((string ballon-unit "ballon")))
  (sem-cat (prototype))))               (syn-cat (noun))))
```

2.2.4 Application of a construction

Now that we know how a linguistic structure is represented in FCG, we can turn to the application of a construction to build up such a structure. Like a linguistic structure, a construction is also represented as a coupled-feature structure. The semantic pole of a construction specifies how meaning has to be built up in parsing or decomposed in production, and the syntactic pole how the form has to be analysed in parsing or built in production. A construction also typically contains more variables as it should be applicable to a wide range of instantiated linguistic structures.

2 Formalisms for language systems and language strategies

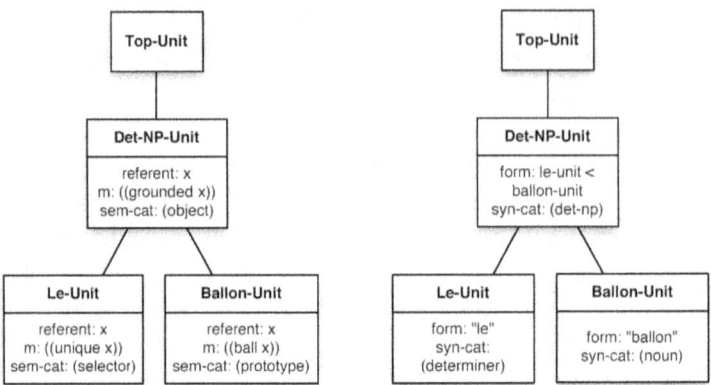

Figure 2.7: A graphical representation of the linguistic structure for *le ballon*. The semantic pole is shown on the left, the syntactic pole on the right. Both poles are structurally very similar, but only contain features that are relevant in their domain.

A construction is applied in three steps: a MATCHING PHASE, a FIRST MERGING PHASE and a SECOND MERGING PHASE. In general, the matching phase checks whether the rule is applicable and the two merging phases add new information to the linguistic structure that is being built up. Although the matching phase is the most strict one, all other phases can block the application of a rule if conflicting information would already be present in the current structure. More details on how matching and merging is exactly implemented can be found in a background article (Steels & De Beule 2006).

In production, it is the syntactic pole that is matched to the syntactic pole of the current structure; in interpretation it is the semantic pole that is matched to the current semantic pole. When the matching phase has been successful, both poles of the rule are merged into the current structure. The application of a rule is illustrated in Figure 2.8.

2.2.5 Structure building

The merging phases during the application of a construction can be used to add new features to a unit or to add new values to a particular feature of a particular unit, but more powerful structure building operations are also possible. These

2.2 Construction Grammar using FCG

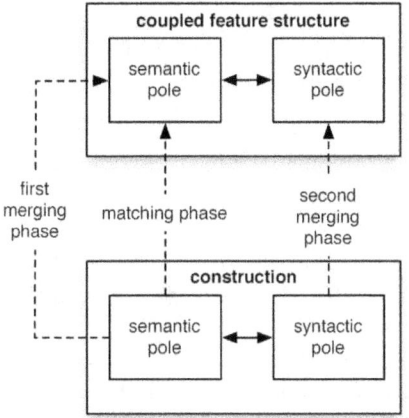 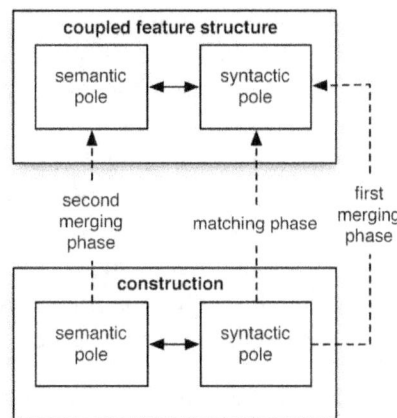

Figure 2.8: Rule application in FCG. Applying a rule consists of three phases: a matching phase and two merging phases. In production (left), the semantic pole is matched to check whether a rule is applicable. In interpretation (right), it is the syntactic pole that is matched. When the matching phase has been successful, both poles are merged into the coupled feature structure.

operations can be used to add new units to the structure, to change the hierarchy relations between units and to move feature-value pairs from one unit to another. All these operations are achieved through two operators: the J-operator (De Beule & Steels 2005) and the TAG-operator. The syntax of these operators is shown below.

─────────────── Syntax of the TAG-Operator ───────────────
```
(?unit
  (TAG ?tag-variable (feature-name feature-value)))
```

─────────────── Syntax of the J-operator ───────────────
```
((J ?focus-unit ?parent-unit (?child-unit-1 ... ?child-unit-n))
 ?tag-variable-1
 ...
 ?tag-variable-n
 (feature-name-1 feature-value-1)
 ...
 (feature-name-n feature-value-n))
```

2 Formalisms for language systems and language strategies

Units that are marked by the J-operator, or J-UNITS for short, are ignored in the matching phase, but receive special treatment during the merging phase. The TAG-operator allows a construction to bind a certain variable, ?tag-variable, to a certain feature-value pair. Whenever this variable appears inside a J-unit of the same rule, the bound feature-value pair will be moved to this J-unit. The special treatment of a J-unit in the merging phase is as follows:

1. If ?focus-unit is bound to a unit-name in the current structure, it will consider this unit to be in focus; if this variable is unbound, a new unit is created that will be in focus of this J-unit.

2. The focus-unit will become a subunit of ?parent-unit and the optional ?child-units will become children of the focus-unit.

3. The listed feature-value pairs will be merged into to the focus-unit.

4. The feature-value pairs that are bound to the ?tag-variables will be moved from their original unit to the focus-unit.

2.2.6 Linking through variable equalities

Once relations between several entities can be expressed in language, hearers face an additional problem in figuring out what these relations are. This is typically considered to be conveyed through grammar. For example in a sentence like *Jack hits Jill* English grammar clearly conveys it is Jack who is the agent and Jill the unfortunate recipient of the event, unlike the sentence *Jill hits Jack* in which the roles are reversed. Another example would be *the big block and the red ball* in which the hearer would need to figure out it is the block which is big and the ball which is red. This problem has been identified as the linking problem (Steels, De Beule & Neubauer 2005).

In FCG this problem has been solved by first assuming that variables introduced by different rules are different, but can be made equal during the application of other grammatical rules. Let us consider the phrase *red ball* and assume the meaning is represented in predicate logic. In parsing, the lexical constructions would introduce two predicates, "red(?x)" and "ball(?y)", each introducing a different variable. Another grammatical construction, which specifies that all predicates referred to by adjectives and nouns that are part of the same noun phrase should share the same variable, will make these variables equal. The application of this rule transforms the interpreted meaning in "red(?x)" and "ball(?x)" and hence solves the linking problem for this small example.

2.2 Construction Grammar using FCG

2.2.7 Application of an example construction

I will now show the application of an example Noun-Adjective-construction in interpretation. It illustrates both the structure building operators and the linking problem. It will search for two units, one of syntactical category "noun" and the other of syntactical category "adjective" that occur next to each other in the utterance parsed so far. When it has found two such units, it introduces an intermediary unit and makes the variables of the predicates in these two units equal through the referents of their units. The coupled feature structure before and after application of the construction is shown in Figure 2.9.

I will now step through the rule application of the rule in more detail. In interpretation the utterance is de-rendered into a set of form constraints: a set of strings, one for each word, and a set of *meets* constraints between each consecutive pair of words. An example for *le ballon rouge* is given in the initial structure below. Note that the semantic pole and syntactic pole are now shown under each other and separated by a double arrow.

─────────────────────── Initial Structure ───────────────────────
```
((top-unit))
<-->
((top-unit
  (form
    ((string le-unit "le")
     (string ballon-unit "ballon")
     (string rouge-unit "rouge")
     (meets le-unit ballon-unit)
     (meets ballon-unit rouge-unit)))))
```
───

Next the lexical constructions apply, which introduce for each string a different unit (using the J-operator), which on the semantic side introduces the corresponding meaning predicate together with their referent and semantical category and on the syntactic side introduces the appropriate syntactical categories. The coupled feature structure after application of lexical constructions is shown below in bracketed notation and in Figure 2.9 (top).

──────── Structure before application of the Noun-Adjective construction ────────
```
((top-unit
  (sem-subunits (rouge-unit le-unit ballon-unit)))
 (rouge-unit
  (meaning ((red ?x)))
  (referent ?x)
  (sem-cat ((pom category))))
 (ballon-unit
  (meaning ((ball ?y)))
```

2 Formalisms for language systems and language strategies

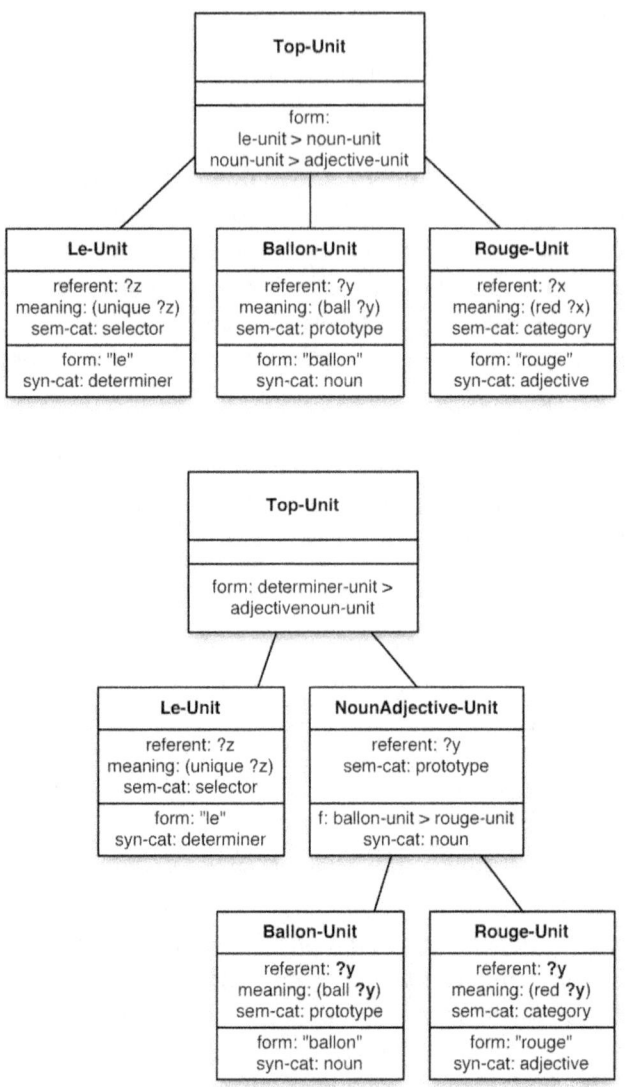

Figure 2.9: Coupled feature structures before (top) and after (bottom) the application of the Noun-Adjective construction in interpretation. It introduces a new unit which combines a Noun and an Adjective unit and makes the variables of their predicates equal through their referents. The coupled feature structures are now mapped on one structure which both contains semantic and syntactic information.

2.2 Construction Grammar using FCG

```
    (referent ?y)
    (sem-cat ((pom prototype))))
   (le-unit
    (meaning ((unique ?z)))
    (referent ?z)
    (sem-cat ((pom selector)))))
<-->
 ((top-unit
   (syn-subunits (rouge-unit le-unit ballon-unit))
   (form
    ((meets ballon-unit rouge-unit)
     (meets le-unit ballon-unit))))
  (rouge-unit
   (form ((string rouge-unit "rouge")))
   (syn-cat ((pos adjective))))
  (le-unit
   (form ((string le-unit "le")))
   (syn-cat ((pos determiner))))
  (ballon-unit
   (form ((string ballon-unit "ballon")))
   (syn-cat ((pos noun)))))
```

We are now ready to apply the Noun-Adjective construction which is shown below. The first phase is the matching phase and as we are in interpretation, this means the syntactic pole of the construction will be matched against the syntactic pole of the current coupled feature structure, which succeeds. There is only one adjective-unit and one noun-unit, so this results one set of possible bindings: ((?parent-unit . top-unit) (?noun-unit . ballon-unit) (?adjective-unit . rouge-unit)).

Matching succeeded, so we can now continue to the first merge phase, in which the syntactic pole of the construction is merged into the current feature structure. The syntactic pole contains only one J-unit which will now be applied. As there is no binding for ?adj-noun-unit yet, it will create a new unit that will be a child of ?parent-unit (which in this application will be top-unit as can be seen in the bindings of the unification phase) and which will have two children: ballon-unit and rouge-unit. The feature-value pairs specified in the J-unit, namely the syntactical category noun, will be added to this unit. Finally the tag-variable ?form will be handled, which moves the meets constraint between the ballon-unit and the rouge-unit from top-unit to the newly created unit.

―――――――――――――― The Noun-Adjective construction ――――――――――――――

```
((?parent-unit
  (sem-subunits (== ?noun-unit ?adjective-unit)))
 (?noun-unit
```

2 Formalisms for language systems and language strategies

```
   (referent ?x)
   (sem-cat (==1 (pom prototype))))
  (?adjective-unit
   (referent ?x)
   (sem-cat (==1 (pom category))))
  ((J ?adj-noun-unit ?parent-unit (?noun-unit ?adjective-unit))
   (referent ?x)
   (sem-cat (==1 (pom prototype)))))
<-->
((?parent-unit
   (syn-subunits (== ?noun-unit ?adjective-unit))
   (tag
    ?form
    (form (== (meets ?noun-unit ?adjective-unit)))))
  (?noun-unit
   (syn-cat (==1 (pos noun))))
  (?adjective-unit
   (syn-cat (==1 (pos adjective))))
  ((J ?adj-noun-unit ?parent-unit (?noun-unit ?adjective-unit))
   ?form
   (syn-cat (==1 (pos noun)))))
```

In the final merging phase, the semantic pole of the construction is merged into the semantic pole of the current feature structure. Next to creating a new unit similar to the unit created in the syntactic pole, it ensures the variables of the predicates for ball and red will be made equal. In the current structure they are available as the referent of the `ballon-unit` and the `rouge-unit`, which are equal in the `?adjective-unit` and the `?noun-unit` of the Noun-Adjective construction. The merging phase will ensure that these variables are equalised in the resulting feature structure, which is shown below and in Figure 2.9 (bottom).

——————————— Structure after application in interpretation ———————————

```
((top-unit
  (sem-subunits (noun-adj-unit le-unit)))
 (noun-adj-unit
  (sem-subunits (rouge-unit ballon-unit))
  (referent ?y)
  (sem-cat ((pom prototype))))
 (le-unit
  (meaning ((unique ?z)))
  (referent ?z)
  (sem-cat ((pom selector))))
 (ballon-unit
  (meaning ((ball ?y)))
  (sem-cat ((pom prototype)))
  (referent ?y))
```

2.2 Construction Grammar using FCG

```
 (rouge-unit
  (meaning ((red ?y)))
  (sem-cat ((pom category)))
  (referent ?y)))
<-->
((top-unit
  (syn-subunits (noun-adj-unit le-unit))
  (form ((meets le-unit noun-adj-unit))))
 (noun-adj-unit
  (form ((meets ballon-unit rouge-unit)))
  (syn-subunits (rouge-unit ballon-unit))
  (syn-cat ((pos noun))))
 (rouge-unit
  (form ((string rouge-unit "rouge")))
  (syn-cat ((pos adjective))))
 (le-unit
  (form ((string le-unit "le")))
  (syn-cat ((pos determiner))))
 (ballon-unit
  (form ((string ballon-unit "ballon")))
  (syn-cat ((pos noun)))))
```

Part II

Language strategies for colour

Introduction

In the first part of this book, I will introduce the semantic and syntactic templates of various language strategies that have been introduced in §1.1. For each of these strategies, I will implement a predefined language system that will allow me to evaluate the performance of the proposed semantic and syntactic templates. The strategies will be compared to human language systems using NAMING BENCHMARKS, and these strategies will be compared to each other in a BASELINE EXPERIMENT.

A compositional approach is applied to both semantic and syntactic templates. This implies that parts of the templates will be shared by various strategies. The semantic templates will be represented by semantic constraint networks (see §2.1.2). These networks consist of semantic primitives which will be explained in more detail for each strategy. The syntactic templates will be presented as a general approach to expressing these semantic networks in language. These templates will be illustrated by giving examples of coupled feature structures (see §2.2.3), which allow to express the semantic constraint networks in language. Example constructions are described that can build up these coupled feature structures (Bleys 2006; Steels & Bleys 2007; Bleys 2008).

Natural language systems are implemented by providing actual ontologies and linguistic inventories to express these ontologies in language. Concerning the basic colour strategy, this boils down to providing agents with an ontology of categories that are reported in literature, the lexical rules for that ontology, and the grammatical rules to express the instantiated semantic template.

The implementation of natural language systems will allow for the evaluation of the proposed templates. A first evaluation method is to name a set of colour samples whose names have been reported in literature in a naming benchmark. Comparing the names produced by the strategy to the expected names gives a rough idea of how well the templates reflect the natural system. A second evaluation method is a baseline experiment in which agents, equipped with the implementation of the natural language system, involve in colour naming games (see §1.2.1). This allows for a comparison of the performance of the templates across language strategies.

3 Basic colour strategy

The basic colour strategy is by far the most studied language strategy for the domain for colour. It stipulates that a colour should be described using a single colour term that refers to a single colour category. At the semantic level it specifies how the categorisation process should be organised; at the syntactic level it specifies how these categories should be expressed in language. As this strategy has been studied extensively in the domain of artificial language modelling, it allows me to establish a solid common base before moving on to the other strategies.

3.1 Related research

3.1.1 Colour categories

Colour categories are considered to be prototypical in nature (Rosch 1973). One colour sample, the PROTOTYPE, is considered to be the best example of a certain category and membership to this category is graded: some samples are considered to be better members of a certain category than others. A bluish shade of green is for example considered to be a worse example of the category of green than the natural colour of grass.

Part of the research in colour cognition aims at locating the typical member of each colour category of the category systems in different natural languages, such as Spanish (Lillo et al. 2007), English (Boynton & Olson 1987; Sturges & Whitfield 1995) and Russian (Safuanova & Korzh 2007). These experiments typically involve naming a set of individual colour samples.

In colour literature, the distinction is made between the FOCUS (the colour sample which is named fastest) and the CENTROID (the colour central to all colours that belong to the category) of a colour category. Interestingly, a discrepancy exists between the locations of these two (Sturges & Whitfield 1995). Some of the experiments also reported on CONSENSUS SAMPLES, which are samples that were consistently named by all participants in the experiment. The consensus samples for English (Sturges & Whitfield 1995) are shown in Figure 3.1.

3 Basic colour strategy

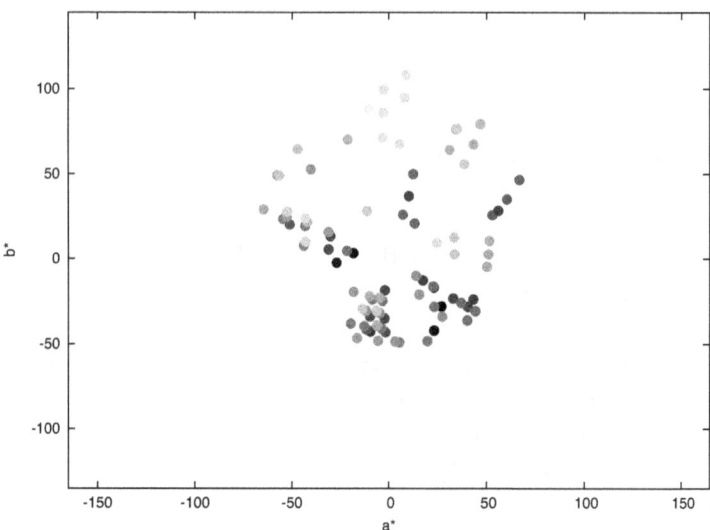

Figure 3.1: The consensus chips (all samples that were consistently named by all participants) for English (Sturges & Whitfield 1995)

3.1.2 Models

The basic colour strategy has received attention within the field of artificial language evolution. Most of these studies adhere to the language game paradigm and use the colour naming game (see §1.2.1) to study how a population of agents could coordinate their own colour category system. Although there seems to be a high coherence in the models that have been proposed for this game, different implementation choices have been made. Colour categories were represented either as radial basis function networks (Steels & Belpaeme 2005), single points in a three dimensional conceptual space (Belpaeme & Bleys 2005b; 2007) or a set of points sharing the same linguistic label in a one dimensional conceptual space (Puglisi, Baronchelli & Loreto 2008; Baronchelli et al. 2010). A comparison between the different implementations of the basic colour strategy is shown in Table 3.1.

Table 3.1: Comparison of the different models for the basic colour strategy

	Steels & Belpaeme (2005)	Belpaeme & Bleys (2005b)	Puglisi, Baronchelli & Loreto (2008)	Bleys & Steels (2009)
CONCEPTUAL- ISATION	most similar; winner-takes-all; discriminatory	most similar; winner-takes-all; discriminatory	most similar; winner-takes-all; discriminatory	most similar; winner-takes-all; non-discriminatory
PRODUCTION	highest associative score	highest associative score	last successful or last created	one-on-one mapping
PARSING	highest associative score	highest associative score	union of all categories that share label	one-on-one mapping
INTER- PRETATION	most similar; non-discriminatory	most similar; non-discriminatory	random choice	most similar; non-discriminatory

3.2 Semantic template

In previous models of the colour naming game (Steels & Belpaeme 2005; Belpaeme & Bleys 2005b; Puglisi, Baronchelli & Loreto 2008) the speaker selected the category that was most similar to the topic entity. Additionally this category needed to be discriminatory in the current context: no other entity in the context should be categorised as belonging to the same category as the topic. In general, the hearer was more lenient: it selected the entity that was most similar to the interpreted category, regardless of whether it would actually be classified as the interpreted category and whether other entities would be classified as the same category. So for example, the hearer would select an orange entity when interpreting the yellow colour category even if it would know a colour category for orange. Previous research has shown the negative impact of applying the discriminatory criterion as a hearer, especially when the category systems of the agents are not aligned (Belpaeme & Bleys 2007).

The semantics I propose in this book adhere to the main ideas proposed by the previous models, but with a minor difference. The speaker still selects the category that is most similar to the topic entity and the hearer will point to the entity that is most similar to the interpreted category. The speaker however is a bit more lenient as it does not apply the discriminatory criterion. This will result in a higher level of communicative success, as the speaker will now be able to successfully name entities that are most similar to a category, even if this category is not discriminatory. For example, if the context contains two green colour samples, the sample that is most similar to the green colour category can still be successfully named.

3 Basic colour strategy

The semantic template of the basic colour strategy can be summarised in three steps: profiling, categorisation and selection. These processes are represented separately in semantics as this will enhance possible re-use of these primitives in other strategies.

3.2.1 Profiling

During the categorisation process, some dimensions of the colour domain might have a bigger impact than others (see §1.1.1). In order to represent this in semantics, I need primitives that will *profile*, or highlight, some dimensions of a particular colour sample before the categorisation process. For each strategy reported in the literature review, I define a different primitive.

This profiling could also instruct the vision system of a robotic agent to process the colour information of the objects. This could defer the computation of the different features of the objects until they become absolutely necessary.

3.2.2 Categorisation based on colour

As the main psychological theory for categorisation, I have chosen to follow the prototype-based approach to colour categories as advocated by Rosch (1973). In this theory, a category is defined by its prototype. This prototype serves as the best sample of a category and is compared to a particular colour sample to determine the graded membership of this sample to this category.

Both colour samples and prototypes of colour categories are represented in the CIE $L^*a^*b^*$ (see §A.2) colour space. This colour space turned out to be the best space in a related model of colour naming (Lammens 1994) and is *equidistant*: Euclidean distance between colours represented in this space reflects psychological differences as perceived by humans.

Similarity can thus be expressed as an exponentially decaying function (Shepard 1987; Gärdenfors 2004) of the weighted distance between the prototype of a colour category and a colour sample (as shown in equation 3.1). In this function, c is a sensitivity parameter. As in the current simulations this parameter is identical for all colour categories, the actual value of this parameter does not result in any qualitatively different results. It is possible to imagine simulations in which the sensitivity parameter is different for each colour category, so that some categories cover a relatively larger area of the colour space than others. The distance is weighted in each dimension by the product of the current profile of the entity and the weights of the prototype of the colour category. The weights of a prototype reflect the importance of each dimension for that category. Some categories, such as the basic colour categories, are defined in all dimensions, whereas others are only defined in some dimensions (such as the lightness dimension for the categories for light and dark). The exact equation is shown in Equation 3.2.

$$s(i,j) = e^{-cd_w(i,j)} \tag{3.1}$$

$$d_w(x,y) = \sqrt{\sum_{k=1}^{n} w_{x_k} w_{y_k} (x_k - y_k)^2} \tag{3.2}$$

3.2.3 Selection based on activation

An activation value is assigned to each entity, which reflects the similarity of that entity to the category that was used during the categorisation process. The more similar the entity was to the category, the higher the activation will be. The entity with the highest activation will be selected as the outcome of the complete process.

3.2.4 Semantic constraint network

The semantic constraint network for the basic colour strategy is shown in Figure 3.2. The EQUAL-TO-CONTEXT primitive introduces all entities in the sensory context of the agent. The PROFILE-COLOUR-DIMENSIONS primitive sets the focus to each entity in the context based on the dimension profiler that is bound to its third slot. The FILTER-BY-COLOUR-LENIENT primitive performs the categorisation process based on the colour categories known to the agent and assigns an activation score of the remaining entities. Finally, SELECT-MOST-ACTIVATED selects the entity with the highest activation from the set of activated entities.

Whether the FILTER-BY-COLOUR-LENIENT primitive selects a subset of entities from its input set depends on whether the argument for its colour category is already bound. During conceptualisation, the argument for the colour category will typically be unbound and hence the primitive will divide the entities of the context in different subsets. In interpretation, however, the colour category is already known and will be used to set the activation of all the entities in the context.

3 Basic colour strategy

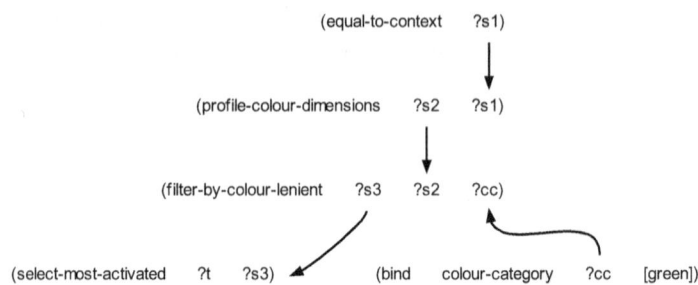

Figure 3.2: The semantic constraint network for the basic colour strategy. The PROFILE-COLOUR-DIMENSIONS primitive profiles some dimensions in the context. FILTER-BY-COLOUR-LENIENT performs the the categorisation process and assigns activation values to the entities. The SELECT-MOST-ACTIVATED primitive will select the entity with the highest activation.

3.2.5 Semantic primitives

3.2.5.1 Semantic primitive EQUAL-TO-CONTEXT

description	Retrieves all entities from the sensory context and collects them in an entity set.
arguments	?context (of type entity-set)
revision specs	∅: collects all entities in the sensory context in an entity set and binds it to ?context

3.2.5.2 Semantic primitive PROFILE-COLOUR-DIMENSIONS

description	Profiles the colour dimensions of the entities in an entity set.
arguments	?profiled-set (of type entity-set) ?source-set (of type entity-set)
revision specs	?source-set: profiles all colour dimensions of the entities in the entity set and binds the resulting entity-set to ?profiled-set

note	Other variants of this primitive which profile other dimensions are defined as well. Profile-Brightness-Dimension profiles only in the L^* dimension and Profile-Brightness-and-Red-Green-Dimensions profiles both the L^* and a^* dimension.

3.2.5.3 *Semantic primitive* Filter-by-Colour-Lenient

description	Applies a colour category to a set of entities. When the colour category is known, this primitive sets the activation of each entity in the set to the similarity between the entity and the category. When the colour category is unknown, it categorises the entities in the set to the category that is most similar to it.
arguments	?categorised-set (of type entity-set) ?source-set (of type entity-set) ?colour-category (of type colour-category)
revision specs	?source-set ?colour-category: sets the activation of the entities in the source set to the similarity to the colour category and binds the resulting entity-set to ?categorised-set ?source-set: categorises each entity in the source set to the category that is most similar to it and returns pairwise bindings for ?colour-category and ?categorised-set

3.2.5.4 *Semantic primitive* Select-Most-Activated

description	Selects the entity from an entity-set that has the highest activation.
arguments	?entity (of type entity) ?entity-set (of type entity-set)
revision specs	?entity-set: selects the entity from the entity-set with the highest activation and binds it to ?entity

3.3 Syntactic templates

The next question I have to address is how these semantic constraint networks will be expressed in a serial utterance. When the hearer parses this utterance, it should be able to fully reconstruct the constraint network that the speaker wanted to transfer.

3 Basic colour strategy

The main approach adopted to express semantic networks in language is outlined as follows. The semantic network is divided in three layers of units: (a) entity units containing the semantic entities, (b) functional units which make direct use of such a semantic entity and (c) contextual units which contain any remaining operations of the semantic constraint network that do not make direct use of any semantic entity. This division is illustrated in Figure 3.3.

As a rule of thumb, the reader can assume that each rule introduces one new unit in the linguistic structure. In production, syntactic information is added to the structure: which words will be used to express certain semantic entities, to which syntactic category does each unit belong and which word order should be applied when this tree is transformed into an utterance. During interpretation, each word in the utterance introduces a new semantic entity. Based on the lexical categories of these entities, the hearer is able to add the layer of functional units. Finally, the information on the word order constraints augmented with the information of the syntactic categories allows the agent to select the right contextual rule. This rule adds extra primitive constraints to the network, but more importantly also connects all primitive constraints by introducing variable equalities (for example between the first argument of Filter-by-Colour-Lenient and the second argument of Select-Most-Activated) in the network shown in Figure 3.2.

The syntactic templates specify the rules to express a semantic network in a serial utterance. I will now discuss each step in more detail. Three templates (1.1 to 1.3) take care of creating the rules that ensure the default division in three layers of units: (a) entity units containing the semantic entities, (b) functional units which contain primitives that make direct use of such a semantic entity and (c) contextual units which contain any other primitives that do not make direct use of semantic entities.

3.3.1 Syntactic template 1.1: Semantic entities

A semantic entity is an entity from the ontology used by a primitive, such as a category, a prototype, a relation, etc. They have an identifier which is created when the entity itself is constructed and which can be used in a lexical rule. In parsing, the resulting rule will also introduce a new variable that will allow the entity to be used by other primitives in the network. To ensure this linking is possible, the variable needs to be part of the link feature of that unit.

An example of a lexical rule for the colour category yellow is given below. The main association is between the category for yellow and the string "yellow". Additionally, the rule adds a link feature to the semantic side that enables other units

3.3 *Syntactic templates*

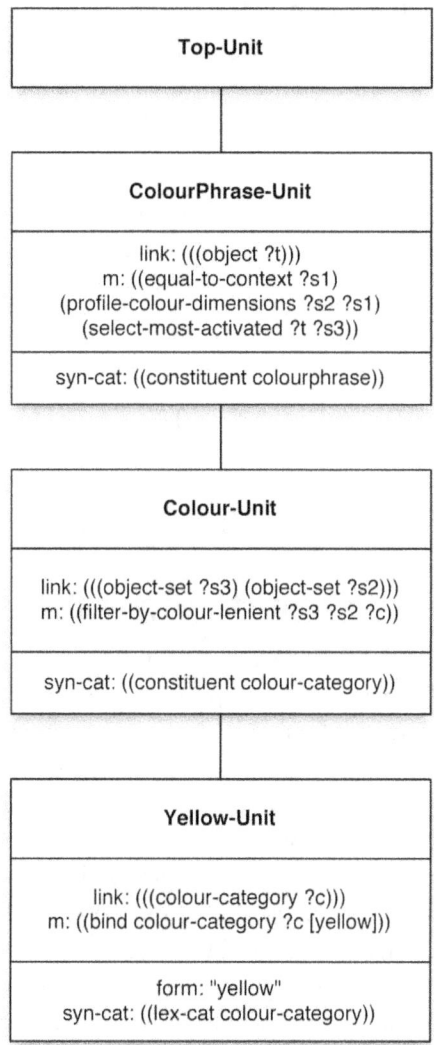

Figure 3.3: Example linguistic structure for colour-network 1. The semantic constraint network is divided over three layers of units: one for the semantic entity [yellow], one for the functional primitive FILTER-BY-COLOUR-LENIENT and one contextual unit for all other primitives of the semantic constraint network. The link feature links the variables for the entities and entity-set. Similarly, the c-link feature passes the variables for colour categories and sets of colour categories.

3 Basic colour strategy

to incorporate this semantic entity in the rest of the semantic network. This rule is responsible for introducing the Yellow-Unit in Figure 3.3 both in production and in parsing.

──────────────── Entity rule for yellow ────────────────
```
((?top-unit
  (tag ?meaning
       (meaning ((bind colour-category ?c [yellow]))))))
 ((J ?yellow-unit ?top-unit)
  ?meaning
  (link (((colour-category ?c))))))
<-->
((?top-unit
  (tag ?form
       (form ((string ?yellow-unit "yellow")))))
 ((J ?yellow-unit ?top-unit)
  ?form
  (syn-cat ((lex-cat colour-category))))))
```

3.3.2 Syntactic template 1.2: Functional primitives

Functional units, created by functional rules, handle the primitives in a semantic network that directly use a semantic entity. For each such primitive a separate functional rule is created. The template to express such primitives has a subunit for each of its arguments. The functional unit that will be introduced by this rule contains the functional primitive that needs to be covered. As the other arguments of the primitive are not provided by the entity unit, these arguments become available in the link of the new functional unit. This link ensures the encapsulated primitive can be incorporated in a larger semantic network.

An example of such a rule for the FILTER-BY-COLOUR-LENIENT primitive is given below. It uses a colour-category $?c$, for example the prototype for yellow, from the set of colour categories cs to filter some elements from a source set $?s2$ to yield a subset of blocks $?s1$. It associates this primitive to a newly invented syntactic constituent category (constituent colour-category). The variable of the colour category is linked in through the link feature specified in the subunit. The new unit will have the two object-sets, $?s1$ and $?s2$, as values for the link feature as these yet need to be covered by another rule. The resulting rule is shown below.

──────────── Functional rule for Filter-by-Colour-Lenient ────────────
```
((?top-unit
  (sem-subunits (?colour-category-unit))
  (tag ?meaning
```

3.3 Syntactic templates

```
       (meaning ((filter-by-colour-lenient ?s3 ?s2 ?c)))))
 (?colour-category-unit
   (link (((colour-category ?c)))))
 ((J ?filter-by-colour-unit ?top-unit (?colour-category-unit))
   ?meaning
   (link (((entity-set ?s3) (entity-set ?s2))))))
<-->
((?top-unit
   (syn-subunits (?colour-category-unit)))
 (?colour-category-unit
   (syn-cat ((lex-cat colour-category))))
 ((J ?filter-by-colour-unit ?top-unit (?colour-category-unit))
   (syn-cat ((constituent colour-category)))))
```

3.3.3 Syntactic template 1.3: Contextual primitives

The primitives that do not make direct use of semantic entities are grouped together in a contextual unit. This unit is introduced by the application of a contextual rule, which contains subunits for each of the functional primitives. It uses the link feature of each of its subunits to ensure the primitives will be incorporated in the primitives it contains. The unit that is introduced will have as link feature the target entity of the semantic constraint network it captures.

An example of such a rule for the contextual primitives of the semantic network shown in Figure 3.2 is given below. It encapsulates three primitives, EQUAL-TO-CONTEXT, PROFILE-COLOUR-DIMENSIONS and SELECT-MOST-ACTIVATED. It requires one subunit to be present in the structure which belongs to the syntactic category Constituent Colour-Category and which has a link feature of two object sets. In parsing, it will ensure the variables in these links are made equal to the variables of the semantic primitives it contains. The newly introduced unit will be of a newly invented syntactic category, Constituent ColourPhrase, and will have as link feature the first argument of the SELECT-MOST-ACTIVATED primitive.

─────────────── ColourPhrase rule for basic colour strategy ───────────────

```
((?top-unit
   (sem-subunits (?colour-unit))
   (tag ?meaning
        (meaning ((select-most-activated ?t ?s3)
                  (profile-colour-dimensions ?s2 ?s1)
                  (equal-to-context ?s1)))))
 (?colour-unit
   (link (((entity-set ?s3) (entity-set ?s2)))))
 ((J ?colourphrase-unit ?top-unit (?colour-unit))
   ?meaning
```

3 Basic colour strategy

```
(link (((colour-entity ?t))))))
<-->
((?top-unit
  (syn-subunits (?colour-unit)))
 (?colour-unit
  (syn-cat ((constituent colour-category))))
 ((J ?colourphrase-unit ?top-unit (?colour-unit))
  (syn-cat ((constituent colourphrase))))))
```

3.4 Baseline experiment

A first test whether the proposed templates are valid is provided by a naming benchmark. It involves naming all consensus chips for English (Sturges & Whitfield 1995) and verifying whether the resulting names correspond to those reported in the literature. This benchmark is only performed for the language system that is based on the centroids of English (Sturges & Whitfield 1995). The results are shown in Table 3.2. The benchmark reaches only around 83% success. This suggests that, although capable of accounting for more than three quarters of the consensus chips, the one-nearest neighbour classification algorithm might be too general to capture all the richness of human colour categories.

Table 3.2: Number of correctly named consensus samples broken down by category: white (WE), grey (GY), black (BK), green (GN), yellow (YW), blue (BL), red (RD), purple (PU), brown (BR), orange (OR) and pink (PK). The total number of consensus chips is shown on top.

WE	GY	BK	GN	YW	BL	RD	PU	BR	OR	PK	TOTAL
2	6	3	22	8	25	4	14	4	6	6	100
2	6	3	17	8	18	4	9	4	6	6	83

3.4.1 Measures of communicative success

The communicative success is the ratio of successful interactions in the last cs_n games. The communicative success has a maximum of 1 and minimum of 0. In all reported experiments the value of cs_n is set to 250.

3.4 Baseline experiment

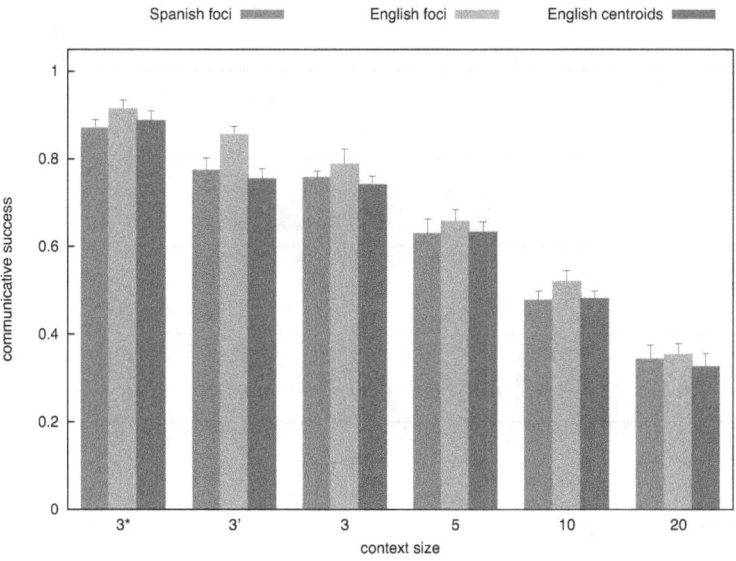

Figure 3.4: The baseline communicative success of three predefined language systems: one is based on the Spanish foci (Lillo et al. 2007) and the others are based on the foci and centroids of English (Sturges & Whitfield 1995). Baseline communicative success is inversely related to the context size increases. The context size for 3' is 3, but an additional constraint on the minimal interstimulus distance is imposed. Additionally, in 3* only the subset of Munsell chips that are faithfully reproducible are considered. These results are averaged over 8 runs.

3.4.2 Results

The communicative success of the baseline experiment is shown in Figure 3.4. The more samples in one context, the lower the corresponding communicative success. The language system based on the English foci seems to perform slightly better than the ones based on other language systems.

Imposing a minimal interstimulus distance of 50 in the CIE $L^*a^*b^*$ colour space (3' in Figure 3.4) does not appear to have a significant impact on the resulting communicative success, but the additional limitation to a particular subset of the Munsell chip does (3* in Figure 3.4).

The main reason why some interactions still fail is that some samples in a context could not be successfully discriminated because another sample in the

3 Basic colour strategy

context was more similar to the prototype of the category that the selected topic would belong to. For example, the sample to the right in the context shown in Figure 3.5, will not be successfully named as the middle sample is more similar to the prototype of the green colour category.

Figure 3.5: Example context in which the basic colour strategy fails. The sample to the right can not be successfully named as the middle sample is more similar to the prototype of the green colour category.

3.5 Conclusion

In this chapter I have shown how the semantic and syntactic templates of the basic colour strategy can be defined. I have proposed semantics that builds upon previous research, both in psychology and artificial language evolution, and have extended it to accommodate for several substrategies in which some dimensions of the colour domain are more relevant as accounted by documented language systems. I have proposed a mapping to language that encodes these semantics.

4 Graded membership strategy

Colour categories are assumed to be prototypical in nature (Rosch 1973), which implies that some colour samples are better examples of a category than others. Some languages allow the users to mark how well a particular sample represents the prototype. In English this marking is optional and achieved through the adverb *very* and the modifying *-ish* suffix, such as in the expression *greenish*. In Russian, the suffix *-ato* indicates a similar meaning (Safuanova & Korzh 2007). In other languages, such as Tarahumara, an indigenous language spoken in Northern Mexico, this marking is obligatory. This language has an elaborate system of modifiers that distinguishes three levels of membership: *-kame* which could be translated as 'very', *-name* which could be glossed as 'somewhat' and *-nanti* for the lowest degree of membership. An example of how this system is used for the Turahumara colour category for red: *Sitá-* is shown in Figure 4.1 (Burgress, Kempton & MacLaury 1983).

In this chapter, I will propose a compositional semantic template that is capable of modelling these observations. I will also introduce the grammatical syntactic templates that allow agents to express this strategy in language. I will use Tarahumara as the main guiding example.

4.1 Related research

Although most models within artificial language evolution and colour naming models represent the graded nature of membership of a colour sample to a colour category, almost none of them deploy syntax to express this membership. One exception is the colour naming model of Mojsilovic, which includes names for modifiers and different lightness values (Mojsilovic 2002; 2005). The semantics of this model, however, is quite limited as each compositional colour name is stored as a different prototype based on a dictionary of colour names compiled by the National Bureau of Standards (Kelly & Judd 1955). It is unclear how this model could be extended to allow for creative language use, for example when names are not explicitly listed in the dictionary.

4 Graded membership strategy

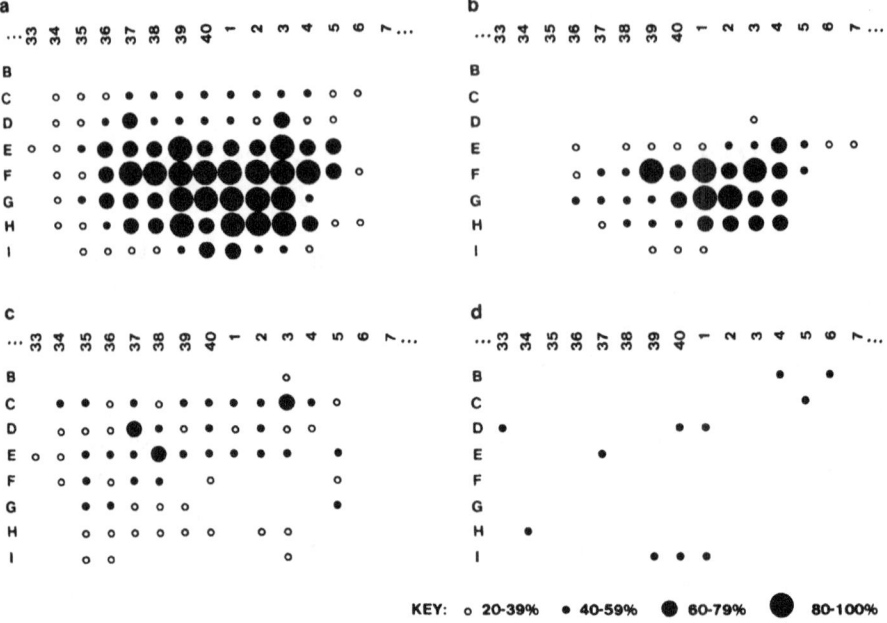

Figure 4.1: The use of modifiers to express graded membership in Tarahumara shown on the Munsell array. The bigger the circle, the more it represents a particular colour expression. (a) aggregate of all expressions using the *Sitá* root (b) *Sitákame* ('very red') (c) *Sitáname* ('somewhat red') (d) *Sitánanti* ('only slightly red'). Note how each modifier specifies a region that is further removed from the prototypical colour of *Sitá*. Figure from Burgress, Kempton & MacLaury (1983).

4.2 Semantic template

Degree modifiers make the degree of membership of a particular entity in the world to a category in the ontology of an agent explicit in language. They split the continuous domain of membership into more or less discrete categories. In order to propose semantics that capture these observations, I need to make two choices: how the membership function is computed and how the categorisation process based on this membership function is implemented.

The membership function corresponds to the similarity function introduced in §3.2.2. The similarity of the colour of an entity to a colour category maps directly on the membership function: the more similar the colour of entity to the prototype of the category, the higher the membership. The maximum value of the membership function is one (when the colour of the entity is exactly equal to the prototype of the category) and approaches zero when they are very dissimilar.

The MEMBERSHIP CATEGORIES are implemented as prototypical categories. Each category has a prototypical value of the membership and classification is organised following a standard nearest-neighbour algorithm. Each entity is assigned to the membership category that is most similar to it. Other approaches, such as discrimination trees (Steels 1996b), could have been chosen, but the prototype theory is sufficient to cover the main principles of the graded membership strategy.

This approach results in the definition of absolute ranges between a colour sample and colour category due to the properties of the membership function and how the membership categorisation process is organised. The membership function is only dependent on the category that is most similar to the sample and the membership categories are defined as prototypical values of this membership function. As a net result, a membership category defines an absolute range in distance between the colour sample and the colour category. A schematic representation of this approach is provided in Figure 4.2.

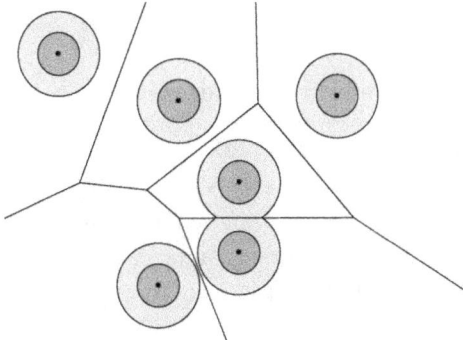

Figure 4.2: Schematic representation of the semantics of the graded membership. The categorisation based on colour categories results in a Voronoi tessellation of the conceptual space. The membership categories (marked in different shades of grey) define a fixed range starting from the prototype of the category.

The semantics of the graded membership strategy can be summarised as follows: first the entities are categorised as in the basic colour strategy. This process stores membership information in the entities as a side-effect. Unlike the basic colour strategy, not just the best member will be selected from this set, but the re-

4 Graded membership strategy

sulting set will be categorised again based on the membership information stored in the entities. This second categorisation process changes the activation stored in the entities. Selection will be based on this activation.

4.2.1 Profiling and categorisation based on colour

The categorisation process is similar to the one introduced for the basic colour strategy, except that this categorisation process is now more strict. Even in interpretation, it assigns each entity to the nearest known colour category. This is identical to the categorisation during conceptualisation.

This modification is based on the observation that whenever the graded membership strategy is used, the base category will be the category that is the most similar to the named sample. For example, a sample that is named "greenish" is still more similar to the prototype for green than to the prototype of brown.

Although strict interpretation is known to decrease the expected communicative success when categories are not aligned between individual language users (Belpaeme & Bleys 2007), it ensures the categorisation process applied by the speaker and hearer are symmetrical. This is especially useful when processes become dependent on each other. Asymmetrical processing might be another source of potential communicative failures.

4.2.2 Categorisation based on membership

Each membership category is represented by its most prototypical membership value. The membership value of each entity is compared to the membership value stored in the category. Each entity is assigned to the membership category that is most similar to it. More than one entity can be categorised as the same category. This categorisation process changes the activation in the entities.

4.2.3 Selection based on activation

This second categorisation process based on membership changes the activation stored in the entities. The entity with the highest activation will be selected as the outcome of the complete process.

4.2.4 Semantic constraint network

The semantic constraint network for the graded membership strategy is shown in Figure 4.3. The EQUAL-TO-CONTEXT and PROFILE-COLOUR-DIMENSIONS primitives are the same ones as introduced before. The FILTER-BY-COLOUR primitive

4.2 Semantic template

is similar to the FILTER-BY-COLOUR-LENIENT except that during interpretation it applies a strict categorisation as well. The FILTER-BY-MEMBERSHIP categorises the resulting sets based on the membership information stored by the FILTER-BY-COLOUR primitive. Finally, SELECT-MOST-ACTIVATED selects the entity with the highest activation.

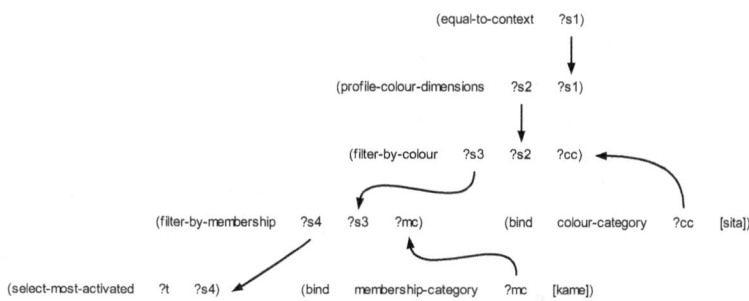

Figure 4.3: The semantic constraint network for the graded membership strategy, which is similar to the one of the basic colour strategy. The FILTER-BY-MEMBERSHIP now categorises the resulting sets further. SELECT-MOST-ACTIVATED selects the entity with the highest activation.

4.2.5 Semantic primitives

4.2.5.1 *Semantic primitive* FILTER-BY-COLOUR

description	Categorises each entity in a source set as the most similar colour category known to the agent. The membership of each entity is set to be the similarity to the category it belongs to.
slots	?filtered-set (of type entity-set) ?source-set (of type entity-set) ?colour-category (of type colour-category)
revision specs	?source-set: categorises each entity of source set and returns pairwise bindings for the remaining slots; categories to which no entities are assigned are ignored ?source-set ?category: computes the categorisation of the source set based on all colour categories known to the agent and when the resulting set for the provided colour category is not empty, it gets bound to ?filtered-set

4.2.5.2 Semantic primitive FILTER-BY-MEMBERSHIP

description	Categorises each entity in a source set as the most similar membership category known to the agent.
arguments	?filtered-set (of type entity-set)
	?source-set (of type entity-set)
	?membership-category (of type membership-category)
revision specs	?source-set: categorises each entity in the source set as one of the known membership categories and returns pair-wise bindings for membership-category and ?filtered-set
	?source-set ?membership-category: computes the categorisation of the source set based on all membership categories known to the agent and when the resulting set for the provided membership category is not empty, it gets bound to ?filtered-set

4.2.6 Alternative approaches to semantics

Several alternative approaches to the proposed semantics exist. One alternative that has been used in previous models is to model basic colour categories as one or more multidimensional "normalised" Gaussian functions (Lammens 1994; Steels & Belpaeme 2005). The similarity measure between a colour category and a colour sample is weighted by the inverse of the standard deviation in each dimension. This distance measure is also known as the Mahalanobis distance.

It might be tempting to model graded membership by modifying the standard deviation of a category: intensifiers such as *very* could be implemented as decreasing the standard deviation and diminutives like *slightly* could increase the standard deviation. This corresponds to the idea that intensified categories should be interpreted more strictly, which is reflected by a lower standard deviation. This however leads to the unwanted outcome that the diminutive will always be preferred among the three variants (intensifier, diminutive and unmodified) as it results in the lowest distance and hence the highest similarity to a particular colour sample. This is due to the Mahalanobis measure which divides the distance in each dimension by its standard deviation. The higher the standard deviation, the lower the distance. A different similarity or distance function would be needed to extend this approach to modifiers.

Another approach that has often been pursued for modelling categories is based on the fuzzy set theory (Kay & McDaniel 1978; Benavente, Vanrell & Baldrich 2008). Some features of language, including modifiers, have been studied using this approach (Hersh & Caramazza 1976). These studies suggested that the probability of the membership of an intensified category is a power of the membership of the unintensified category. This again reflects the intuitive idea that membership of an intensified category should decrease faster than membership of the original category, but fails to account for why intensified categories should be favoured over orginal categories for the best members of the fuzzy set.

4.3 Syntactic templates

The templates to express this network in language are in general similar to the one used for the basic colour strategy in §3.3: the semantic network is divided in three layers of units: (a) entity units containing the semantic entities, (b) functional units which make direct use of such a semantic entity and (c) contextual units which contain any remaining operations of the semantic constraint network that do not make direct use of any semantic entity. The main difference is that in order to express both the basic colour strategy and the graded membership strategy, an additional template can be used to allow the re-use of the contextual rule introduced for the basic colour strategy.

The linguistic structure for *sita-kame* is shown in Figure 4.4. Besides introducing the colour category for *sita*, the lexicon rules now also introduce the membership category for *kame*. Functional rules take care of the FILTER-BY-COLOUR and FILTER-BY-MEMBERSHIP primitives. All other parts of the semantic network are grouped in a contextual rule, which also ensures that the two functional primitives are linked into the other primitives of the network.

4.3.1 Syntactic template 1.1: Semantic entities

The entity rules for membership categories are very similar to the one I introduced in the previous chapter for colour categories. During parsing it will introduce the membership category. In production, it will introduce the string that is associated with this category. In both modes a new unit is introduced that encapsulates this information. On the semantic side, the *link* feature will allow other rules to incorporate the membership category in the semantic network during parsing.

―――――――――――――――――――― Entity rule for kame ――――――――――――――――――――
```
((?top-unit
  (tag ?meaning
       (meaning ((bind membership-category ?c [kame])))))
 ((J ?kame-unit ?top-unit)
```

4 Graded membership strategy

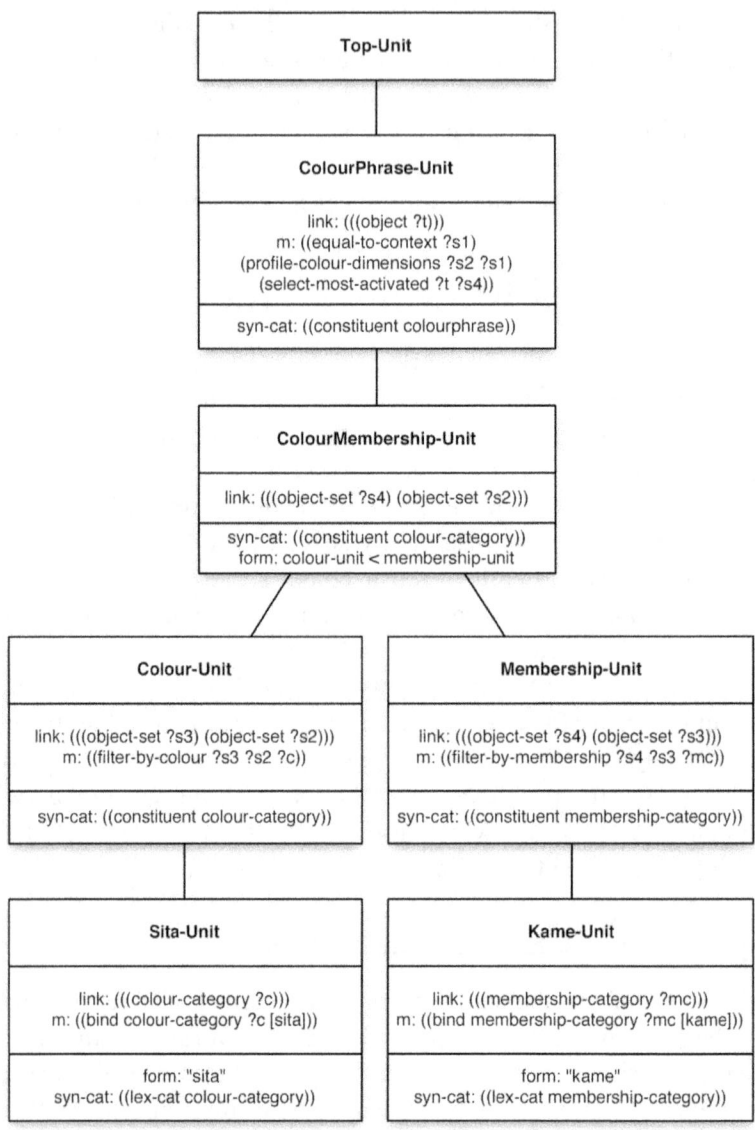

Figure 4.4: Linguistic structure for graded membership strategy. Both semantic and syntactic poles are shown in the same structure. Semantic information is shown in the top part of each unit, the syntactic information in the bottom part of each unit. The structure consists of four layers: one for the semantic entities, one for the functional primitives and the top one represents the contextual rule introduced in the previous chapter. The additional ColourMembership-Unit is introduced by a rule based on Syntactic template 2.

```
  ?meaning
  (link (((membership-category ?mc))))))
<-->
((?top-unit
  (tag ?form
       (form ((string ?yellow-unit "kame")))))
 ((J ?kame-unit ?top-unit)
  ?form
  (syn-cat ((lex-cat membership-category)))))
```

4.3.2 Syntactic template 1.2: Functional primitives

The functional rules for FILTER-BY-COLOUR and FILTER-BY-MEMBERSHIP are similar to the functional rule for FILTER-BY-COLOUR-LENIENT in the previous chapter. An example of such a rule for FILTER-BY-MEMBERSHIP is shown below.

```
─────────────────── Functional rule for Filter-by-Membership ───────────────────
((?top-unit
  (sem-subunits (?membership-category-unit))
  (tag ?meaning
       (meaning ((filter-by-membership ?s4 ?s3 ?mc)))))
 (?membership-category-unit
  (link (((membership-category ?c)))))
 ((J ?filter-by-membership-unit ?top-unit
     (?membership-category-unit))
  ?meaning
  (link (((entity-set ?s4) (entity-set ?s3))))))
<-->
((?top-unit
  (syn-subunits (?membership-category-unit)))
 (?membership-category-unit
  (syn-cat ((lex-cat membership-category))))
 ((J ?filter-by-membership-unit ?top-unit
     (?membership-category-unit))
  (syn-cat ((constituent membership-category)))))
```

4.3.3 Syntactic template 2.1: Re-use of constructions

Re-use also occurs when the agent already knows a construction which covers part of the meaning to be conveyed. Such a template fixes the glitches that prevent other rules to apply. Let us consider the situation in which an agent needs to be able to express both the strict basic colour strategy and the graded membership strategy. The strict basic colour strategy is identical to the normal basic colour strategy, except that it uses FILTER-BY-COLOUR primitive instead of

4 Graded membership strategy

a FILTER-BY-COLOUR-LENIENT primitive for categorisation. The semantic templates of both strategies share the same contextual primitives, so re-use of the same contextual rule could be achieved. In order to do so, a new unit needs to be introduced to the structure that combines two subunits into one and that also takes care of variable equalities between the subunits and contextual rule. An example of such a "glue"-rule is shown below. This rule allows the agents to re-use the contextual rule for the basic colour strategy to express the graded membership strategy.

────────────────── ColourMembership rule ──────────────────
```
(((?top-unit
   (sem-subunits (?membership-unit ?colour-unit)))
  (?membership-unit
   (link (((entity-set ?s4) (entity-set ?s3))))))
  (?colour-unit
   (link (((entity-set ?s3) (entity-set ?s2))))))
  ((J ?colourmembership-unit ?top-unit
      (?membership-unit ?colour-unit))
   (link (((entity-set ?s4) (entity-set ?s2)))))))
<-->
(((?top-unit
   (syn-subunits (?membership-unit ?colour-unit))
   (tag ?form
        (form ((meets ?colour-unit ?membership-unit)))))
  (?membership-unit
   (syn-cat ((constituent membership-category))))
  (?colour-unit
   (syn-cat ((constituent colour-category))))
  ((J ?colourmembership-unit ?top-unit
      (?membership-unit ?colour-unit))
   ?form
   (syn-cat ((constituent colour-category))))))
```
──

4.4 Baseline experiment

In the baseline experiment, I will compare three different predefined language systems: the first two will only be able to categorise based on the basic colour categories, while the third language will additionally be able to express the degree of membership in language through modifiers.

The first two language systems are based on English (Sturges & Whitfield 1995) and Central Tarahumara (Burgess, Kempton & MacLaury 1983). Although in Tarahumara the use of modifiers is obligatory to express a colour sensation, the

4.4 Baseline experiment

artificial language system in which they are not allowed to do so will allow me to assess the actual impact of the categorisation based on membership and to assess the impact of the number of basic colour categories on the resulting communicative success. English has 11 basic colour categories, whereas Tarahumara only has 5 (Kay & Maffi 2008).

As the exact location of the basic colour categories in Tarahumara are not readily available in the literature, I have made an estimation based on the data reported in the World Color Survey (Kay et al. 2010). More than 5 colours terms have been reported for Tarahumara in this study, from which I have selected the 5 most common ones as being the basic colour terms. In these data, the foci indicated by each informant are noted as chips indicated on the Munsell array. The Munsell chip that was indicated by the highest number of the 9 informants was selected as the focus of that category. An overview of the resulting category system can be found in Figure 4.5.

Figure 4.5: The basic colour categories for Central Tarahumara. These are the estimated foci of each category based on data from the World Color Survey (Kay et al. 2010). From left to right (including the corresponding Munsell chip): *rosá* (7.5R 9 2), *chó* (5.0R 2 8), *sitá* (5.0R 5 14), *siyó* (2.5BG 4 8) and *sawaró* (5.0YR 7 14).

As no exact data for the modifiers in Tarahumara are available, I have estimated their prototypical membership values in such a way that each of them cover a reasonable number of colour chips (560 for *-kame*, 1445 for *-name* and 643 for *-nanti*). Due to the absolute nature of the membership categories, the proportion of the chips that will be classified as each membership category depends on the colour category they modify and its surrounding colour categories. The actual prototypical values are provided in Table 4.1.

A first test whether the proposed membership categories are valid is provided by a naming benchmark. This benchmark involves naming each of the Munsell chips and grouping the samples based on the resulting name. The results for two roots, *sitá* and *sawaró*, are shown in Figure 4.6. In this figure, the samples for one root are separated in more or less equal parts using the three modifiers. These results are qualitatively similar to the reported use of modifiers in Tamahumara as shown in Figure 4.1.

4 Graded membership strategy

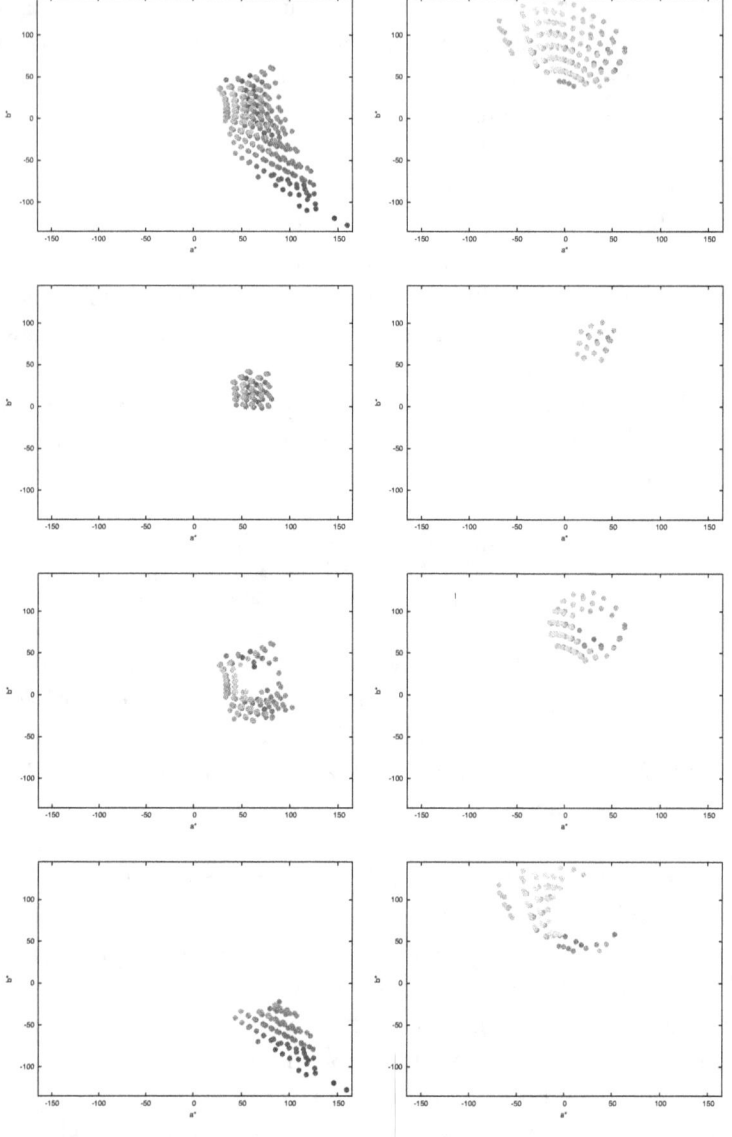

Figure 4.6: Example of modelled graded membership for *sitá* ('left') and *sawaró* ('right') in Tamahumara. The top row shows the aggregate of all uses of the corresponding term as root, the second row the uses of the *-kame* ('very') modifier, the third row the uses of *-name* ('somewhat') and the bottom row show the uses of *-nanti* ('only slightly'). All diagrams are projections on the hue plane of the CIE $L^*a^*b^*$ colour space.

4.4 Baseline experiment

Table 4.1: Membership categories for Central Tarahumara. The higher the prototypical value, the more similar the colour category and the colour sample have to be.

membership category	prototypical value
-kame	0.2
-name	0.02
-nanti	0.002

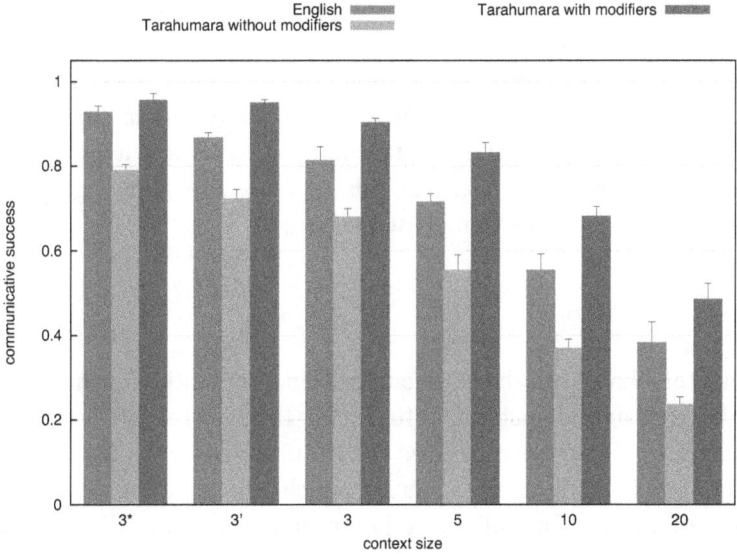

Figure 4.7: The baseline communicative success for graded membership strategy, comparing three different language systems: two are limited to the basic colour strategy and are based on English (11 terms) and Tarahumara (5 terms). The third system is based on Tarahumara as well, but involves the graded strategy using 3 modifiers. The lower number of basic terms has a negative impact on communicative success, but this can be overcome by allowing the use of modifiers.

Results

The resulting communicative success of the baseline experiment is shown in Figure 4.7. A lower number of basic categories has a negative impact on the communicative success (compare English to Tarahumara without modifiers) but this effect can be countered by allowing the use of modifiers (compare Tarahumara with and without modifiers). Most interestingly, by allowing the use of modifiers a system with a lower number of basic categories can become more expressive than systems with a higher number of basic categories that do not allow for modifiers (compare Tarahumara with modifiers and English).

In systems in which only the strict basic strategy is deployed, the chosen sample needs to be discriminable by one category which is enforced by the selection process. The higher the number of categories, the lower the chance another sample will be categorised as the category of the topic. This explains the first observation that a lower number of basic categories results in a lower baseline communicative success.

When modifiers are allowed in the language system, the restriction of a single discriminatory category is somewhat loosened. Instead of a single category it now is the consecutive filtering using a colour category and a membership category that needs to be discriminative. This explains why allowing modifiers has a positive impact on the resulting baseline success.

4.5 Conclusion

In this chapter, I have introduced a compositional semantics for the graded membership strategy and linguistic rules to express the membership categories in language. I have qualitatively compared the resulting names to those reported for the Tarahumara language using a naming benchmark. I have also shown the positive impact of the use of modifiers on the baseline communicative success, which can counter the negative impact of a lower number of basic colour categories.

5 Category combination strategy

Some languages also allow users to compound two colour categories into a new one. This can also be applied to the domain of colour, especially to describe a colour sample that is not a good example of any of the basic colour terms. An example in English would be *blue-green*. This compounding can also be modulated by an additional marker, like for example *-ish* in English as in *brownish-red*. Other languages, such as Vietnamese, allow to repeat one colour term to give it emphasis, as in *yellow yellow* (Alvarado & Jameson 2002).

Safuanova & Korzh (2007) have collected data on the focal colours of compounds in Russian. One of their main findings is that in Russian, the order in which colour terms are combined has an influence on the resulting focal colour: the second term seems to be more important in the expression. This is illustrated in Figure 5.1. The colours between *žëltyj* ('yellow') and *zelëno* ('green') are for example named: *zelenovato-žëltyj* ('greenish-yellow'), *zelëno-žëltyj* ('green-yellow'), *žëlto-zelënyj* ('yellow-green') and *žëltovato-zelënyj* ('yellowish-green') where the suffix *-ato* acts as a modulator.

To summarise, I have to account for three basic observations: category combination can be asymmetrical in the sense that one colour category is deemed more important than the other. This combination can be modulated through markers in language and the same colour category can be repeated in the same utterance to give emphasis to indicate it is a good example of a particular colour category.

5.1 Related research

Several suggestions have been made on how the combination of concepts should be modelled. In certain situations, some compatible properties can be changed in the base concept, such as in *green apple*. In other situations, the mapped properties are not compatible and overrule the corresponding properties in the base concept, such as in *pink elephant*.

But the combination of concepts is actually not as clear cut, as the actual modification depends on the context in which it is used. Consider the Russian example below which states there are many *red cows* in the Ural mountain range. These

5 Category combination strategy

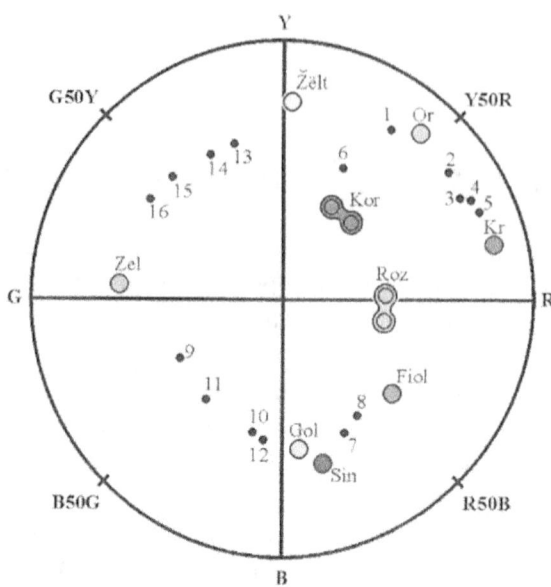

Figure 5.1: Compound chromatic terms projected on the hue plane of the NCS colour space. The second term in the compound clearly has a bigger impact on the resulting focal colour than the first one. The colours between *žëltyj* ('yellow') and *zelënyj* ('green') are for example named: (13) *zelenovato-žëltyj* ('greenish-yellow'), (14) *zelëno-žëltyj* ('green-yellow'), (15) *žëlto-zelënyj* ('yellow-green') and (16) *žëltovato-zelënyj* ('yellowish-green'). Figure from Safuanova & Korzh (2007).

cows are of course not of a bright red colour, but are rather more ginger-coloured (Tribushinina 2008).

(1) Na Urale   mnogo krasnyh   korov.
    On Ural-LOC many red-PL.GEN cows-GEN
    'There are a lot of red cows in the Urals.'

The actual colour implied by the colour adjectives is dependent on the context in which it is used. The actual colour implied by the adjective *red* is different whether it is used in the context of wine, hair, skin, or indeed cows. This is why the use of contrast classes is suggested. These define a subregion of colours that some base class is usually associated with, for example the set of all skin colours. The set of colour categories is transformed into this subregion. For example, *white skin* does refer to a colour that would normally be named pinkish and *black* refers to the darkest colour of skin (Gärdenfors 2004).

Models

The colour naming model proposed by Lammens sorts all categories based on the similarity to the colour sample that needs to be named and deployed some heuristics to include the secondmost similar category using diminutives such as *-ish* and *somewhat x-ish* (Lammens 1994). Other colour naming models store different centroids for each compound colour term, including the combination of basic colour terms (Mojsilovic 2005).

5.2 Semantic template

As I am pursuing a compositional approach to semantics, I start from the semantic network of the basic colour strategy and extend it by adding a second categorisation process. As the first categorisation process is strict, it would be unproductive to use the same category set as it would just return the exact same colour category. In order for the second categorisation process to be useful, the category set needs to be modified.

The most naive way to modify the category set is to remove the category that was used during the first categorisation process. This would allow the second categorisation process to find the category that is secondmost similar to the colour sample that needs to be described. This approach would however not be able to account for the repetitive use of the same colour term to highlight the similarity between the colour sample in the colour category, like in Vietnamese.

The transformation I have implemented is to move all the colour categories in the colour category set towards the category that has been used during the first categorisation process. This will entail that the region of the colour space that was first categorised as the base category will be repartitioned over its adjacent categories. The centre of that region, however, will still be classified as the base category. An illustration of such a transformation is provided in Figure 5.2.

When this second categorisation process would not be constraining enough to single out a particular colour sample in a context, an optional categorisation process based on membership can be added. This process is similar to the one proposed in the graded membership strategy but the membership function is now based on the combined membership of the two categorisation processes instead of one.

5 *Category combination strategy*

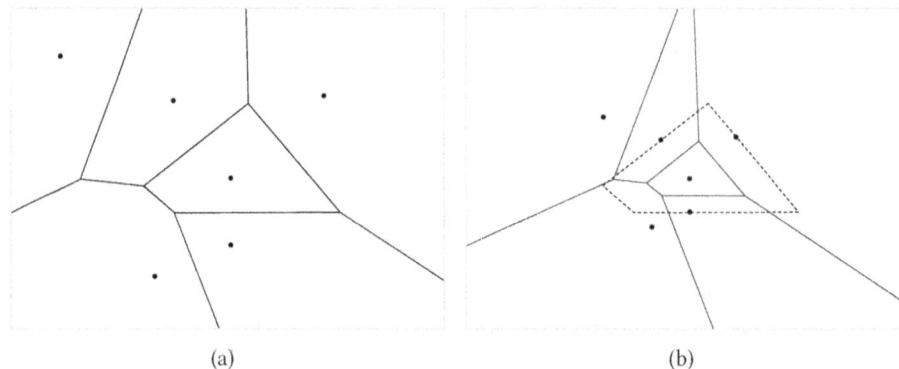

Figure 5.2: Impact of the transformation of the category set in the category combination strategy on the partitioning of the colour space: (a) partitioning of the colour space before the colour category set is transformed; (b) partitioning of the colour space after the category set is transformed towards the central category. The region that was categorised as the base category after the first transformation, is now repartitioned over the categories adjacent to the base categories. As the base category is also a member of the transformed set, the centre of that region will still be classified as the base category.

The semantics of the CATEGORY COMBINATION STRATEGY can be summarised as follows: first all the entities are categorised as in the basic colour strategy. Next, all categories are drawn towards the base category that has been used. This transformed category set is used during the second categorisation process. Optionally a third categorisation process based on membership can be added. From the resulting set the entity with the highest activation is selected.

The proposed semantics satisfy the three requirements outlined at the beginning of this chapter. Asymmetry is achieved through the ordering of the categorisation process based on colour: the first one will define the main region of the conceptual space in which the sample is to be found; the second one specifies a subregion within that region. The modulation of the combination process is realised through the optional categorisation process based on membership. The repetitive use of a colour category refers to the region that is close to the repeated colour category.

5.2 Semantic template

5.2.1 Profiling and first categorisation based on colour

The profiling and the first categorisation process is identical to the one of the graded membership strategy. It is a strict implementation of the categorisation process, as in interpretation only the samples that are most similar to the interpreted category are considered for further processing. This decision is based on the observation that colours that are named using a category combination will always be most similar to one of its constituent categories, as supported by the data of Russian compounds (Safuanova & Korzh 2007).

5.2.2 Transformation of the set of colour categories

The transformation procedure involves moving each colour category known to the agent in the direction of the base category that was used during the first categorisation process. Each colour category is moved to a point on the line segment between the original category and the base category in the conceptual space of the agent. The new location is slightly closer to the base category. An illustration of such a transformation is provided in Figure 5.2.

5.2.3 Second categorisation based on colour

The transformed category set is used for a second categorisation based on colour. In each entity, the resulting membership value of the first categorisation process is overwritten by the second categorisation process, but could also be a function based on these two functions. Although the first categorisation process is important to select some samples from the context, I have chosen to overwrite the value as the actual membership of the second categorisation process is independent of the membership of the first categorisation process. For example, a *green-blue* colour sample would have a low membership during the categorisation with the category for blue, but could be a very good member of the green category that is transformed for the category for blue.

This process allows for a further specification of the region in the conceptual space that was originally categorised as the base category.

5.2.4 Optional categorisation based on membership

An optional categorisation process based on membership can be added to the chain of processes, which would allow for further specification of the colour sample. As the membership values stored in the entities now reflect the second

5 Category combination strategy

categorisation process, this will specify regions within the regions that were defined by the previous categorised process.

5.2.5 Selection based on activation

The selection process is based on the notion that each categorisation process changes the activation values of each of the entities in the resulting set. The entity with the highest activation is selected as the entity resulting from the complete process.

5.2.6 Semantic constraint network

The semantic network for the category combination strategy is shown in Figure 5.3. The EQUAL-TO-CONTEXT and PROFILE-COLOUR-DIMENSIONS primitives are the same as the ones before. The FILTER-BY-COLOUR primitive is like the one introduced before, but now has a specific argument of the colour category set it is applying, as this set might be modified by other primitives. This requires another primitive GET-BASIC-COLOUR-CATEGORY-SET to retrieve all the categories known to the agent to mimic the old behaviour of FILTER-BY-COLOUR. This category set is also provided to the DRAW-CATEGORY-SET-TO-CATEGORY primitive which draws all the categories in the direction of the category that is used during the first categorisation process based on colour. Next another FILTER-BY-COLOUR primitive applies the transformed category set to the sets filtered by its first instantiation. Finally SELECT-MOST-ACTIVATED returns the most activated entity from this set as the value for the complete process. An optional FILTER-BY-MEMBERSHIP primitive can be added between the last two primitives (not shown in figure).

5.2.7 Semantic primitives

5.2.7.1 *Semantic primitive* GET-BASIC-COLOUR-CATEGORY-SET

description	Retrieves all colour categories known by the agent.
slots	?colour-category-set (of type category-set)
revision specs	∅: collects all colour categories known to the agent and binds it to ?colour-category-set

5.2 Semantic template

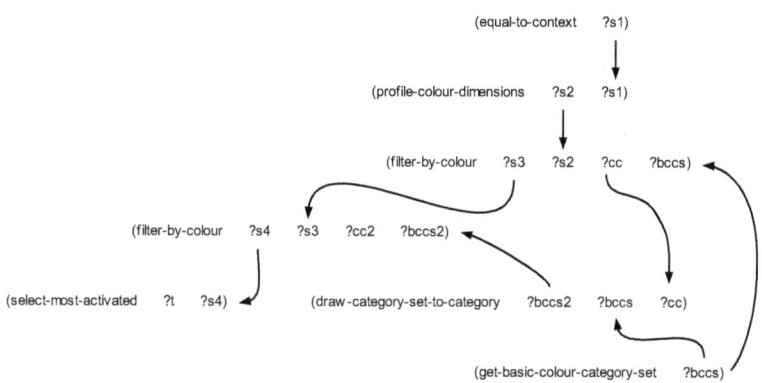

Figure 5.3: The semantic constraint network for the category combination strategy. Consists of two FILTER-BY-COLOUR primitives of which the second one deploys a transformed category set. This transformation is computed by the DRAW-CATEGORY-SET-TO-CATEGORY primitive.

5.2.7.2 *Semantic primitive* FILTER-BY-COLOUR

description	Categorises each entity in a source set as the most similar colour category in its argument category set. The membership of each entity is set to be the similarity to the category it belongs to.
slots	?filtered-set (of type entity-set) ?source-set (of type entity-set) ?colour-category (of type colour-category) ?colour-category-set (of type category-set)
revision specs	?source-set ?colour-category-set: categorises each entity of the source set and returns pairwise bindings for the remaining slots; categories to which no entities are assigned, are ignored. ?source-set ?colour-category-set ?category: computes the categorisation of the source set based on all colour categories in the category set and when the resulting set for the provided colour category is not empty, it gets bound to ?filtered-set

77

5 Category combination strategy

5.2.7.3 Semantic primitive DRAW-CATEGORY-SET-TO-CATEGORY

description	Draws all categories in a category set towards a particular member of this category set. When this category is not a member of this set, this operation is undefined.
slots	?transformed-category-set (of type category-set) ?category-set (of type category-set) ?category (of type colour-category)
revision specs	?category ?category-set: draws all categories in the category set towards ?category bound to ?category so that they are on the line segment between of ?category and the original location of the category; the linear factor that determines the resulting position is set to 0.4 (where 0 would be equal to ?category and 1.0 would be the original location of the category)

5.2.8 Alternative approaches to semantics

Although not implemented nor tested, it has been suggested that fuzzy sets could support category combinations in a quite natural way. Some samples belong with full probability to one fuzzy set representing one basic colour category, but others will be members of more than one set. If a sample would have a membership of 0.5 to blue and one of 0.5 to green, it could be named *blue-green*. The *-ish* suffix could be used for samples with a high membership of one category and up to a certain membership of another (e.g. samples with memberships 0.7 to green and 0.3 to blue could be named *bluish green* (Benavente, Vanrell & Baldrich 2008)).

5.3 Syntactic templates

The syntactic templates that can be used to express this semantic network are similar to the templates introduced in the previous chapter. The main difference to the previous templates is that the rules don't only need to link the variables of the different entity sets, but also the variables that deal with colour category sets and colour categories. This is most clear when observing the arguments of the DRAW-CATEGORY-SET-TO-CATEGORY primitive, which requires the colour category that is used in the first categorisation process to compute a new colour category set that will be used during the second categorisation process. The variables related to colour categories will be dealt with in the COLOUR LINK, c-link feature for short.

5.3 Syntactic templates

The linguistic structure for *zelëno-žëltyj* ('green-yellow') is shown in Figure 5.4, in which some morphological issues are ignored.

5.3.1 Syntactic template 1.1: Semantic entities

The semantic entities are dealt with in a similar way as before. I kindly refer the reader to the previous chapters for examples of entity rules.

5.3.2 Syntactic template 1.2: Functional primitives

The functional rule for FILTER-BY-COLOUR is similar to the one introduced before, but now also provides a c-link feature in which the variables of its colour category and the colour category set are stored. The category needs to be available to the rest of the semantic network for when it should be needed for a transformation of the colour category set. The colour category set is required to allow for transformed colour category sets to be used by the filtering process.

```
────────────── Functional rule for Filter-by-Colour ──────────────
((?top-unit
  (sem-subunits (?colour-category-unit))
  (tag ?meaning
       (meaning ((filter-by-colour ?s3 ?s2 ?c ?cs)))))
 (?colour-category-unit
  (link (((colour-category ?c)))))
 ((J ?filter-by-colour-unit ?top-unit (?colour-category-unit))
  ?meaning
  (link (((entity-set ?s3) (entity-set ?s2))))
  (c-link (((colour-category ?c) (colour-category-set ?cs))))))
<-->
((?top-unit
  (syn-subunits (?colour-category-unit)))
 (?colour-category-unit
  (syn-cat ((lex-cat colour-category))))
 ((J ?filter-by-colour-unit ?top-unit (?colour-category-unit))
  (syn-cat ((constituent colour-category)))))
```

5.3.3 Syntactic template 1.3: Contextual primitives

The basic colour strategy is now redefined using the FILTER-BY-COLOUR primitive as defined in this chapter. The contextual rule that is needed for this strategy is very similar to the contextual rule in §3.3.3, except that it now also encapsulates a GET-BASIC-COLOUR-CATEGORY-SET primitive of which the argument is part of the c-link of the subunit.

5 Category combination strategy

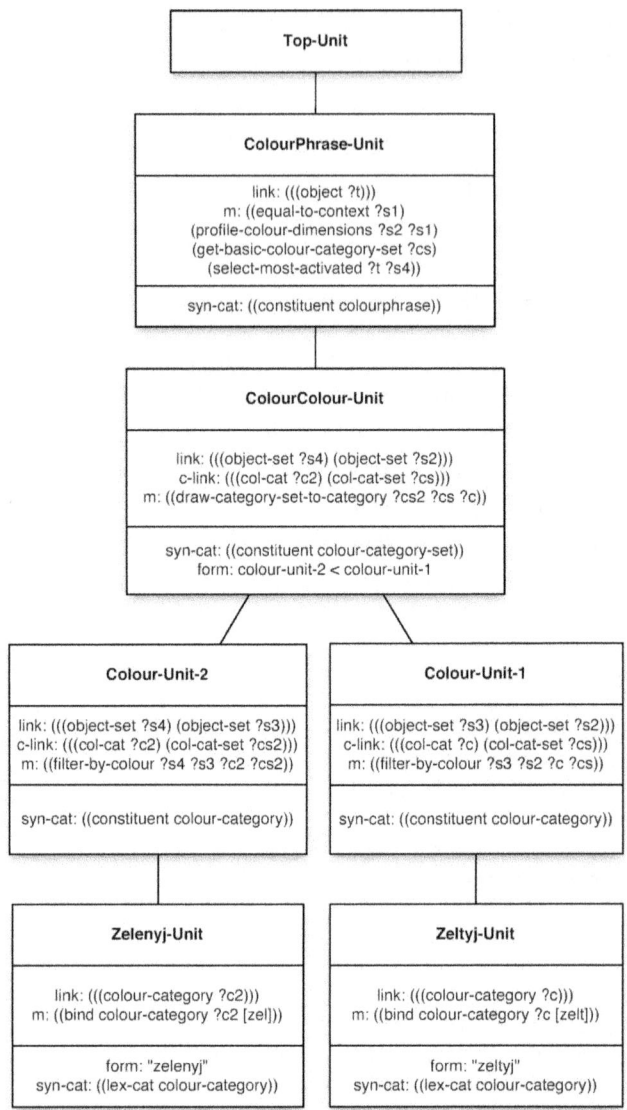

Figure 5.4: Linguistic structure for category combination strategy. Both semantic and syntactic poles are shown in the same structure. Semantic information is shown in the top part of each unit, the syntactic information in the bottom part of each unit. Next to the link features that have been used before to link the entity-sets of the primitives together, a c-link feature is required to establish variable equalities between primitives for the colour categories and the colour category sets.

5.3 Syntactic templates

---------- ColourPhrase rule for Basic Colour Strategy ----------
```
((?top-unit
  (sem-subunits (?colour-unit))
  (tag ?meaning
       (meaning ((select-most-activated ?t ?s3)
                 (profile-colour-dimensions ?s2 ?s1)
                 (equal-to-context ?s1)
                 (get-basic-colour-category-set ?cs)))))
 (?colour-unit
  (link (((entity-set ?s3) (entity-set ?s2))))
  (c-link (((colour-category ?c) (colour-category-set ?cs)))))
 ((J ?colourphrase-unit ?top-unit (?colour-unit))
  ?meaning
  (link (((colour-entity ?t))))))
<-->
((?top-unit
  (syn-subunits (?colour-unit)))
 (?colour-unit
  (syn-cat ((constituent colour-category))))
 ((J ?colourphrase-unit ?top-unit (?colour-unit))
  (syn-cat ((constituent colourphrase)))))
```

5.3.4 Syntactic template 2.2: Re-use of constructions

An extended version of syntactic template 2.1 needs to be introduced. The resulting rule looks similar to the one introduced before, but additionally the rule needs to take care of two additional aspects. First it needs to be able to cover some meaning. For the current semantic template, this would be the DRAW-CATEGORY-SET-TO-CATEGORY primitive. And second, it needs to provide the correct colour link of the new unit.

---------- ColourColour rule ----------
```
((?top-unit
  (sem-subunits (?unit-2 ?unit))
  (tag ?meaning
       (meaning ((draw-category-set-to-category ?cs2 ?cs ?cc)))))
 (?unit-2
  (link (((entity-set ?s3) (entity-set ?s2))))
  (c-link (((colour-category ?cc2) (colour-category-set ?cs2)))))
 (?unit
  (link (((entity-set ?s2) (entity-set ?s1))))
  (c-link (((colour-category ?cc) (colour-category-set ?cs)))))
 ((J ?colourcolour-unit ?top-unit (?unit-2 ?unit))
  ?meaning
  (link (((entity-set ?s3) (entity-set ?s1))))
```

5 Category combination strategy

```
(c-link (((colour-category ?cc2) (colour-category-set ?cs))))))
<-->
((?top-unit
  (syn-subunits (?unit-2 ?unit))
  (tag ?form
       (form ((meets ?unit-2 ?unit)))))
 (?unit-2
  (syn-cat ((constituent colour-category))))
 (?unit
  (syn-cat ((constituent colour-category))))
 ((J ?colourcolour-unit ?top-unit (?unit-2 ?unit))
  ?form
  (syn-cat ((constituent colour-category))))))
```

5.4 Baseline experiment

In the baseline experiment, I will compare three different language systems. All language systems are based on the Russian basic colour categories (Safuanova & Korzh 2007). The first one is based on the strict version of the basic colour strategy, the second one is based on the variant of the category combination strategy without the additional categorisation based on membership and the third language system is based on the graded variant of this strategy.

The exact location of the chromatic colour terms in Russian have been determined (Safuanova & Korzh 2007). These categories were reported in the Natural Color System and have been converted to the CIE $L^*a^*b^*$ colour space using the method described in Appendix A.5. Only the location of the chromatic colour categories has been determined which include two hues for the region English speakers would call *blue*: *sinij* ('dark blue') and *goluboj* ('light blue'). The basic colour categories are shown in Figure 5.5.

Figure 5.5: The basic chromatic colour categories for Russian based on the work of Safuanova & Korzh. From left to right: *krasnij* 'red', *oranževyj* 'orange', *žëltij* 'yellow', *zelënyj* 'green', *sinij* 'dark blue', *goluboj* 'light blue', *rozovyj* 'rose', *fioletovyj* 'purple' and *koričnevyj* 'brown'.

The same study reports on the exact location of some chromatic compounds. As a first qualitative test, I will verify whether the proposed semantics and syntax

5.4 Baseline experiment

will name the reported locations in a similar way. An example from the study lists the chromatic compounds between *žëltyj* ('yellow') and *zelënyj* ('green') which are reproduced in Figure 5.6.

Figure 5.6: Example of colour compounds in Russian (Safuanova & Korzh 2007). From left to right: (a) *žëltyj* 'yellow', (b) *zelenovato-žëltyj* 'greenish-yellow', (c) *zelëno-žëltyj* 'green-yellow', (d) *žëlto-zelënyj* 'yellow-green', (e) *žëltovato-zelënyj* 'yellowish-green', (f) *zelënyj* 'green'.

For this naming benchmark, I use an agent that is knowledgeable about the basic colour strategy and the category combination strategy (both the graded and the ungraded variant) and an implementation of the basic colour categories of Russian (as shown in Figure 5.5). Next, I run the production procedure and check what utterances are produced for the chips shown in Figure 5.6. When more than one strategy is capable of reaching the communicative goal, the strategy in which the topic entity has the highest activation is selected. This activation reflects the membership of the last categorisation process.

The results of this naming benchmark are shown in Table 5.1. Five out of six colour samples are named correctly. The one chip that (d) cannot be named is the yellow-green one. This is due to the first categorisation process based on colour, which categorises the (a-d) as *žëltyj*. Only (a-c) are discriminable by one of the provided language strategies. This example does not include the morphological complexities of the Russian language.

Results

The resulting baseline communicative success is shown in Figure 5.7. The communicative success for the system in which agents are allowed to combine categories is higher than when they are restricted to their basic usage. The communicative success for the system in which an additional categorisation process based on the membership is added, is even higher. The richer the semantics the agents are allowed to use, the higher the resulting communicative success.

As the number of colour samples in one context increases, the performance of each of the strategies decreases. The basic colour strategy is most prone to this phenomenon. Being able to combine colour categories compensates for most of

5 Category combination strategy

Table 5.1: Naming benchmark for Russian colour compounds. Five out of six samples are named correctly. The one sample that can not be named is wrongly categorised as *zeltyj* during the first categorisation process based on colour.

	expected name	produced name
(a)	*žëltyj*	*zeltyj*
(b)	*zelenovato-žëltyj*	*zelenyj -ato zeltyj*
(c)	*zelëno-žëltyj*	*zelenyj zeltyj*
(d)	*zelto-zelenyj*	–
(e)	*žëltovato-zelënyj*	*zeltyj -ato zelenyj*
(f)	*zelënyj*	*zelenyj*

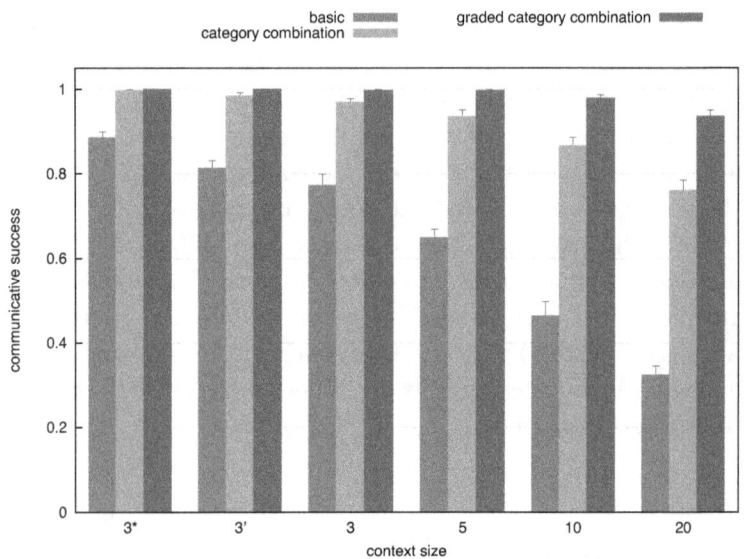

Figure 5.7: The baseline communicative success for category combination strategy, comparing three different language systems based on Russian (9 terms). The first system is based on the basic colour strategy, the second on the category combination strategy and the third one on the graded category combination strategy. Allowing agents to combine basic categories results in higher communicative success. This effect is increased by adding another categorisation process based on membership.

the loss. An additional categorisation process based on membership results in a language system that is quite successful, even in very large contexts.

Compared to the English basic colour system (shown in Figure 4.7), the baseline communicative success for Russian is lower. This is due to the lower number of basic colour categories that are reported for the Russian system (9 compared to 11 for English). The study on Russian colour categories only reports on chromatic colour categories, and therefore does not specify locations of the achromatic colour categories (white, grey and black).

5.5 Conclusion

In this chapter, I have introduced a compositional semantics for the category combination strategy and linguistic rules to express this semantics in language. Using a naming benchmark, I have qualitatively compared the resulting names to these reported for the Russian language. I have shown the positive impact of combining colour categories on the baseline communicative success. This impact was even higher when the category combination process was extended to include a categorisation process based on membership.

6 Basic modification strategy

Next to the basic colour strategy, most languages allow to specify certain aspects of a colour through the use of modifiers. In English and Chinese, the use of "basic" modifiers accounts for a high number of colour descriptions in unconstrained naming experiments (Simpson & Tarrant 1991; Lin et al. 2001). The basic modifiers are defined as the ones that are the most frequently used, which in English correspond to *bright, dull, light, pale*, etc. In general they specify the lightness or the chromaticity aspect of a certain colour.

Although basic modifiers are quite commonly used, only a few papers report on the exact transformation that is implied by these modifiers. One exception to this rule is a study on the Russian language, for which the location of the modified categories has been determined. An example of such an analysis is shown in Figure 6.1. The modifiers *tëmno-* ('dark') and *svleto* ('light'), modify the focus of the basic category parallel to the blackness dimension (W-S). The modifiers *bledno-* ('pale') and *jarko-* ('bright') shift the chromaticity of the basic colour category. This shift is parallel to the W-C dimension for lighter colours and parallel to the S-C dimension for darker colours (Safuanova & Korzh 2007).

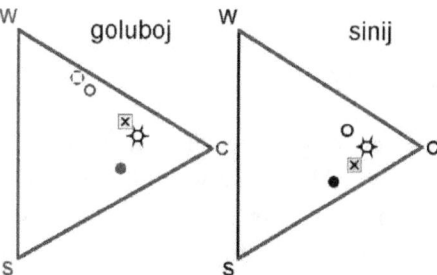

Figure 6.1: Location of modified basic colour foci in Russian projected into the NCS blackness-chromaticity triangle. *tëmno-* 'dark' (solid circle), *jarko-* 'bright' (sun), *svetlo-* 'light' (open circle) and *bledno-* 'pale' (dashed circle). Figure from Paramei (2005).

6 Basic modification strategy

6.1 Related research

The suggestions made in the literature about how to implement the combination of a basic modifier and a basic colour category are similar to those reported for the category combination strategy (see §5.1) as the basic modification strategy could be thought of as a special case of that strategy.

The process of mapping a set of properties to a specific category can not be seen as a straightforward overwriting of a specific property in the base category. For example, a light brown sample is still darker than a dark yellow sample. So instead of overwriting the lightness value of the base category with an absolute value, the modifiers alter the values specified by the base category. As a result, basic modifiers are relative to the base category they modify.

Alternatively, the semantics of a combination of a basic modifier and a basic colour category could be thought of as a context dependent filtering operation. First, all entities that are categorised as the basic colour category would be selected from the context. Next, the average lightness value of the remaining entities could be used to decide which entity should be named "dark" and which should be named "light". Although this could be a productive strategy, using average lightness values of the remaining entities might yield unwanted results. For example, if the contexts would consist for example of only two very light green colour samples, it would be unlikely one would be called "light green" and the other one "dark green". Moreover, human subjects are able to assign prototypical colour samples to each description independent of the context in which the colour samples are presented (Safuanova & Korzh 2007).

6.2 Semantic template

I hypothesise that the agents maintain different sets of categories, which each specify a mutual exclusivity relation between its members. One such set is the set of basic colour categories. For example, a colour can not at the same time be red and green. A similar relation holds for the lightness modifiers *light-* and *dark-*: a colour is considered to be either light or dark and can never be light and dark at the same time. This relation is represented by organising colour categories in different sets. Another set of categories could be those that specify the chromaticity of a particular colour, like *pale-* and *bright-*.

The approach of agents maintaining several category sets, ensures a uniform treatment of each of these sets in all of the strategies introduced before. This allows for example to only specify some dimensions of a colour sample, as in *bright green*, or to specify graded membership, as in *darkish red*.

6.2 Semantic template

As I am still pursuing a compositional semantics, I will start from the semantics of the category combination strategy, as this is already quite similar to the semantics needed for the current strategy. The transformation proposed for that strategy can not be applied anymore, as the modifier category is not a member of the basic colour category set.

The transformation I propose, shifts the modifiers to the borders defined by the other basic colour categories. So for example, let us suppose the base category is yellow. The light modifier will now be shifted to the border with the white category and the dark modifier to the border with the brown category. A schematic representation of this operation is shown in Figure 6.2.

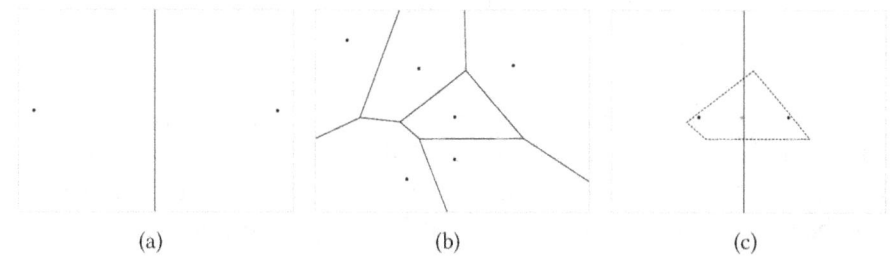

(a) (b) (c)

Figure 6.2: Schematic representation of the transformation for basic modifiers: (a) the partitioning of the colour space based on two basic modifiers; (b) the partitioning of the colour space based on the basic colour categories; (c) the transformation of the basic modifiers towards one of the basic colour categories. The transformed basic modifiers lie on the border of the basic colour category.

The semantics of the basic modification strategy can be summarised as follows: first a normal categorisation similar to the one in the basic colour strategy is performed. Before the basic modifiers are applied, they are transformed corresponding to the base category that is used during the first categorisation process. Next the most activated entity is selected from the resulting set. This process can potentially be extended by a categorisation process based on activation.

6.2.1 Profiling and first categorisation based on colour

The profiling and the first categorisation process is identical to the one of the graded membership strategy. It is a strict implementation of the categorisation process, as in interpretation only samples that are most similar to the interpreted category are considered for further processing. This decision is based on the

6 Basic modification strategy

observation that for basic modifiers, the base category is always the one that is most similar to the colour sample (Safuanova & Korzh 2007).

6.2.2 Transformation of set of modifying categories

Based on the category used during the first categorisation process, the basic modifiers are transformed in such a way they represent the partitioning defined by the basic colour categories. This operation is based on an iterated estimation procedure in which the location of the modifier is estimated on the line section between the modifier and the base category. Each time the new location is estimated, it is reified as a colour sample that is classified using the basic colour category set. This procedure stops when the new location is close to the borders of the base category.

The modifying categories are represented as any other colour category, but also specify a weight for each dimension representing how relevant this dimension is. For the lightness modifiers, this would mean that only the lightness dimension is relevant (L^* in the CIE $L^*a^*b^*$ colour space). For the chromaticity modifiers, this would be the two hue dimensions (a^* and b^* in the same colour space). When there are two categories the resulting coordinates are determined based on these weights: the lower the weight, the less a particular category contributes to that dimension.

6.2.3 Second categorisation based on modifiers

Once the modifier categories are transformed, they are used for a second categorisation process. Like in the category combination strategy the membership value of the first categorisation process is overwritten by the one resulting from the second categorisation process for similar reasons. A "light-brown" colour sample could have a low membership for the base category brown, but might be a very good member of the light modifier after it is transformed for brown. This second categorisation process allows the agent to further specify the subregion of the conceptual space that was classified as the base category.

6.2.4 Optional categorisation based on membership

An optional categorisation process based on membership can be added to the process, which allows for a further specification of the subregion of the colour space. This additional process allows to describe samples as "darkish green" or

6.2 Semantic template

"very light yellow" and could be added when the subsequent categorisation process is not sufficient to discriminate a particular colour sample in a context.

6.2.5 Selection based on activation

The selection is based on the membership value that can be altered by each of the categorisation processes. The entity with the highest activation is selected as the entity resulting from the complete process.

6.2.6 Semantic constraint network

The complete semantic network for the basic modification strategy is shown in Figure 6.3. It is very similar to the one for the category combination strategy. The first categorisation process based on the basic colour category set is entirely identical. The GET-LIGHTNESS-CATEGORY-SET retrieves the lightness modifiers known to the agent. The SCALE-CATEGORY-SET-TO-CATEGORY transforms this category set to the category that was used during the first categorisation process.

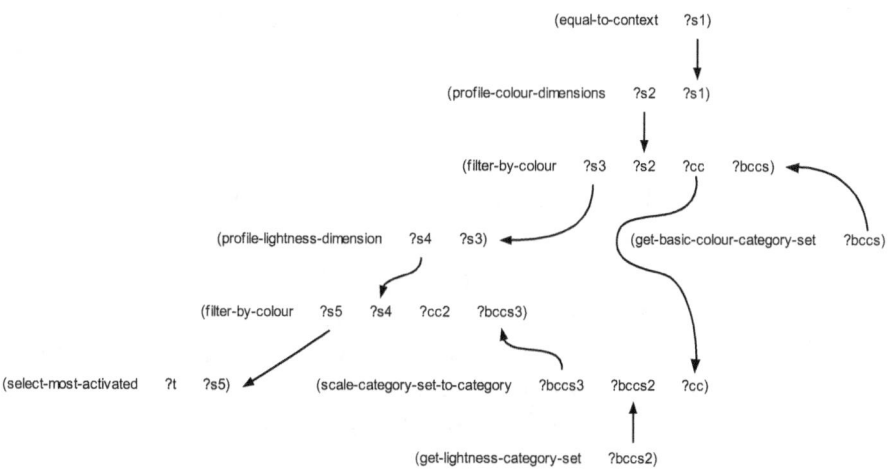

Figure 6.3: Semantic constraint network for basic modifiers. The network consists of two FILTER-BY-COLOUR primitives. The first uses the basic colour category set, the second the lightness modifiers which are transformed into the category used by the first categorisation process. This transformation is computed by the SCALE-CATEGORY-SET-TO-CATEGORY primitive.

91

6 Basic modification strategy

The resulting category set is used by the second FILTER-BY-COLOUR operation. Finally, SELECT-MOST-ACTIVATED returns the entity with the highest entity from the resulting set. An optional FILTER-BY-MEMBERSHIP primitive can be added between the last two primitives.

6.2.7 Semantic primitives

6.2.7.1 *Semantic primitive* GET-LIGHTNESS-COLOUR-CATEGORY-SET

description	Retrieves all lightness known by the agent.
slots	?colour-category-set (of type category-set)
revision specs	∅: collects all lightness modifiers known to the agent and binds it to ?colour-category-set

6.2.7.2 *Semantic primitive* SCALE-CATEGORY-SET-TO-CATEGORY

description	Scales all categories in a category set so that they fit into a specific category. The borders of that category are determined by the other categories in the category set to which that category belongs. The category does not need to be a member of the category set that is transformed, but the categories of both sets should be compatible so they can be successfully combined, like for example scaling a set of colour categories to another colour category from another category set.
slots	?transformed-category-set of type *category-set* ?category-set of type *category-set* ?category of type *colour-category*
revision specs	?category ?category-set: scales all categories in the category set towards ?category bound to ?category so that they are on the border of ?category

6.3 Syntactic templates

The templates introduced in the previous chapter can be used to cover each part of the semantic constraint network in Figure 6.3. The linguistic structure for *tëmno-rozovyj* is shown in Figure 6.4.

6.3 Syntactic templates

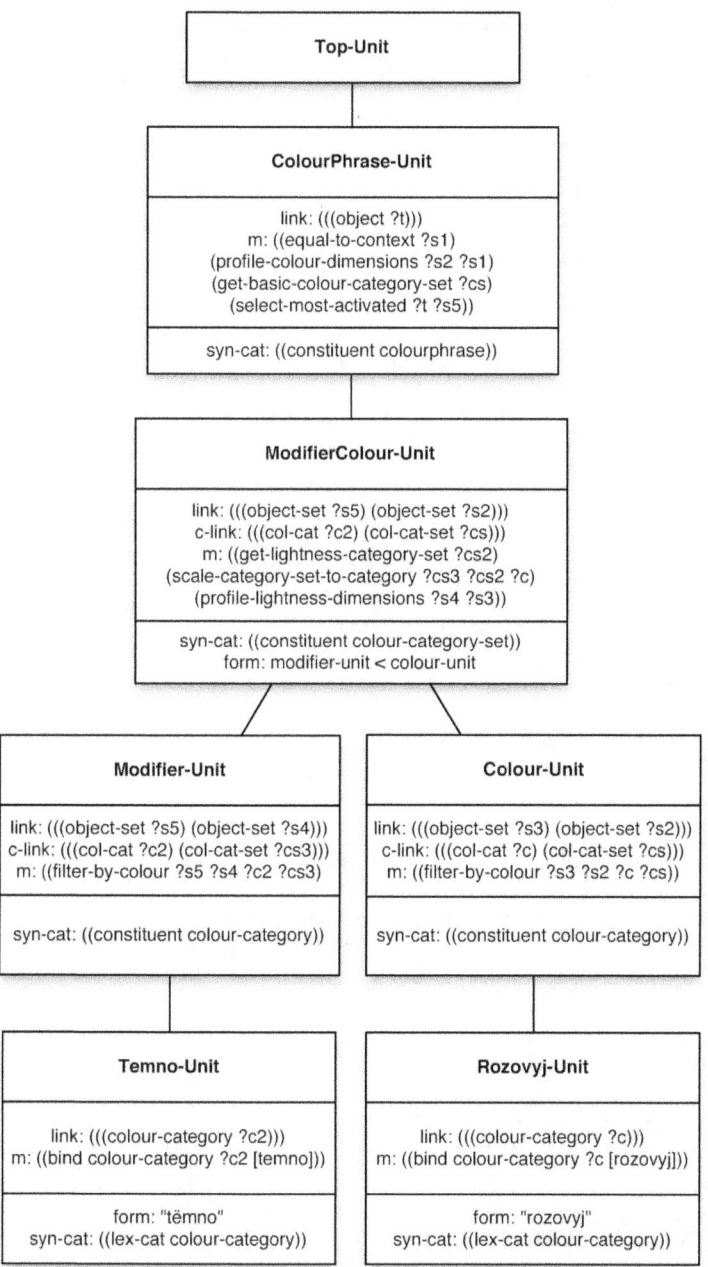

Figure 6.4: Linguistic structure for basic modifiers. The structure is similar to the one presented in the previous chapter, but with a different instantiated rule based of Syntactic template 2.1 that introduces the Modifier-Colour unit to the structure.

6 Basic modification strategy

Syntactic template 2.2: Re-use of constructions

The syntactic template 2.2 that was introduced in the previous chapter can also be used to express the parts of the basic modification strategy that are not yet covered by any of the other rules. It encapsulates all remaining primitives t and takes care of all the needed variable equalities between its subunits and the contextual rule of the basic colour strategy. It is responsible for introducing the ModifierColour-unit in Figure 6.4 in both producing and parsing.

```
―――――――――――――――――――――― ModifierColour rule ――――――――――――――――――――――
((?top-unit
  (sem-subunits (?modifier-unit ?colour-unit))
  (tag ?meaning
       (meaning ((scale-category-set-to-category ?cs3 ?cs2 ?cc)
                 (get-lightness-category-set ?cs2)
                 (profile-lightness-dimensions ?s3 ?s2)))))
 (?modifier-unit
  (link (((entity-set ?s4) (entity-set ?s3))))
  (c-link (((colour-category ?cc2) (colour-category-set ?cs3)))))
 (?colour-unit
  (link (((entity-set ?s2) (entity-set ?s1))))
  (c-link (((colour-category ?cc) (colour-category-set ?cs)))))
 ((J ?modifiercolour-unit ?top-unit (?modifier-unit ?colour-unit))
  ?meaning
  (link (((entity-set ?s4) (entity-set ?s1))))
  (c-link (((colour-category ?cc2) (colour-category-set ?cs))))))
<-->
((?top-unit
  (syn-subunits (?modifier-unit ?colour-unit))
  (tag ?form
       (form ((meets ?modifier-unit ?colour-unit)))))
 (?modifier-unit
  (syn-cat ((constituent colour-category))))
 (?colour-unit
  (syn-cat ((constituent colour-category))))
 ((J ?modifiercolour-unit ?top-unit (?modifier-unit ?colour-unit))
  ?form
  (syn-cat ((constituent colour-category)))))
```

6.4 Baseline Experiment

The baseline experiment will compare three different predefined language systems. Each of them is based on the Russian colour category system (Safuanova & Korzh 2007). The first one is based on the strict version of the basic colour strategy. The second one is based on the basic modification strategy using 2 basic modifiers: *svleto* ('light') and *tëmno* ('dark'). The modifiers are specified as maximal and minimal lightness values and are only specified in the lightness dimension. The third language system is based on the basic modification strategy which includes a categorisation process based on membership using the same basic semantic entities.

The foci of the basic and modified colour categories have been reported in the Natural Color System (Safuanova & Korzh 2007) and have been converted using the method described in Appendix A.5. The resulting foci are shown in Figure 6.5.

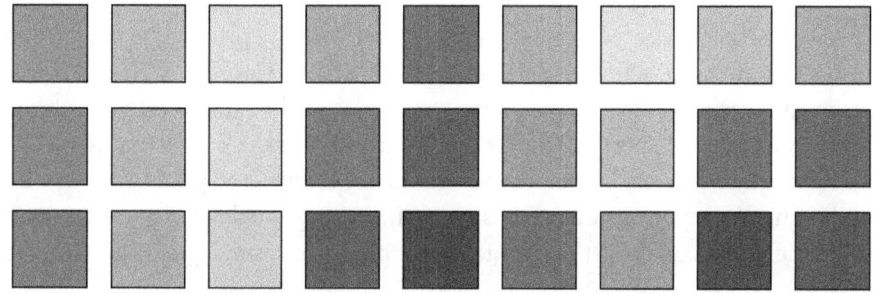

Figure 6.5: Foci of modified basic colour categories in Russian. The basic colour categories are shown in the middle. The top row shows these categories modified with *svleto-* 'light' and the bottom row shows the same categories modified with *tëmno-* 'dark'. From left to right: *krasnij* 'red', *oranževyj* 'orange', *žëltij* 'yellow', *zelënyj* 'green', *sinij* 'dark blue', *goluboj* 'light blue', *rozovyj* 'rose', *fioletovyj* 'purple' and *koričnevyj* 'brown'.

As a first test of the proposed semantics, I run a naming benchmark over all the colour chips reported in the study (shown in Figure 6.5). I run the production procedure and compare the resulting names to the ones reported by the study. The results for this benchmark are quite good: 15 out of 18 modified chips are named correctly. The chips that were named incorrectly are shown in Table 6.1

tëmno-žëltij could not be named, as it is still considered a light shade of yellow. The names for the colours samples for *tëmno-goluboj* ('dark light blue') and *svleto-sinij* ('light dark blue') were mixed up, as the former is lighter than the second, which is also reported in literature (Safuanova & Korzh 2007). All other colour samples were named correctly.

6 Basic modification strategy

Table 6.1: Naming benchmark for Russian lightness modifiers. Only the three samples that were named incorrectly are shown.

expected name	produced name
tëmno-žëltij	–
tëmno-goluboj	*svleto-sinij*
svleto-sinij	*tëmno-goluboj*

Results

The results of the baseline experiment are shown in Figure 6.6. The language system in which agents can use basic modifiers reaches a higher level of baseline communicative success when compared to the basic colour strategy. This positive impact is even higher when agents are allowed to grade the resulting membership (compare results of basic modifiers to graded basic modifiers). The higher the expressivity of the agents, the higher the resulting baseline communicative success.

When compared to the baseline experiment of the category combination strategy, the resulting baseline communicative success is slightly lower. This is probably due to the lower number of categories that can be used to modify the basic categorisation process. In the current experiment, only two such categories are present, whereas in the category combination experiment, all adjacent colour categories could be used.

6.5 Conclusion

In this chapter I have proposed a semantic template that allows agents to use basic modifiers. This template is based on observations in natural language and is highly compositional. This compositionality allows agents to re-use the semantic primitives and constructions that have been introduced in previous chapters.

The proposed semantic template in which the lightness categories are represented in a set of colour categories separate from the basic colour categories, allows for the re-use of each of the previous language strategies using these lightness categories. Representing the semantics of descriptions like *light* or *very light* requires the simple replacement of the primitive that retrieves the colour category set from the ontology of an agent.

6.5 Conclusion

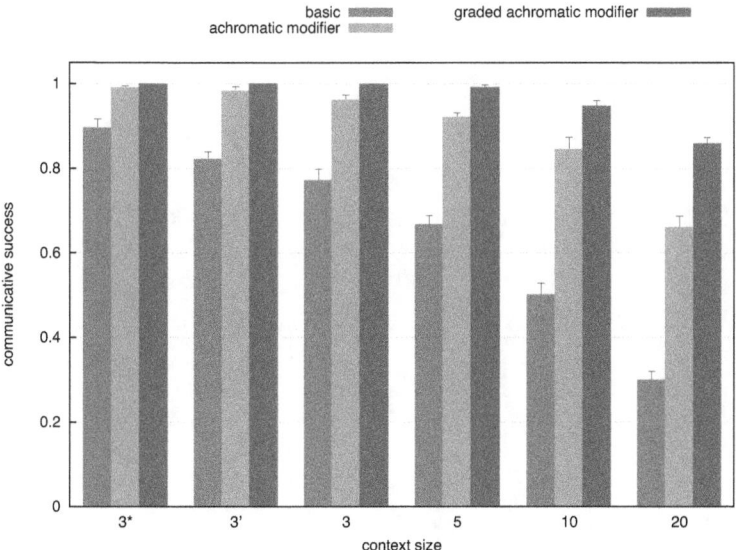

Figure 6.6: Baseline communicative success for basic modification strategy. The baseline success of the basic colour strategy is lower than the success of the basic modification strategy. When this strategy is extended with a categorisation process based on membership, the resulting baseline success is even higher.

Part III

Self-organisation of language systems

Introduction

In the third part of this book, I will study the self-organisation of language systems that are based on a single strategy. In order to do so, I need to introduce the adoption, alignment and invention operators for that strategy. The ADOPTION OPERATOR specifies how language users can pick up items of the language system. The ALIGNMENT OPERATOR specifies how agents should update their linguistic knowledge after a communicative interaction. The INVENTION OPERATOR is triggered when the (current knowledge of) the language system is insufficient or when the current language system is considered to be inefficient (Steels & Wellens 2006).

The performance of the adoption and the alignment operator can be evaluated in an ACQUISITION EXPERIMENT in which one agent acquires a predefined language system through playing language games. This evaluation is achieved by comparing the communicative success of the learner to the communicative success of two agents that share the predefined language system. The predefined language systems are implemented as in the baseline experiments in Part II.

The invention operator can be evaluated in a FORMATION EXPERIMENT in which a population of agents needs to construct its own language system based on one language strategy and allows agents to extend the current language system. These innovations can be picked up by other agents using the adoption operators. After each interaction agents align their knowledge of the language system using the alignment operator. This alignment operator allows agents to track their (local view on) the communicative success of certain linguistic items, which they can use to prefer one linguistic item over the other. At the system level this mechanism can lead to the dominance of one item over the other and to the disappearance of items that are disused. The complete process of how a language strategy can construct a language system is illustrated in Figure 7.1.

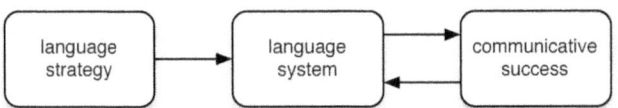

Figure 7.1: The construction of a language system based on a single language strategy. The language strategy allows agents to expand the language system. Based on a feedback loop which reflects success in communication, an agent can prefer linguistic items that are more successful, whereas unsuccessful linguistic items can be removed from the language system.

7 Basic colour strategy

To complete the definition of the basic colour strategy, I need to introduce its adoption, alignment and invention operator. The invention operator allows users to expand the current language system whenever they feel it is insufficient for their communicative needs. This expansion involves the invention of a new colour category and a lexical rule to express this category in language. The adoption operator allows language users to pick up these newly invented terms and the corresponding colour categories. The alignment operator specifies how language users can align their linguistic knowledge both on the syntactic and the semantic level.

7.1 Related models

In Chapter 3, I already introduced various models (Steels & Belpaeme 2005; Belpaeme & Bleys 2005b; 2007; Puglisi, Baronchelli & Loreto 2008; Baronchelli et al. 2010) that adhere to the language game paradigm and use the colour naming game. The goal of these studies was to study how a population of agents could coordinate their own colour category system through local interactions.

Other models for the coordination of a colour category system have been proposed as well. One model is more in line with the iterated learning model (Smith, Kirby & Brighton 2003) in which the burden of the explanation is placed on the idea that a language learner will have to generalise from only a limited number of observations instead of the communicative function. In this model, colour categories are inferred using Bayesian inference and invention is based on a random choice (Dowman 2007).

Another mathematical model focusses on a discrimination task for which the expected outcome depends on the similarity of the colours that need to be discriminated. In this model, a circular conceptual colour space is deployed, in which any typology of categories is as likely to occur as others. Adding heterogeneity to the model breaks this symmetry, either in the population or in the likelihood that a particular colour is presented to the agents or both (Komarova & Jameson 2008).

7.2 Adoption and alignment operators

The main goal of the adoption and alignment operators is to ensure that one agent can acquire the language system of another agent. It needs to learn the private knowledge of the language system that is being used in such a way that is sufficiently coordinated to ensure communicative success.

The adoption operator is used to learn the colour categories of another agent that are unknown to the learning agent. The main trigger for this operator is hearing an unknown colour term. The application of this operator results in learning a new category that is focussed on the colour of the topic of the current interaction. The unknown colour term is associated with this new category. This operator is in line with research in developmental psychology which showed the influence of learning a category upon hearing a new label (Xu 2002). Note that this implementation of the adoption operator implies that no synonyms will be present in the resulting language system.

The alignment operator is implemented by shifting the prototype of the category that was used in the direction of the colour of the topic. It is used by both speaker and hearer after a successful interaction. The rate by which this shift happens is controlled by COLOUR CATEGORY ALIGNMENT RATE (r_a) which linearly specifies the new location of the prototype (c_{n+1}) on the line segment between the old location of the prototype (c_n) and the topic (t). The exact formula is shown in Equation 7.1. If the alignment rate is 0, the prototype does not shift at all, whereas at a rate of 1 the new location would be the topic of the last interaction. In all experiments reported in this book, the alignment rate is fixed to 0.05 unless stated otherwise. An illustration of an alignment rate is given in Figure 7.2.

$$c_{n+1} = (1 - r_a)c_n + r_a t \qquad (7.1)$$

7.2.1 Acquisition experiment

In the acquisition experiment, one agent needs to acquire the language system known by another agent. This will allow me to assess the effectiveness of the acquisition operators. The language system I have chosen as target is the one based on English centroids (Sturges & Whitfield 1995). The contexts will consist of three randomly chosen Munsell chips (Newhall, Nickerson & Judd 1942) without any additional constraints. Other language systems and environmental conditions exhibit similar dynamics and are not shown.

7.2 Adoption and alignment operators

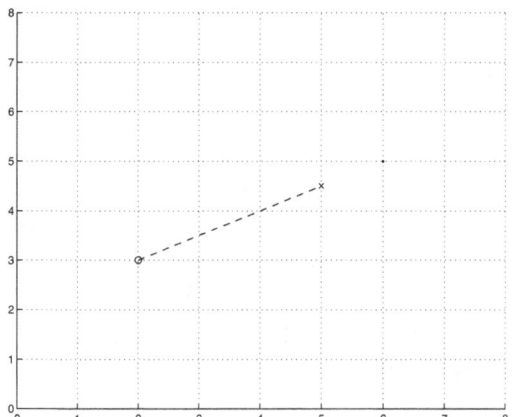

Figure 7.2: Illustration of the alignment rate. Before the game the prototype of the category was at (2,3). The colour of the topic sample was located at (6,5). Given that the interaction was successful and the alignment rate is 0.75, the location of the prototype will become (5,4.5).

7.2.2 Measures

7.2.2.1 Number of categories

The number of categories known to one agent (n_c) simply counts the number of categories known to this agent. At the level of a population P it is understood as the number of categories averaged over all agents in the population.

$$n_c(P) = \frac{\sum_{i=1}^{|P|} n_c(a)}{|P|} \quad (7.2)$$

7.2.2.2 Interpretation variance

Interpretation variance is a measure for the coherence of a population of agents (P) when interpreting a form: the lower the variance, the higher the coherence. For each unique form (f) that exists within the population the interpretation variance is measured within the subset $A_f = \{a_1, a_2, ..., a_n\}$ of agents that know this form, as shown in Equation 7.3. For each pair of agents the distance between the categories that are associated with the form is computed and averaged.

7 Basic colour strategy

$$I_{var}(f) = \frac{2}{n(n-1)} \sum_{i=1}^{n} \sum_{j=i+1}^{n} d(a_i(f), a_j(f)) \qquad (7.3)$$

In order to extend this measure to cover all existing forms in the population F, I need to decide how to combine the interpretation variances of each unique form. In previous research (e.g. Belpaeme 2002), the weight of the interpretation variance of each form was equal to the number of agents (n) that know this form. However, this weight does not reflect the actual probability of such a form being used in a random interaction. This probability depends on two choices: the choice of being selected as the speaker and the number of other forms known to that agent.

Let us consider a population of 4 agents in which one form (A) is shared by all agents, and another form (B) is only shared between two agents. Given a random interaction and that each form known to the agent is as likely to be used, what is the probability that form B will be observed? If an agent that knows B will be selected, it will choose form B with a chance of 1 out of 2. There are two such agents in the population, so the chance of selecting an agent that knows B is 1 out of 2 as well. In total the probability of observing form B is 1 out of 4. A similar reasoning can be made for form A, which will be observed by a probability of 3 out of 4.

The general equation for the interpretation variance within a population is given in Equation 7.4, where $|P|$ is the population size and $|a_i|$ is the total number of forms that are known to agent a_i.

$$I_{var}(P) = \sum_{f \in F} \left(\sum_{i=1}^{n} \frac{1}{|P||a_i|} \right) I_{var}(f) \qquad (7.4)$$

7.2.3 Results

The dynamics of the example acquisition experiment are shown in Figure 7.3. The learner quickly acquires the 11 categories known to the teacher agent and their communicative success reaches a level that is almost as high as in the baseline experiment (around 75% as also shown in Figure 3.4). The interpretation variance decreases and hence coherence increases over time. It reaches an equilibrium at a value of around 10, but still fluctuates slightly as the learner keeps adapting its colour categories.

The interpretation variance never drops to zero, which reflects the fact that the prototypes of the learned colour categories never completely match the pro-

7.2 Adoption and alignment operators

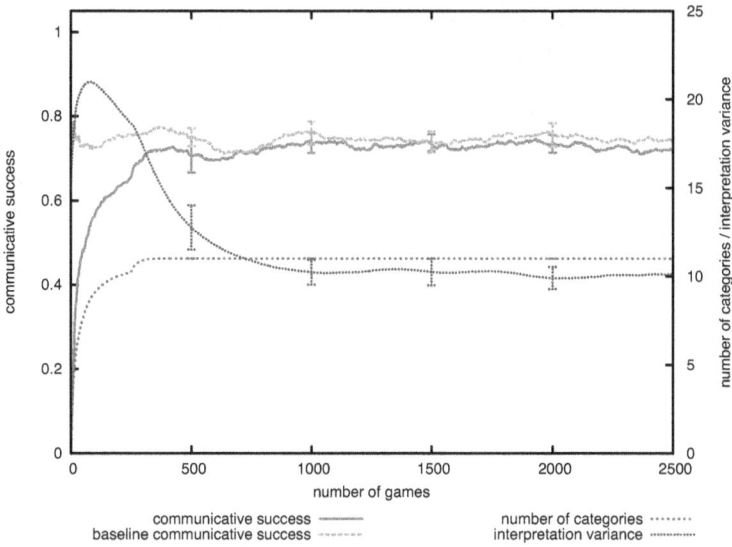

Figure 7.3: Dynamics of an example acquisition experiment in which the learner picks up a colour category system of the teacher. After 500 interactions, the communicative success of the teacher-learner interactions is almost as high as in the baseline experiment. The interpretation variance decreases to a value of around 10.

totypes of the colour categories of the teacher. The learner tries to position the prototype of each category on the centroid of a term – the most central colour of all the colours that will be named by the teacher using the same term. Hence the nonzero interpretation variance can be explained if the prototypes used by the teacher are not exactly at the centre of all colour samples that belong to the same category. One possible explanation could be that my model uses a different colour space than the one in which the centroids were reported and computed in literature. Sturges & Whitfield (1995) report their centroids in Munsell Colour System, whereas in my model the CIE $L^* a^* b^*$ colour space is used. As the transformation between these two spaces is not linear (see Appendix A.2 and A.4) a discrepancy between the prototypes of the teacher and the prototypes of the learner is to be expected.

The impact of the alignment rate on the interpretation variance is explored in Figure 7.4. It shows a trade-off between accuracy and speed of learning. A learner agent that uses a low alignment rate will align more slowly but will end up with

7 Basic colour strategy

a category system that more accurately represents the system of the teacher. The variance of agents that do not align their categories remains high.

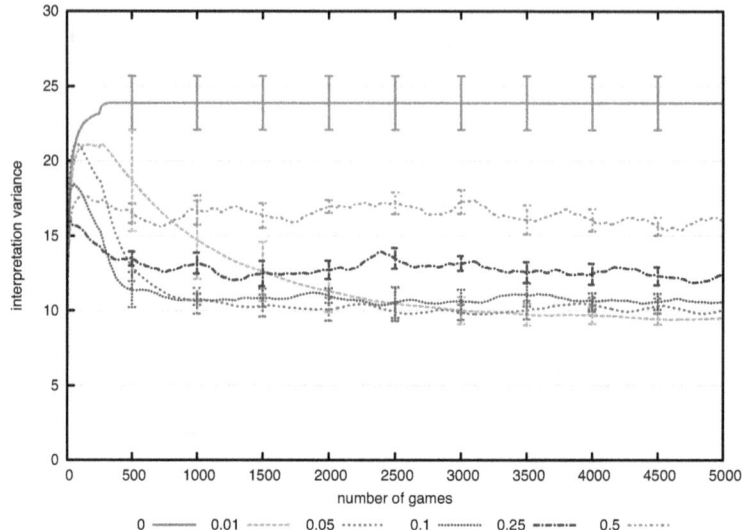

Figure 7.4: Parameter study for the alignment rate in relation to the interpretation variance between the resulting category system and the predefined language system. Higher alignment rates will result in faster but less accurate alignment.

Figure 7.5 shows an example acquisition process of a colour category system next to the target colour system. After 100 interactions, the learning agent has already learned the 11 different colour terms, but the prototypes of the corresponding categories do not yet fully resemble the target colour system. At the end of the acquisition experiment the alignment of the colour system is better.

7.3 Invention operator

The invention operator is triggered on the basis of not being able to discriminate the randomly selected topic colour sample in a context. Whenever this occurs, an agent might invent a new colour category focussed on the current topic to which a newly invented form will be associated. This form will be used to express this category in language.

7.3 Invention operator

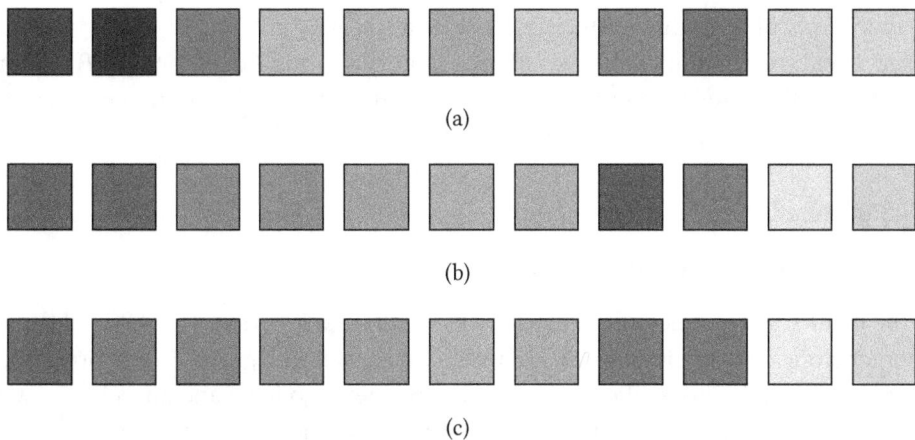

Figure 7.5: Example of acquired colour system: after 100 interactions (a) and after 2500 interactions (b). The target colour system is shown for comparison (c).

The rate at which new categories are invented is controlled by the COLOUR CATEGORY INVENTION RATE parameter. If it is set to a low value, it ensures that categories get a chance to spread into the population before another category gets invented. In the reported experiments, this rate is constant and set to 0.005.

Previous models (Steels & Belpaeme 2005; Belpaeme & Bleys 2005b; 2007) did not use an invention rate, but instead implemented mechanisms in which several terms could compete to express the same colour category. This competition was coordinated using a lateral inhibition scheme, which decreased the chances of competing terms being used whenever a successful interaction took place. It has been shown that such a mechanism leads to a one on one mapping between terms and colour categories. Typically, these models also included the functionality to merge two colour categories into one whenever they became too similar to each other.

The proposed use of an invention rate does not have a significant impact on the reported results and could be thought of as a simplification of previous models.

7.3.1 Formation experiment

In the formation experiment a population of agents needs to form their own colour category system from scratch. One context will consist of three randomly chosen Munsell chips (Newhall, Nickerson & Judd 1942), but with the additional

7 Basic colour strategy

constraints of a minimal interstimulus distance of 50 in the CIE $L^*u^*v^*$ colour space and the reproducibility of colour categories in the Adobe 1998 RGB colour system. Other environments display similar dynamics, but require more colour categories and more time to align. The population size is 10.

7.3.2 Results

7.3.2.1 Brightness and hue strategy

The resulting dynamics of the BRIGHTNESS AND HUE STRATEGY, in which all three dimensions of the colour space are used, are shown in Figure 7.6. The proposed strategy is sufficient to allow a population of agents to form and align their own colour category system. As in the acquisition experiment, the interpretation variance decreases over time but has not stabilised yet. The communicative success even surpasses the baseline communicative success (which is estimated in Figure 3.4 to be just below 90%). This however comes at the cost of a few more colour categories than in the baseline which consisted of 11 categories. As the adoption operator is implemented to not consider synonymy, the number of categories (shown in ontology size) is equal to the number of lexical entries in the lexicon (shown in lexicon size).

An example of the self-organisation of a colour category system in a population of 5 agents is shown in Figure 7.7. Initially, a lot of variability between the colour categories exists but this variability decreases over time due to the alignment operator. The final colour system is sufficiently coordinated to support successful communication.

7.3.2.2 Brightness strategy

The BRIGHTNESS STRATEGY, in which only the brightness dimension is profiled, is equally suitable to form a category system that is adequate for the communicative challenge posed by the environment as shown in Figure 7.8, although a slightly higher number of categories is required to achieve a slightly lower communicative success. The main difference is that the invented colour categories now do not possess any hue information and hence the colour categories are shades of grey, as illustrated in Figure 7.9.

7.3 Invention operator

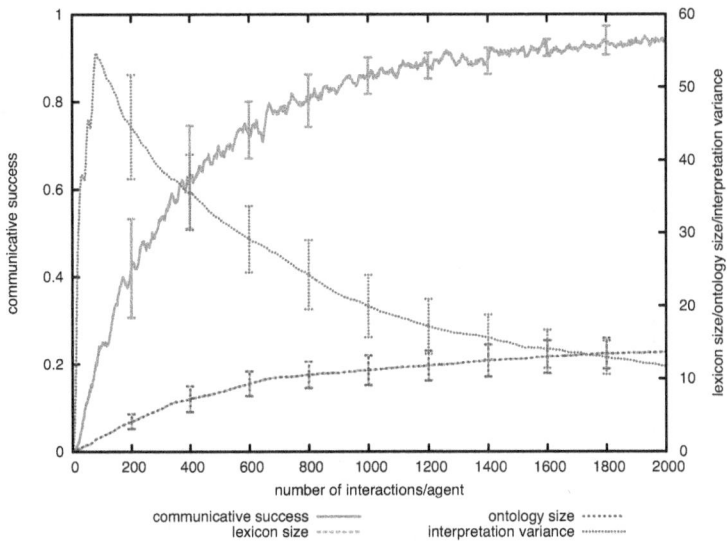

Figure 7.6: Dynamics of the formation experiment for the brightness and hue strategy. The agents are able to coordinate a colour category system that is successful in the communicative environment.

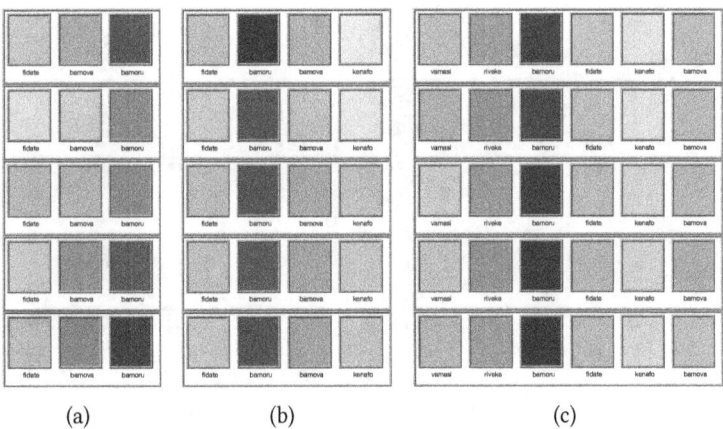

Figure 7.7: An evolving colour system for the basic colour strategy of a population of five agents after 200 (a), 400 (b) and 600 (c) interactions per agent. Each row shows the lexicon of one agent and the columns show the prototypes associated with a shared form.

7 Basic colour strategy

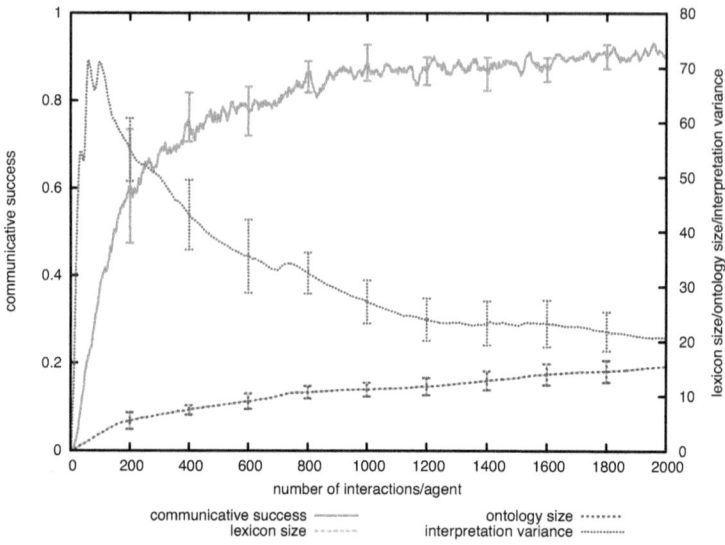

Figure 7.8: Dynamics of the formation experiment for the brightness strategy. The agents are able to coordinate a colour category system that is successful in the communicative environment.

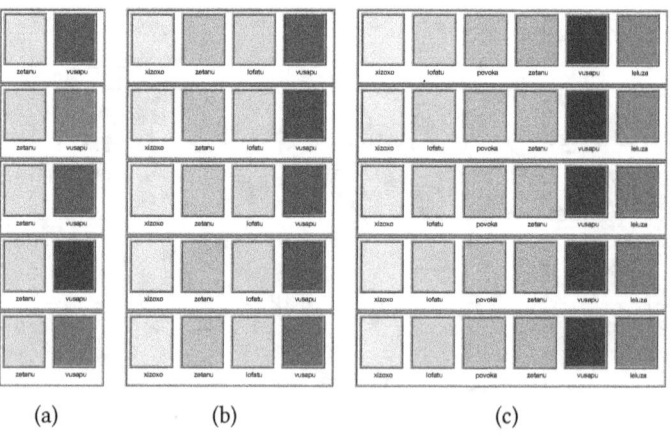

Figure 7.9: An evolving colour system for the brightness strategy of a population of five agents after 200 (a), 600 (b) and 800 (c) interactions per agent. Each row shows the lexicon of one agent and the columns show the prototypes associated with a shared form.

7.4 Conclusion

By specifying the acquisition and invention operators of a language strategy, it becomes possible to study the self-organisation of a language system based on that language strategy. The acquisition operators allow simulated agents to acquire a basic colour language system from one another and invention operators that allow a population of agents to invent their own language system. The performance of the acquisition operator can be evaluated by comparing the communicative success of an agent that acquires a predefined language from another agent. In a formation experiment, a population of agents need to invent a language system from scratch. This experiment allows to check the performance of the invention operators.

8 Graded membership strategy

As in the previous chapter for the basic colour strategy, the implementation of the graded membership strategy can be completed by defining its adoption, alignment and invention operator. Instead of inventing and acquiring colour categories, the graded membership strategy allows agents to invent and acquire membership categories. The invention operator allows users to expand the current language system with a new membership category and a new lexical rule to express this category in language whenever they feel the current system is insufficient for their communicative needs. The adoption operator allows users to pick up these newly invented terms and the corresponding membership categories. The alignment operator specifies how language users can align the prototypical values of the membership categories they are using.

8.1 Adoption and alignment operators

The main goal of the adoption and alignment operators of the graded membership strategy is to ensure that an agent can acquire the membership categories of another agent. The learner needs to be able to figure out how many membership categories are used by the other agent, and what the prototypical membership values of these categories are.

The adoption operator of the graded membership strategy is triggered whenever an agent hears an unknown term in combination with a known term which is associated with a colour category. The agent determines the membership value of topic's colour to the interpreted colour category and learns a new membership category based on this value. The resulting membership category is associated with the previously unknown term.

After each interaction in which a membership category is used the alignment operator for the graded membership strategy is used to ensure the prototypical membership values become aligned between agents. This operator involves determining the membership value of the current topic to the colour category used and adapting the membership value of the used membership category to this value. The rate at which this alignment happens is based on the MEMBERSHIP CATEGORY ALIGNMENT RATE, which linearly determines how much the prototypical

8 Graded membership strategy

value of the membership category should be adapted to the current situation. In this chapter the membership category alignment rate is set to 0.05 unless stated otherwise.

8.1.1 Acquisition experiment

In the acquisition experiment, one agent needs to learn the membership categories used by another agent through interactions based on a set of shared basic colour categories. These membership categories are identical to the ones used in the baseline experiment of the graded membership strategy for Tarahumara as described in §4.4. The contexts about which the agents have to communicate consist of five randomly chosen Munsell chips (Newhall, Nickerson & Judd 1942), without any additional constraints.

8.1.2 Measures: Membership category variance

The membership category variance is defined similarly to the interpretation variance for basic colour categories, but instead of computing the distance between the different colour categories in a conceptual space, the difference between the prototypical values of the membership categories is used in this measure. The lower the variance, the higher the coherence between the membership categories of the agents.

For each unique form (f) that is associated with a membership category in a population of agents P, the membership category variance is computed within the subset $A_f = \{a_1, a_2, ..., a_n\}$ of agents that know this form, as shown in Equation 8.1. For each pair of agents the difference between the prototypical values of the membership categories is computed and averaged.

$$I_{mcv}(f) = \frac{2}{n(n-1)} \sum_{i=1}^{n} \sum_{j=i+1}^{n} d(a_i(f), a_j(f)) \tag{8.1}$$

Following an identical reasoning as for the interpretation variance, the formula for computing the membership category variance for all forms (F) that are associated with a membership category within a population, is defined in Equation 8.2, where $|P|$ is the population size and $|a_i|$ is the total number of forms that are known to agent a_i.

$$I_{mcv}(P) = \sum_{f \in F} \left(\sum_{i=1}^{n} \frac{1}{|P||a_i|} \right) I_{mcv}(f) \tag{8.2}$$

8.1.3 Results

The resulting dynamics are shown in Figure 8.1. Initially the communicative success of the learner is lower than the baseline communicative success. This is due to the initial guesses made by the learner on the prototypical membership values of the membership categories used by the teacher. After some interactions, the alignment of the membership categories improves, as shown by a decrease in the membership category variance measure. This is also reflected by an increase of the communicative success of the learner which in the end of the experiment matches the baseline communicative success. The number of membership categories known to the learner is not shown, as this would obscure the details of the membership category variance, but in each run the learner quickly picks up the three different membership categories used by the teacher.

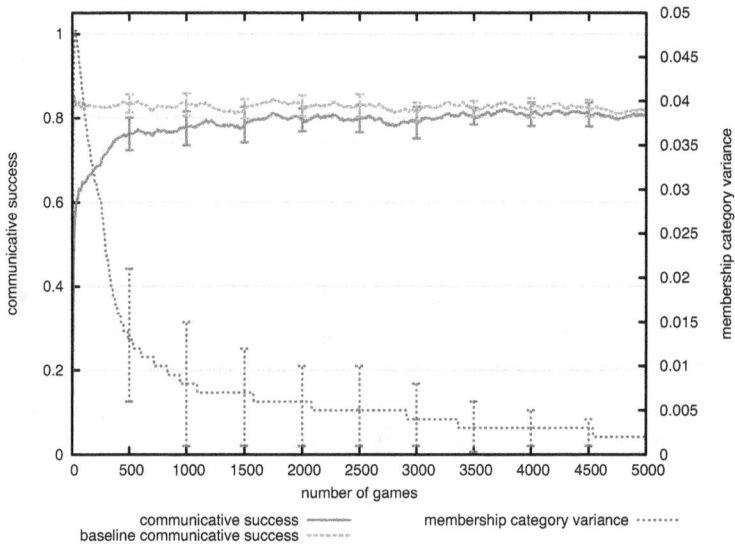

Figure 8.1: Dynamics of the acquisition experiment for the graded membership strategy. The learner is able to pick up the membership categories used by the teacher, as shown by its communicative success. This success matches the baseline communicative success as the membership category variance decreases. The results are averaged over 10 independent runs.

8 Graded membership strategy

Another way of verifying the performance of the adoption and alignment operators is by tracking the prototypical membership values of the categories known to the learner over time. An example of a graph tracking these values is shown in Figure 8.2 and the target values are shown in Table 4.1. Although the initial guesses of the prototypical values are quite different from the target values, the alignment operator enables the agent to learn the correct values over time.

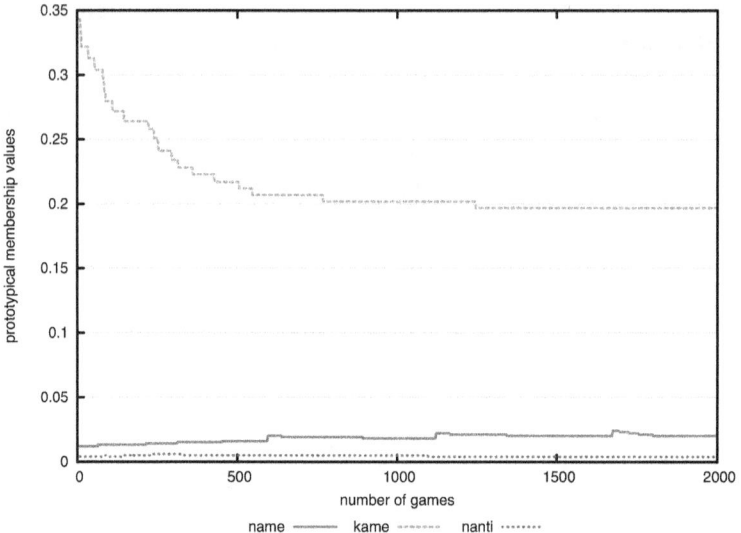

Figure 8.2: Prototypical membership values learned in an acquisition experiment based on the Tarahumara language system. Initially, the prototypical membership values of these categories are quite different from the teacher. After around 1000 interactions, the values approach those of the teacher until they match almost perfectly.

8.2 Invention operator

The invention operator can be triggered whenever a speaker is not able to discriminate the colour of the randomly selected topic. Whenever this occurs, the agent can extend the current language system with a new membership category based on the membership value of the topic of the current interaction. The rate at which an agent chooses to do so, is controlled by the MEMBERSHIP CATEGORY INVENTION RATE. The lower this rate, the lower the chance of an agent inventing a new membership category.

8.2 Invention operator

8.2.1 Formation experiment

The goal of the formation experiment is to let a population of agents develop its own system of membership categories. As the use of these categories depends on the use of basic colour categories, the set of basic colour categories is assumed to be shared within the population, before they start inventing membership categories.

The formation experiment is run in two different environments: an unconstrained one and a constrained one. Unconstrained contexts consist of five randomly drawn Munsell chips (Newhall, Nickerson & Judd 1942). Constrained contexts will be introduced later on. The basic colour category system that is shared by all agents at the onset of the experiment is based on the Tarahumara language system (but without the membership categories). The invention rate is set to 0.005.

8.2.2 Measures: Number of membership categories

The number of membership categories of an agent (n_{mc}) simply corresponds to the number of membership categories known to this agent. At the level of a population P it is understood as the average number of known membership categories over all agents in the population.

$$n_{mc}(P) = \frac{\sum_{i=1}^{|P|} n_{mc}(a)}{|P|} \qquad (8.3)$$

8.2.3 Results

The resulting dynamics of the experiment in an unconstrained environment are shown in Figure 8.3. The agents reach a level of communicative success that is higher than the baseline experiment. The variance between the membership values of the membership categories between agents is quite low. The higher level of communicative success comes at the cost of a higher number of membership categories (around 13 where in the baseline experiment there were only 3). Moreover, this number does not seem to stabilise.

The main reason why the agents keep inventing new membership categories in an unconstrained environment, is that the continuous nature of the membership function. Agents keep on encountering situations in which their current repertoire of membership categories is insufficient to discriminate the topic based on its membership value.

8 Graded membership strategy

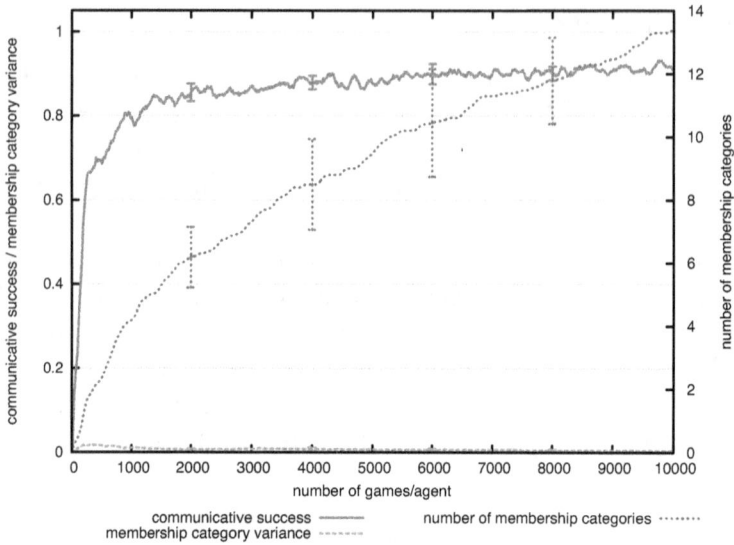

Figure 8.3: Dynamics of the formation experiment in an unconstrained environment. The agents reach a level of communicative success that is higher than the baseline experiment, but this comes at the cost of a higher number of membership categories. The results are averaged over 10 independent runs.

In order to verify this hypothesis, I have run exactly the same model in a constrained environment: the difference between the membership values of entities that belong to the same basic colour categories is guaranteed to be above a certain threshold, which is set to 0.2. As the agents are expected to invent only a limited number of membership categories, the invention rate is set to 0.5.

The resulting dynamics are shown in Figure 8.4. The communicative success reached by the agents is higher than in the previous experiment and the membership variance is slightly higher than before. Most importantly the average number of membership categories stabilises around 5. This number corresponds exactly to the expected number of required membership categories, as the membership function ranges from zero to unity and a minimal difference of 0.2 in membership value is guaranteed.

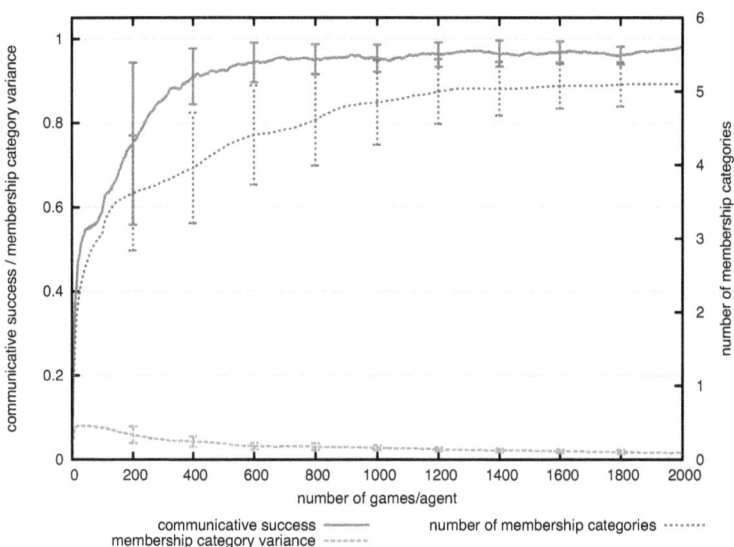

Figure 8.4: Dynamics of the formation experiment in a constrained environment in which the difference in membership values of entities categorised as the same basic colour categories is guaranteed to be more than 0.2. This additional constraint results in a stable number of membership categories. The results are averaged over 10 independent runs.

8.3 Conclusion

In this chapter, I have shown how the methodology that was used for completing the basic colour strategy can readily be extended to cover other language strategies, such as the graded membership strategy. I have introduced the adoption and alignment operators that allow one agent to pick up the membership categories used by another agent. The performance of these operators is evaluated in an acquisition experiment. Finally, I introduced the invention operator for the graded membership strategy, which allows a population of agents to invent and coordinate its own system of membership categories.

9 Further experiments on basic colour systems

Once all the operators have been provided for a particular language strategy, several in-depth studies on various aspects of language systems based on that language strategy are possible. In this chapter, I will study language systems that are based on the basic colour strategy. First, I will study the impact of colour distributions in the environment of the agents on the similarity between individually learned colour systems and human colour systems in §9.1 (Belpaeme & Bleys 2009). Next, I will investigate the impact of language on the similarity between universal trends that have been reported in literature in §9.2 and colour systems that result from simulation (Belpaeme & Bleys 2005a,b; 2007). Both these experiments have been conducted in collaboration with Tony Belpaeme. Finally, I will examine the impact of embodiment on the performance of the adoption, alignment and invention operators of the basic colour strategy in §9.3 (Bleys et al. 2009).

9.1 Impact of environment on similarity to natural systems

Ever since Berlin & Kay (1969) observed that colour categories show a remarkable cross-cultural similarity, there has been an ongoing debate on what the main cause of this universal character of colour categories might be. Some authors (Van Wijk 1959; Shepard 1992; Yendrikhovskij 2001) claim that this cross-cultural similarity is due to the shared environment in which individuals use their colour categories. These environments exhibit statistical distributions by which colours occur, which are not uniform. It is claimed that these distributions limit the number of possible configurations of the colour category systems.

Yendrikhovskij (2001) presented computational simulations that support this view. He demonstrated how the distribution of colours in natural images can be used to extract colour categories that resemble human colour categories. For this purpose, the colour information of 10k pixels drawn from images of natural

9 Further experiments on basic colour systems

scenes was converted to a perceptual colour space (CIE $L^*u^*v^*$) and an unsupervised clustering algorithm was used to extract a number of clusters. Yendrikhovskij showed how these clusters resemble the colour categories of American subjects (Boynton & Olson 1987). This was shown by matching the cluster centroids to the English colour categories and computing the correlations between each dimension of the CIE $L^*u^*v^*$ colour space, the chroma C^*_{uv} and the hue h^*_{uv}. The correlations were high, ranging from $r = 0.762$ for lightness to $r = 0.999$ for hue.

Without denying the importance of Yendrikhovskij's work, we would like to critically assess the evidence and extend his work. In order to truly validate the claim that the high correlations to human colour categories are mainly due to the colour distributions in the environment, it is essential to compare the reported results starting from a control dataset in which no such distribution is present (i.e. each colour occurs with the same probability). Only if the correlations between the centroids found in the latter dataset are significantly lower than those originally reported, one can conclude that the high correlation in the original study is due to the colour distribution present in the original dataset. In order to measure the importance of the colour distribution, one could also start from a different set of pictures and compare the results to those reported in the original study.

9.1.1 Data sets

Two sets of photographs have been collected, one containing natural images and the other urban images. The nature collection was compiled from image databases on the internet, and contains imagery of animals, flowering plants and landscapes. The urban collection contains photographs shot with a digital camera (Olympus C-4000 ZOOM) in a Northern European environment; it contains imagery of buildings, people and urban activities, both indoor and outdoor; both collections contain 300 images.

From both image sets 25k RGB-pixels were randomly selected, one which I will call the NATURAL DATA SET and the other which I will indicate as the URBAN DATA SET. I also added a control dataset, called UNIFORM DATA SET which consists of 25k random RGB values, to test the null-hypothesis that categories are not influenced by the chromatic distribution in the environment. All RGB values have been converted to both the CIE $L^*a^*b^*$ and CIE $L^*u^*v^*$ colour space. A projection of the three data sets on the a^*b^* plane are shown in Figure 9.1.

A first analysis of the data reveals that natural and urban data sets indeed contain a non-random structure. Figure 9.2 shows histograms of the CIE $L^*a^*b^*$

9.1 Impact of environment on similarity to natural systems

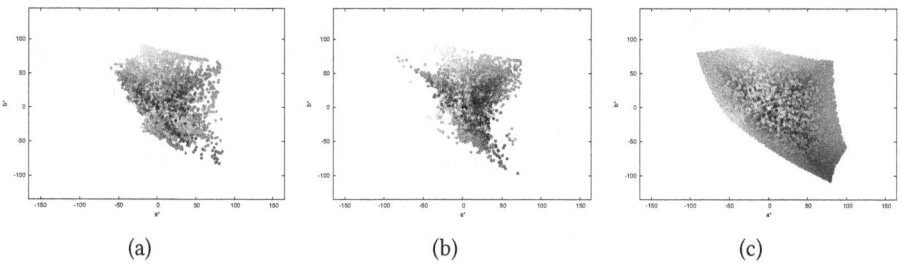

Figure 9.1: Three different simulated data sets, projected on the a^*b^* hue plane of the CIE $L^*a^*b^*$ colour space: (a) the natural data set; (b) the urban data set; (c) the uniform data set

values of the data sets. While the uniform data set has a quasi uniform distribution, the natural and urban data sets have a higher distribution of lowly saturated colours. This confirms previous observations of the chromatic content of natural scenes (Howard & Burnidge 1994) that natural occurring colours occupy a restricted area of the chromaticity diagram.

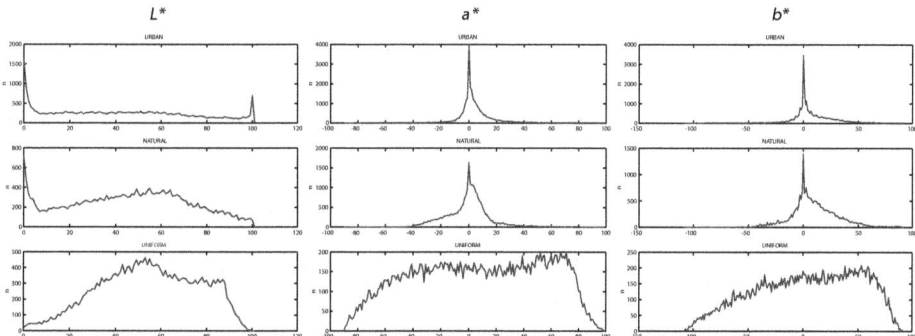

Figure 9.2: Histogram of the three different simulated data sets per channel. The urban and natural data set contain more unsaturated colours than the uniform data set.

9.1.2 Extracting colour categories

As clustering algorithm I used the k-means clustering algorithm (Lloyd 1982). k-means clustering uses an iterative re-estimation procedure. Initially, k data points are selected as initial centroids. All data points are assigned to the nearest

9 Further experiments on basic colour systems

centroid (according to the distance between the sample and the centroid). The centroids are recalculated to be the mean of all the samples that are associated to it. After the recalculation all the samples are classified again and the centroids are recomputed. This algorithm continues until a stop criterion is met, usually when there is no further change in the assignment of the data points.

As k-means clustering is not deterministic (a random seed is needed to select the initial centroids), the clusters found by each run of the algorithm might vary. How much the clusters vary depends on the structure of the data. To deal with possible variation in the found clusters, the colour data was clustered 1000 times. The variation in the outcome of the centroids found by the algorithm for the datasets I am using, is illustrated in Figure 9.3. The $1000 \times k$ centroids are then clustered again using k-means clustering, but now the initial points are each time chosen to be equal to the outcome of one run in the previous phase. From these solutions, the one in which the average distance between the $1000 \times k$ centroids and the nearest centroid in the solution is minimal, is chosen to be the final k clusters. The goal of this additional step is to avoid some algorithm specific problems due to outliers in the original dataset (Bradley & Fayyad 1998).

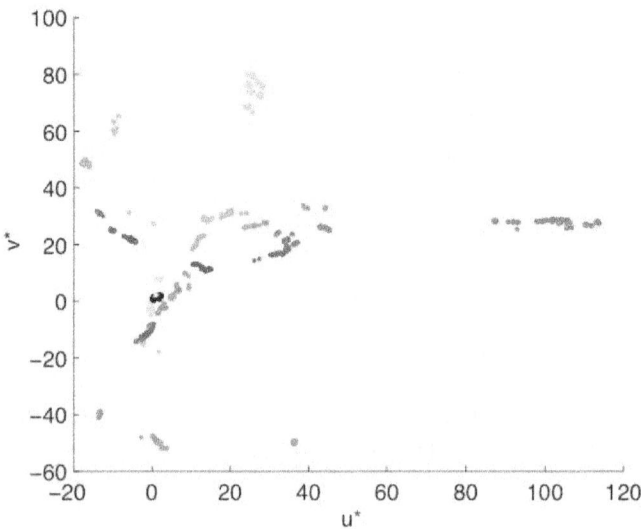

Figure 9.3: Typical example of the variation of the centroids found after running the standard k-means clustering algorithm. The collection of the centroids of 1000 independent runs of the algorithm is projected on the u^*v^*-plane for the natural data-set for k = 11.

9.1 Impact of environment on similarity to natural systems

9.1.3 Comparison to human colour categories

To compare the impact of the statistical distribution on the resulting centroids several analyses can be performed. I provide the results of two such analyses.

The first analysis is based on a correlation measure (Kendall's Tau) for each dimension. This non-parametric test does not require data to have a certain distribution (Conover 1999). The test returns values between -1 and 1. A value of 1 indicates that the correlation is complete and -1 that the correlation is complete, but inverse. A value of 0 indicates that no linear correlation could be found, while values closer to 1 or -1 indicate an increasing correlation. The correlation was computed for 11 clusters. Table 9.1 reports the correlations between the centroids extracted from the natural, urban and uniform data sets and the English categories, both for CIE $L^*a^*b^*$ and CIE $L^*u^*v^*$.

Table 9.1: Correlation between cluster centroids and human colour categories in the CIE $L^*a^*b^*$ and CIE $L^*u^*v^*$ colour space.

	L^*	u^*	v^*	C^*_{uv}	H_{uv}
NATURAL	0.561*	0.673*	0.636*	0.709*	0.745*
URBAN	0.972*	0.564*	0.673*	0.636*	0.636*
UNIFORM	0.187	0.418	0.745*	0.491*	0.818*
	L^*	a^*	b^*	C^*_{ab}	H_{ab}
NATURAL	0.785*	0.200	0.745*	0.709*	0.636*
URBAN	0.935*	0.382	0.745*	0.491*	0.345
RANDOM	0.411	0.309	0.782*	0.600*	0.709*

* Correlation is significant at the 0.05 level.

The high correlations between the centroids extracted from the natural and urban data sets and the English colour categories (Sturges & Whitfield 1995) confirm the results of Yendrikhovskij. However, the correlation remains high (although somewhat lower) for the uniform dataset. As the uniform data set contains no chromatic structure, as opposed to the natural or urban data sets, one would expect the correlation for this set to be zero on average. Nevertheless, the uniform data set still results in clusters having a remarkably positive correlation with human colour categories, which allows me to reject the explanation offered by Yendrikhovskij. This can only be explained by the structure of the colour space and the nature of the clustering algorithm.

9 Further experiments on basic colour systems

For the second analysis, I created a benchmark test to compare the performance of each resulting set of centroids in more detail. This benchmark consists of naming one hundred consensus chips (i.e. chips for which there was unanimous agreement in colour naming) of the study of Sturges & Whitfield (shown in Figure 3.1). In order to name these chips, a matching process is required to associate each centroid to one of the English colour categories. Each consensus chip is named using the colour term of the associated English colour category, using a nearest neighbour algorithm based on the centroids. The results, broken down by each category, are summarised in Table 9.2.

Table 9.2: Number of correctly named consensus samples broken down by category: white (WE), grey (GY), black (BK), green (GN), yellow (YW), blue (BL), red (RD), purple (PU), brown (BR), orange (OR) and pink (PK). The total number of consensus chips is shown on top. The top part represents the results in CIE $L^*a^*b^*$, the bottom part in CIE $L^*u^*v^*$. The results are shown for the categories found in English (s&w) and all three datasets: natural (NAT), urban (URB) and uniform (UNI). Only the results for 11 centroids are shown.

	WE	GY	BK	GN	YW	BL	RD	PU	BR	OR	PK	TOTAL
	2	6	3	22	8	25	4	14	4	6	6	100
s&w	2	6	3	17	8	18	4	9	4	6	6	83
NAT	2	1	3	8	8	11	4	6	2	0	0	45
URB	2	4	2	5	8	18	4	2	0	0	3	48
UNI	2	0	3	2	0	5	4	0	0	1	3	20
s&w	2	6	3	18	8	18	4	9	4	6	6	84
NAT	2	5	3	15	8	24	4	6	0	0	1	68
URB	2	5	3	5	8	24	4	6	2	0	2	61
UNI	2	0	3	13	8	0	4	1	0	4	4	39

A first important observation from these results is that even when the English categories of the same study are used, the benchmark only reaches about 83% of success. This suggests that, although capable of accounting for more than three quarters of the consensus chips, the one-nearest neighbour classification algorithm might be too general to capture all the richness of human colour categories. This first result sets the maximal level of success one might hope to achieve when using this particular classification algorithm.

The performance of the centroids resulting from the uniform data set is still quite good, from a quarter to a half of the maximal expected performance, depending on the used colour space. This can only be accounted for by the shape of the colour spaces and the clustering algorithm that were used but not by any statistical distribution in the environment. However, if such a distribution is present in a data set, such as in the natural and urban data sets, it significantly improves the performance of the benchmark by about a third of the maximal expected performance. When using the CIE $L^*a^*b^*$ or CIE $L^*u^*v^*$ colour space, about half or a quarter of the maximal expected performance remains unaccounted for.

9.1.4 Conclusion

The chromatic structure in the environment has a positive impact on the correlation of the resulting centroids of the clustering algorithm and colour categories of human subjects. However, even if there is no chromatic structure in the environment, our model still manages to extract categories which correlate well with human colour categories. This suggests that while there is an impact of the environment on resulting colour categories, the perceptual colour space and the clustering algorithm that are used have a more profound influence.

9.2 Impact of language on universal trends

In order to discern the impact of language on the coordination of colour categories, I compare two experiments. The first one is a regular formation experiment (see §7.3.1) in which a population of agents needs to construct their own category system. In the discrimination experiment on the other hand, there is a population of agents which needs to learn to discriminate different colours in a particular context through a series of discrimination games without using any language (Steels 1997; Belpaeme, Steels & van Looveren 1998).

As the only difference between the formation and discrimination experiment are the linguistic constraints, I can compare the outcome of the two types of experiments to quantify the influence of language on the formation of a colour category system.

9.2.1 Discrimination game

In contrast to a normal naming game, a DISCRIMINATION GAME is played by a single agent to whom a context consisting of several objects is presented. The agent selects a random object for which it needs to find a discriminative category:

9 Further experiments on basic colour systems

no other object in the context might be categorised as belonging to the same category as the chosen object. Whenever it is able to find such a category, the game is considered to be a success; otherwise, it is considered to be a failure.

When a discrimination game fails, the decision to either deploy the invention operator or the alignment operator, for which the learning rate is set to 0.7, depends on a number of conditions. When the agents do not know any categories so far, the invention operator is used. Otherwise, the choice depends on its *discriminative success*, which tracks the rate of success by the agent in the game so far. If this rate is above a certain threshold (in this experiment it is set to 0.9), the agent will use the alignment operator, otherwise it will deploy the invention operator. This ensures that after a sufficient number of games, the agent will end up with a set of categories that allow it to reach the level of discriminatory success indicated by the threshold.

9.2.2 Alignment within one population

To investigate the impact of language on the coordination of colour categories within one population, I used the random data sets from the previous experiment (see §9.1.1) and compared the resulting categories at the end of one formation experiment to the categories at the end of one discrimination experiment. This comparison confirms the earlier results from Steels & Belpaeme (2005): cultural acquisition of categories under the influence of language results in categories which are coordinated among all agents in a population. Figure 9.4 shows the prototypes of each category of all agents of one population at the end of a simulation projected on the a^*b^*-plane. The formation experiment results in categories which are clustered; the discrimination experiment results in colour categories which are randomly scattered across the colour space. This clearly shows that the coordination of the categories should be credited to the cultural influence on the formation process.

9.2.3 Alignment over different populations

In their groundbreaking research, Berlin & Kay (1969) studied colour naming of 20 different languages around the world, which showed remarkable cross-cultural similarities. Some colour samples from the Munsell chart seemed to be more likely to become named by a colour term than others which moreover correspond to the 11 basic colour terms in English. This study received heavy criticisms, such as eliciting information only from a very low number of informants. Most of these criticisms have been addressed in a follow-up study, which

9.2 Impact of language on universal trends

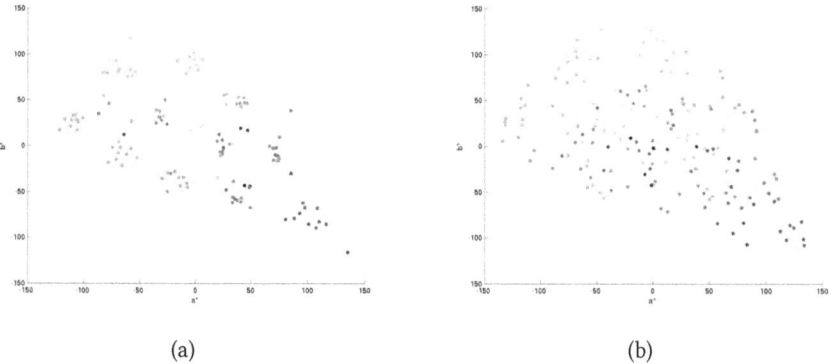

Figure 9.4: Resulting categories of (a) all agents in a population of 10 agents at the end of a formation experiment and (b) 10 agents learning categories individually in a discrimination experiment.

studied 110 pre-industrial languages (Kay et al. 2010). The resulting typology of these 110 languages are shown in a contour plot over the histogram of the Munsell chart in Figure 9.5. Some regions in the chart are more likely to become the foci that are named in a language. These regions are claimed to correspond to the English colour foci. Analysis of the resulting data has confirmed the existence of universal trends (Regier, Kay & Cook 2005). These results are, however, still controversial (see for example Roberson, Davies & Davidoff (2002); Roberson (2005)).

One of the main questions is whether the proposed implementation of the *basic colour strategy* in which the focus is put on the linguistic/cultural constraints, is capable of reproducing such trends. If culture is largely arbitrary, then colour categories are expected to be largely arbitrary as well (Roberson 2005). Two separate populations will end up with different colour categories, even if these populations start out under the same conditions.

I compare two experiments: a discrimination experiment, in which language has no impact on the formation of the colour category system, and a formation experiment, in which language does apply some pressure to the formation process. Each experiment is run 105 times in a population of 10 agents in two different environmental conditions: one is based on the natural data set and the other one on the uniform data set (§9.1.1). The context consists of three colour samples and the minimal distance between the different samples in the context varies between 40 and 60 (5 runs for each integer increment) in the CIE $L^*a^*b^*$ colour space.

9 Further experiments on basic colour systems

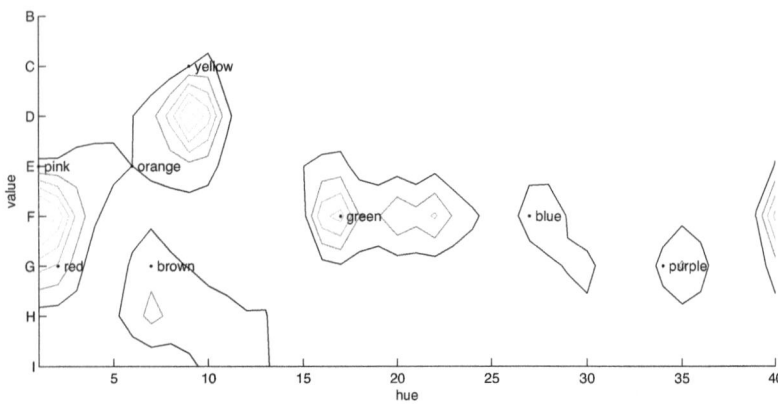

Figure 9.5: Contour plot of the histogram of foci over the Munsell diagram for the 110 languages studied in the World Colour Survey. The lighter the contour lines, the higher the histogram. The foci of the colour categories for English are shown for reference.

The resulting categories of the different runs are collected and presented as a contour plot of the histograms on the Munsell diagram in Figures 9.6–9.9. Interestingly, the histograms that are produced by the experiments are not flat but contain some structure.

To compare the simulation results with the data from the World Color Survey, I first determine the location of the highest peaks in all histograms. This is done by a search for local maxima in the histogram. Local maxima are connected components of histogram values with the same value v, whose external boundaries all have a value less than v. Next I compare the 10 highest peaks of the World Color Survey data with the 10 highest peaks of our simulation data. This is done by computing the undirected Hausdorff distance (Rucklidge 1997). The undirected Hausdorff distance $H(A, B)$ between two sets of coordinates A and B is computed as in Equations 9.1–9.2, with $d(s, t)$ being the Euclidean distance between coordinates s and t.

$$H(A, B) = \max(h(A, B), h(B, A)) \tag{9.1}$$

$$h(S, T) = \max_{s \in S} \left(\min_{t \in T} \left(d\left(s, t\right) \right) \right) \tag{9.2}$$

Table 9.3 shows the distance between the highest WCS peaks and the highest peaks of the simulation results. The best result is obtained when communicative

9.2 *Impact of language on universal trends*

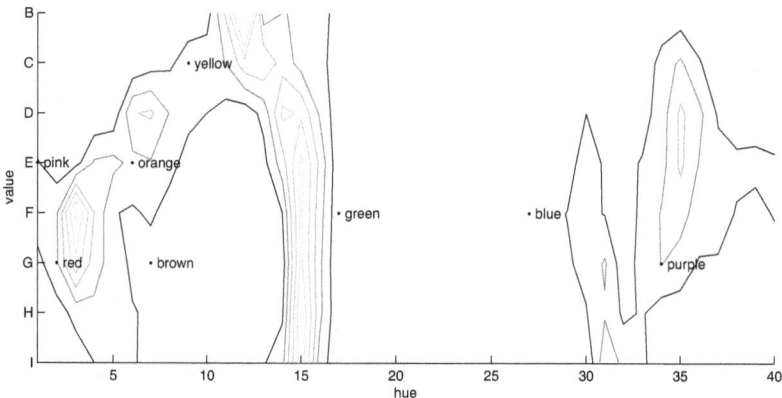

Figure 9.6: Contour plot of the resulting categories of 105 runs of the discrimination experiment using the natural data set.

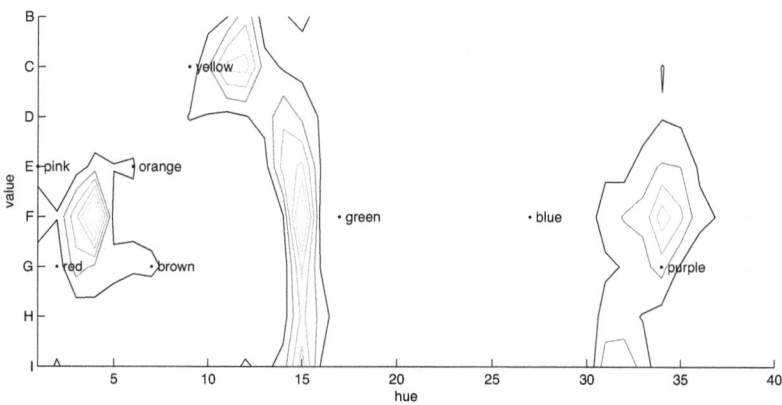

Figure 9.7: Contour plot of the resulting categories of 105 runs of the formation experiment using the natural data set.

9 *Further experiments on basic colour systems*

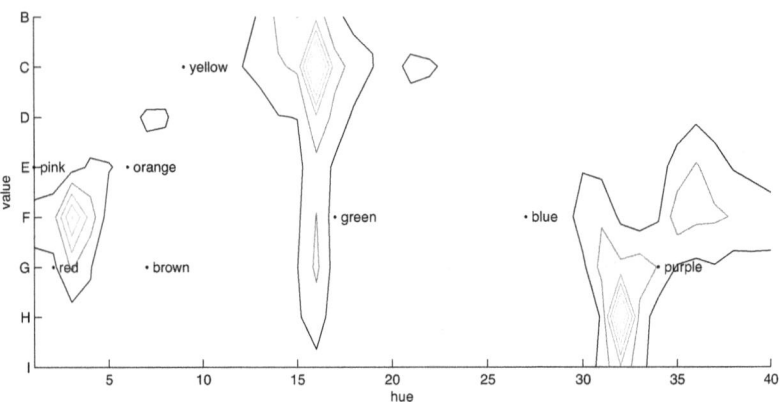

Figure 9.8: Contour plot of the resulting categories of 105 runs of the discrimination experiment using the uniform data set.

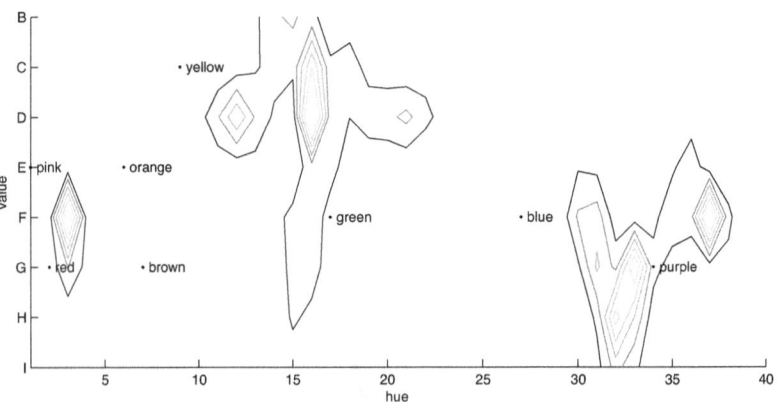

Figure 9.9: Contour plot of the resulting categories of 105 runs of the formation experiment using the uniform data set.

constraints are present but the environmental constraints are absent. This suggests that environmental constraints are more of a burden than a blessing: if the agents are allowed to sample the whole colour gamut, they form categories at locations that are more closely to human colour categories.

Table 9.3: Hausdorff distance between resulting topologies and WCS data. The lower the distance, the more similar to the WCS data.

x	$H(x, WCS)$
discrimination experiment, uniform data set	5.39
discrimination experiment, natural data set	7.00
formation experiment, uniform data set	5.10
formation experiment, natural data set	7.00

9.2.4 Conclusion

I have shown the coordinating role of language which allows agents to align their colour categories. When no linguisic or cultural feedback mechanism is in place, the colour categories of the agents are spread out over the complete conceptual space. The impact of language on the alignment over different populations is less pronounced: although some universal trends seem to pop up, the additional effect of language seems rather limited. I have been able to show that environmental constraints are more of a curse than of a blessing if one wants to explain the universal trends that exist in human colour category systems around the world. Other constraints, for example the structure of the internal conceptual space or properties of the classification algorithm, most likely play a bigger part to explain these trends.

9.3 Impact of embodiment on performance of operators

Most of the previous studies on the formation and coordination of colour category systems have assumed that no difference exists in how interacting agents perceive the colour stimuli in the context. This is not very realistic for embodied interactions in which agents perceive colourful objects around them, using their own vision system. Embodied agents will never share the same position in the world and hence will perceive the objects from their own perspective. The

9 Further experiments on basic colour systems

colours of the objects perceived by the agents will never be identical, due to for example differences in lighting conditions or appearances when perceived from different angles.

To investigate the influence of this PERCEPTUAL DEVIATION, I introduce the Grounded Colour Naming Game in which agents are embodied in humanoid robots (Figure 9.10) and individually perceive scenes through their cameras. The setup is similar to other language game experiments with robots (e.g. Lego robots (Vogt 2003), pan-tilt cameras (Steels 1998), Sony Aibo robots (Steels & Loetzsch 2008; Loetzsch, van Trijp & Steels 2008) and the Sony humanoid robots which are also used in this experiment (Wellens, Loetzsch & Steels 2008)).

Figure 9.10: The Grounded Colour Naming Game. It is similar to the Colour Naming Game but involves embodied agents that perceive the world through their own vision system.

The embodied data used in this experiment was recorded by Michael Spranger and Martin Loetzsch. Michael Spranger also developed the vision system that is used by these robots.

9.3.1 Robotic setup and visual perception

The Sony humanoid robots (Fujita et al. 2003) used in this experiment are about 60 cm high, weigh approximately 7 kg and have 38 degrees of freedom. The robots are placed in a closed office environment in which a set of coloured objects are placed. Before each interaction, the experimenter modifies the current scene by adding or removing an object or by changing the position or orientation of an object in the scene. Each scene contains between two and four coloured objects from a set of 20 objects (Figure 9.11). The main sensor used for perception is one of the three CCD cameras in the head of the robot.

Figure 9.11: Objects that were presented to the robots. Left: ten geometric objects (carton boxes, buckets, foam bricks). Right: ten toy-like objects (cones, a ball, animals).

The main goal of the robot's vision system is to construct persistent internal representations of the objects in the robot's environment. This system involves three sub-systems. First, low-level vision routines process raw camera images to yield basic PERCEPTS (Figures 9.12(a)-9.12(d)). Percepts are connected regions that differ from the background of the environment. The statistics of the environment's background are acquired in a calibration phase.

Second, these foreground regions are tracked in subsequent camera images despite changing positions and appearances of the objects. In order to do so, the vision system needs to establish a correspondence between the internal OBJECT MODEL and the image regions that refer to the same physical object, a process known in robotics as ANCHORING (Coradeschi & Saffiotti 2003). Colour histograms of already established object models are used to classify image regions with respect to their similarity to object models (Figure 9.12(d)). Kalman Filters (Kalman 1960) are used to associate classified regions to object models based on colour similarity and position in the image (Figure 9.12(e)).

Third, when needed in communicative interactions, the vision system encodes a set of visual properties about each object model. These properties are colour, position, height and width, but in this experiment only the colour information of each object is used. The camera of the robot delivers up to 30 images per second with a resolution of 176×144 pixels in the YCrCb colour space. The colour of the object is the average colour of all pixels that make up the object. This average

9 Further experiments on basic colour systems

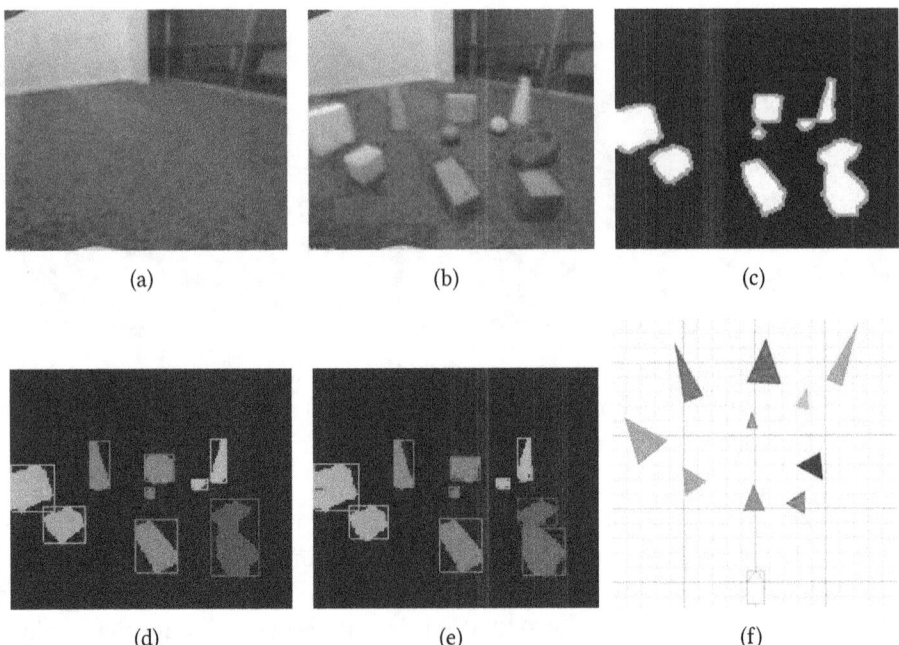

Figure 9.12: The object vision system. (a): a raw camera image taken during the calibration phase. (b): a camera image of a scene containing objects. (c): the result of noise-reduced foreground/ background classification. (d): the segmented foreground regions drawn in their average colour and with bounding boxes. Note that the partially overlapping blue and green blocks in the right bottom of the original image are segmented into the same foreground region. (e): classification of foreground pixels using existing colour models. Pixels are drawn in the average colour of the most similar object model. (f): computation of colour, position and size in a robot-egocentric reference system. The width and height of objects is indicated by the width and height of the triangles.

9.3 Impact of embodiment on performance of operators

colour is transformed into the perceptually equidistant colour space CIE $L^*a^*b^*$ (using the equations described in Appendix A). Furthermore, in order to be able to point to objects, the position of objects is computed in a robot egocentric reference system (Figure 9.12(f)).

The robotic setup, including the vision system and mechanisms to establish JOINT ATTENTION (Tomasello 1995), is described in more detail in other background papers (Spranger 2008; Loetzsch, Spranger & Steels 2010).

9.3.2 Perceptual deviation and structure in embodied data

When moving from simulated to embodied experiments, the colour stimuli differ in two main ways. The first difference is that in embodied experiments, it is very unlikely that both speaker and hearer experience the colours of a physical object in an identical way as lighting conditions and appearances of objects may vary from the different perspectives of the robots. This is what I call PERCEPTUAL DEVIATION, which is illustrated in Figure 9.13. The average difference in perceptual experiences for the same objects in the world across all scenes used in our experiment, is shown in Figure 9.14.

	obj-9	obj-11	obj-17	obj-7	obj-15	obj-10
L^*	35.5	51.2	50.5	35.6	62.2	52.8
a^*	7.7	−17.1	26.7	7.2	27.9	−20.1
b^*	−40.7	−14.0	39.6	−39.0	52.5	−11.3

Figure 9.13: Comparison between the colour perceptions of two robots for an example scene. The robots see the yellow duck (obj-17 for the left robot and obj-15 for the right robot) from different sides and distances and thus perceive very different a^* and b^* values for the same object.

9 *Further experiments on basic colour systems*

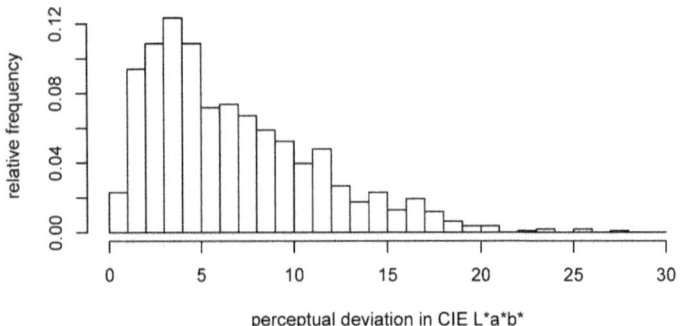

Figure 9.14: A histogram of the perceptual deviation between the speaker and the hearer for the grounded data set used for the experiments reported in this paper (mean = 6.721; st. dev. = 4.575). This distribution is skewed towards lower deviations.

The second main difference between simulated stimuli and embodied data is that the colour stimuli in embodied experiments contain a higher level of *structure*. Because the number of used objects is typically limited in embodied experiments due to practical constraints (in our experiment to 20 objects), some colours do not occur at all while other colours will appear more often than others (Figure 9.15). Using a one nearest-neighbour classification algorithm, I determine the relative frequency of the English colour categories (Sturges & Whitfield 1995) in the grounded data: red (.28), green (.20), purple (.12), black (.11), blue (.10), brown (.09), orange (.04) and yellow (.04). The colour categories pink, grey and white are not represented in the grounded data.

In contrast, artificially generated contexts usually consist of a (constrained) subset of a larger set of stimuli, like for example the set of all Munsell chips within the visual spectrum (Figure A.4) which was originally used in anthropological research (Kay et al. 2010; MacLaury 1997). Such a set possibly reflects the colour distributions of real-world environments based on a series of photographs, such as an urban or natural environment (see §9.1). If no such distribution is reflected, such as for example in the set of Munsell chips, each stimulus will as likely be represented in a shared context. Although stimuli sets that do reflect real-world colour distributions contain more structure than those that do not, the embodied

9.3 Impact of embodiment on performance of operators

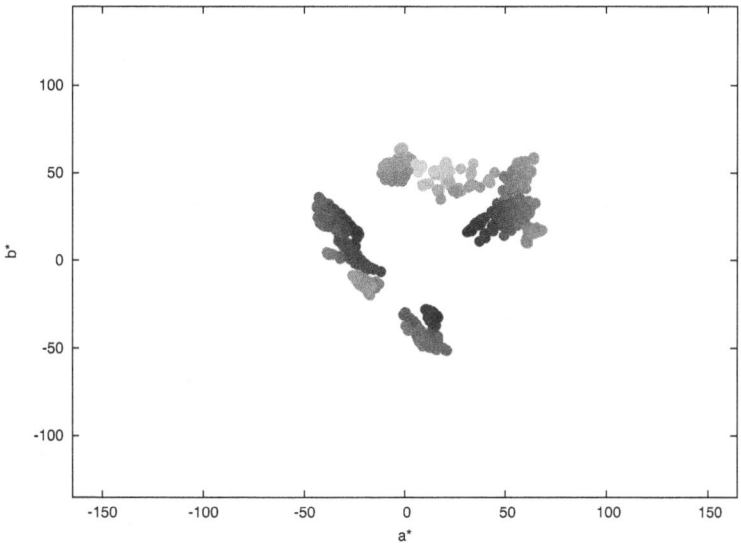

Figure 9.15: The colours of all the objects in all contexts in the dataset used in our experiment projected on the hue plane of the CIE $L^*a^*b^*$ colour space. The colour data in the embodied experiment is clearly structured, with more colours appearing around the actual colour of the objects used.

data set is far more structured, as it reflects the different appearances of a limited number of objects.

9.3.3 Discerning the impact of embodiment

I compare three environmental conditions to discern the influence of the two main differences when moving from simulated to real-world perception. In the first condition (shared simulated perception), agents will perceive artificial contexts which are sets of randomly chosen Munsell chips. In the second (shared grounded perception), both agents artificially share the same grounded perception coming from one robot body. In the third (individual grounded perception), both agents perceive the environment through their individual robot bodies.

In order to measure the influence of the structure in a grounded world, I compare the performance of conditions I and II. Basic characteristics of the scenes in condition II are carefully controlled in condition I. These characteristics are

9 Further experiments on basic colour systems

based on the set of all embodied scenes used and entail the distribution of context sizes, the total number of colour stimuli and the minimal and maximal distance between different colours within one scene/context. The better these characteristics are controlled, the better I can discern the impact of the structure in the embodied data.

To quantify the impact of the perceptual deviation between speaker and hearer, I compare conditions II and III.

9.3.4 Resulting dynamics

The three environmental conditions are compared across four different experiments. The first baseline experiment is similar to the one introduced earlier (§3.4) except that now the predefined language system is based on the English category system (Sturges & Whitfield 1995). This experiment gives an idea about how two English human subjects would perform in the three different environmental conditions. The resulting communicative success is shown in Figure 9.16, which is roughly around 80%. The interactions in which the two agents fail, are those in which the topic could not be discriminated. The presence of structure in the world has a positive impact on communicative success and the additional problem posed by perceptual deviation seems to have negative impact. This negative impact is rather limited and resonates with a previous analysis of the same grounded data which indicated that colour is the least variable when different perspectives are used, unlike for example the spatial positions of the objects (Wellens, Loetzsch & Steels 2008).

In the acquisition experiment, one agent needs to master the English colour lexicon from another agent using the adoption and alignment operators introduced in §7.2. These operators result in a level of communicative success that is almost as high as in the baseline experiment after 2k games using the 8 colour terms for the colour categories that are represented in the grounded data (see §9.3.2). This indicates that the used operators are adequate to acquire an ontology from another agent.

Figure 9.16 shows the communicative success in a formation experiment for a population of 10 agents after 10k games per agent. These agents are more successful than the ones in the baseline and acquisition experiment, mainly due to the higher number of colour categories (around 20 for conditions II and III and 25 for condition I). Figure 9.17 shows the interpretation variance (the average distance between the prototypes of the colour categories associated with the same form within the population) of the population over time. It is significantly lower for conditions II and III because the structure in the environment restricts the

9.3 Impact of embodiment on performance of operators

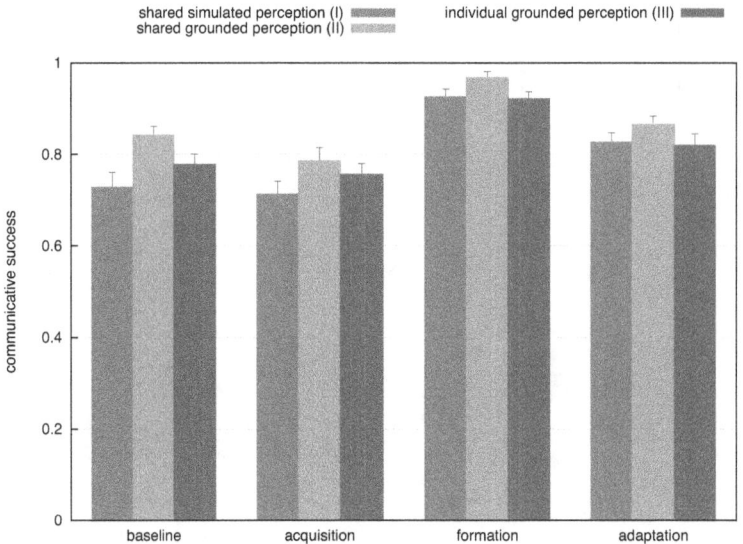

Figure 9.16: Resulting communicative success of four different experiment types for the three different conditions, grouped per experiment type. The predefined language system is based on the English colour category system. The results are shown after 2k games for the acquisition experiment and after 10k games/agent in the formation and the adaptation experiment. The results are averaged over 10 runs.

possible location of the colour categories used by the agents. It is also slightly lower when both agents share their perception.

Finally, I studied the impact of having adaptive colour categories, independent of the ontology size, in an adaptation experiment. In this experiment a population of 10 agents starts out with a colour lexicon based on the English colour categories but is allowed to change these categories to its functional needs using the alignment operator. The invention and adoption operators are disabled. The communicative success after 10k games per agent is shown in Figure 9.16. Compared to the success of the baseline experiment, an overall improvement is observed in all three conditions.

9 *Further experiments on basic colour systems*

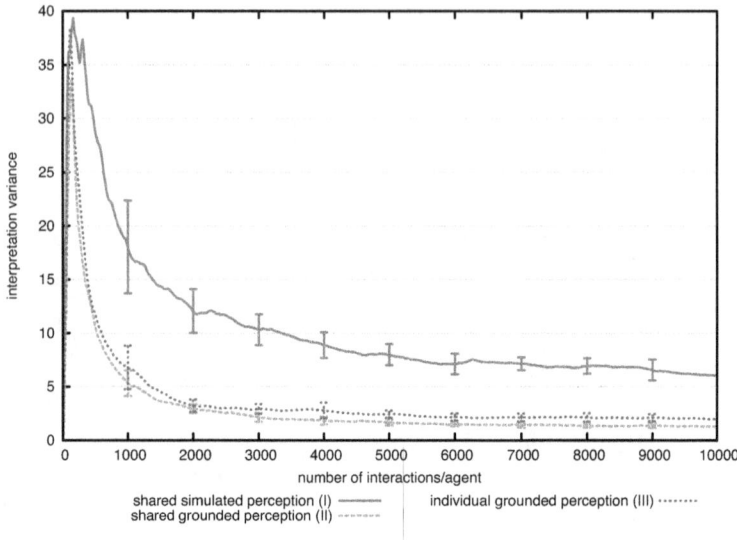

Figure 9.17: The interpretation variance in formation experiments is significantly lower for the grounded conditions than for shared simulated perception. In the grounded condition it is lower when perception is shared between both interacting agents.

9.3.5 Comparison to human categories

I compare the resulting ontologies to the colour categories of English (Sturges & Whitfield 1995) using two different methods: the direct comparison method and a naming benchmark. In the direct comparison method, I compute the distance between the two ontologies in the CIE $L^*a^*b^*$ colour space. The lower this distance, the more similar the two ontologies are. The naming benchmark consists of naming the colour chips that were consistently named by English subjects (Sturges & Whitfield 1995) (shown in Figure 3.1). The higher the performance on this benchmark, the more similar the performance of the agents to human performance is. Both methods require a matching procedure in which each category of the resulting ontology is paired to a category of the English ontology in such a way that the pair-wise distance in the colour space is minimal.

Using these two methods, I compare the ontologies resulting from two different experiment types: the acquisition experiment and the formation experiment. To rule out the impact of ontology size on the comparison, I control the maximum number of colour categories in the formation experiment to be the number

9.3 Impact of embodiment on performance of operators

of categories that are learned in the acquisition experiment. As in the acquisition experiment, the teacher only uses the colour terms that are present in the embodied dataset, which are listed in §9.3.2. This maximum number of colour categories is set to 8. For each experiment type, I compare the three environmental conditions as described in the previous section.

The results of the direct comparison method and the naming benchmark are shown in Figure 9.18 and Table 9.4 respectively. Both methods show that in general, the acquisition experiments lead to ontologies that are more similar to the colour categories of English than the formation experiment. The main reason for this is that in the acquisition experiment the predefined colour lexicon of the speaker is identical to the one I compare to and hence guides the learner to categories that are similar to the English colour lexicon, whereas in the formation experiment no such guidance is present.

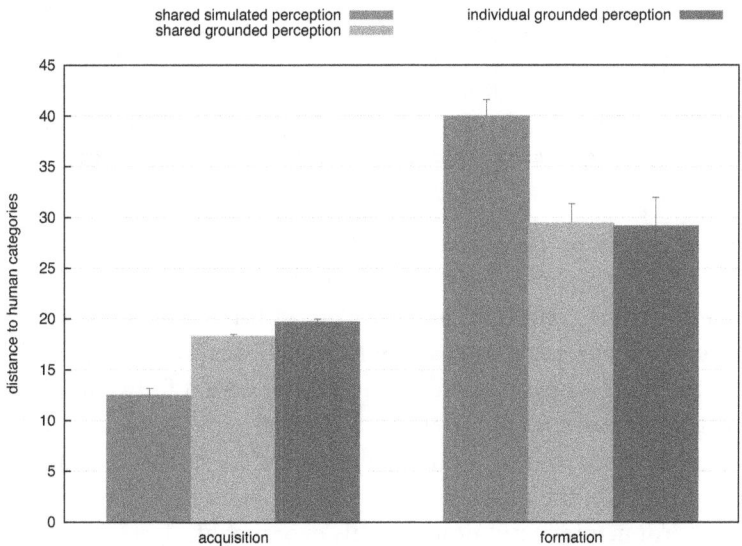

Figure 9.18: Results of the direct comparison method. Two experiment types are compared in three environmental conditions, grouped per experiment type: the acquisition experiment (2k games) and the formation experiment (population of 10 agents; 10k games per agent). The results are averaged over 10 runs.

In the acquisition experiment, condition I seems to yield ontologies that are more similar to human colour categories than conditions II and III, as shown in

9 Further experiments on basic colour systems

Table 9.4: Results of the naming benchmark, broken down by category: red (RE), green (GN), purple (PU), black (BK), blue (BL), brown (BR), orange (OR) and yellow (YL). The top part shows the baseline performance using the centroids of the English colour ontology. The middle and bottom part show the performance of the acquisition experiment, respectively formation experiment, for the three environmental conditions.

	RE	GN	PU	BK	BL	BR	OR	YL	TOTAL
	4	22	14	3	25	4	6	8	86
	4	19	14	3	22	4	6	8	80
I	4	15.7	10.3	3	21.8	3.7	6	8	72.5
II	4	17.5	9.6	3	21.1	4	6	8	73.2
III	4	16.5	10.2	3	21.7	4	6	8	73.4
I	1.6	3	6.7	3	6.2	0	2.8	7.9	31.2
II	1.9	14.3	10.5	1.1	10.3	0.1	3.5	7.6	49.3
III	1.7	13.4	7.7	2	9.7	0.3	3.6	7.4	45.8

the results of the direct comparison method. The prototypes of the categories acquired by the learner are situated on the centre of all stimuli that the speaker has named using the term that is associated with that category. In conditions II and III some colour categories are only partially represented, and hence the location of the prototypes acquired by the learner do not fully correspond to the locations of the prototypes of the teacher. In condition I however, all categories are fully represented, leading to a smaller difference with the ontology of the teacher. The results of the naming benchmark show no clear distinction between the three environmental conditions for this experiment.

In the formation experiment, both comparison methods suggest that conditions II and III produce ontologies that are more similar to English colour categories than condition I. Although no guiding teacher is present in this experiment, the structure in the grounded data partially takes over the guiding role of the teacher. The colours of the objects presented to the robots (Figure 9.11) are better examples of the basic colour categories for English than the stimuli in the simulated world in which no such structure is present.

9.3.6 Conclusion

I have shown that our model for the colour naming game is robust enough to overcome the main difficulties arising from embodiment in an experiment using humanoid robots. In embodied experiments, speaker and hearer perceive the world from a different perspective and hence experience the colours of the objects around them differently. In our experimental setup, the impact of this perceptual deviation is rather limited as the lighting conditions are constant in the office environment.

I have attested the positive impact on the resulting communicative success of adapting categories to the functional needs of the agents, even when compared to an experiment in which static categories are completely shared within a population. This finding resonates with previous studies in experimental psychology (Garrod & Doherty 1994), in which it is shown that humans align their ontologies when interacting with each other, even in the course of a single dialogue.

As the resulting ontologies reflect the structure of the environment in which they are developed, these ontologies will bear more resemblance to the colour categories of English when the environment consists of objects that are good examples of these categories than in an environment in which the colours are uniformly distributed over the colour spectrum.

9.4 General conclusion

I have accounted for a positive impact of the structure in the environment on the similarity between simulated and natural language systems, although part of this impact is accounted for by general categorisation principles that are inherent to the algorithms used. I have shown the coordinating role of language between language users in one community. I have also studied the impact of language and environment on the universal trends observed in language systems around the world. The environmental constraints seem to have a negative impact, whereas language seems to have a slightly positive impact. Finally, I have shown the impact of embodiment on the performance of the adoption, alignment and invention operators and compared the resulting language systems to the English basic colour language system.

Part IV

Evolution and origins of language strategies

Introduction

When one takes a historical perspective on language, one can observe periods in time when the dominating language strategy for one subarea of meaning is replaced by another strategy. This happened for example in the history of the basic colour terms which simultaneously shifted from a strategy that focussed on brightness to another strategy in which the hue dimensions also became relevant. In order to model such shifts, I explore the hypothesis in which agents track the communicative success both at the level of linguistic items and the level of the language strategies (Bleys & Steels 2009).

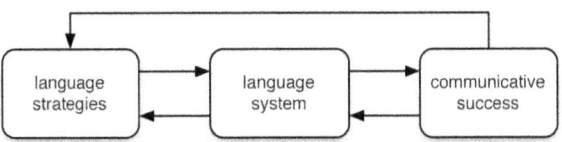

Figure 10.1: Several language strategies can compete to express the same subarea of meaning. This competition can be orchestrated through tracking the communicative success both at the level of the linguistic items in a language system and at the level of language strategies.

The next question is how new language strategies may come into existence. The main theory that I will explore is the recruitment theory (Steels 2007), which states that general cognitive operations can be recruited to solve linguistic problems. This can be achieved through a combinatorial search process of basic cognitive operations. This process is illustrated in Figure 10.2.

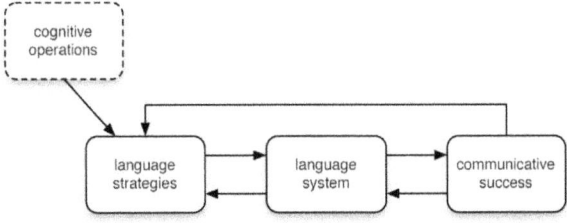

Figure 10.2: A language strategy can be generated through a combinatorial search process of cognitive operators

10 Linguistic selection of language strategies

In the evolution of the basic colour terms in English an interesting meaning shift has occurred: at their Indo-European root most colour terms had primarily a brightness meaning sense. Around the transition from Old to Middle English the hue sense of all basic colour terms became more dominant than the original brightness sense (Casson 1997).

This is illustrated in Figure 10.3 in which the history of the term *yellow* is shown. In Indo-European its syntactic form was *ghel* which was primarily used to refer to the shining (of yellow metals). In Old English the term *geolo* acquired a hue sense and could be used for example to refer to the colour of some silk cloth. In the transition to Middle English *yelou* the hue sense became the more dominant and the term could also be used to refer to, for example, yolk and ripe corn although it could still be used to refer to gold. This same shift happened to all other English basic colour terms. Most interestingly, all colour terms that were introduced to English after this shift, like for example *orange*, never had a brightness sense but only a hue sense (Casson 1997). Similar meaning shifts have been reported in a wide range of languages (MacLaury 1992).

YELLOW

*ghel-2	*Ghel-wo	*gelwaz	geolo	yelou
Indo-European		Germanic	Old English	Middle English
BRIGHTNESS			BRIGHTNESS	HUE
			hue	brightness
to shine (yellow metals)			to shine	fabrics
bite/gall			fine yellow silk cloth	yolk
			linden wood shield	discolored paper
				ripe corn
				sun/gold

Figure 10.3: The evolution of the term *yellow* in English. Like almost all other basic colour terms, its meaning shifted from brightness to hue around the transition from Old English to Middle English (Casson 1997).

10 Linguistic selection of language strategies

The goal of this chapter is to understand and model the competition, selection and evolution of language strategies for this particular language phenomenon. Constructing the model consists of the following steps: identifying and operationalising the language strategies that are involved in this phenomenon and adding an extra layer of linguistic selection at the level of language strategies.

10.1 Language strategies

Although the strategies are commonly referred to as being brightness-based or hue-based in the literature, the hue-based strategy does clearly not ignore the brightness dimension. For example, in contemporary English the colour category for *yellow* clearly refers only to light colours whereas *brown* refers to darker colours of a similar hue. This is commonly attested in literature for a wide range of languages, including English (Sturges & Whitfield 1995; Boynton 1997) and Spanish (Lillo et al. 2007).

The two strategies described above have already been introduced in Chapter 3 of this book as being substrategies of the basic colour strategy: the brightness strategy and the brightness and hue strategy. Both language strategies have been operationalised and have been proven to be sufficient to allow a population of agents to self-organise their own language system (see Chapter 7 for more details).

10.2 Strategy selection

I can now turn to the main question of this chapter: how can I orchestrate the coordination of which language strategy to use in such a way that it optimises expected communicative success but also allows for a shift from one strategy to another so that I am able to study the observed phenomenon?

Starting from the observation that colour terms introduced after the meaning shift only had the hue sense (e.g. *orange* in English), it seems reasonable to hypothesise that agents keep track of the *overall success* of a strategy that should be used whenever the language system is expanded. These overall success rates can also be used to indicate which strategy to use to expand the language system when the default strategy is insufficient to tackle the current communicative challenge. The speaker can use it to utilise its language in a more creative way with low risk of failure in communication, assuming that the hearer has a similar ranking for its strategies.

10.2 Strategy selection

On the other hand, the language system should be able to sustain enough variability to allow for a shift from one strategy to another. It should be possible that a strategy becomes successful for a few terms without hampering overall communicative success so that the system can reach a tipping point. This suggests that agents should also keep track of *term-specific success* of a strategy, which should be preferred over the overall dominant one. The strategy which has the highest term-specific success for a term, is the DEFAULT STRATEGY which will be used when producing or interpreting a specific term. A schematic representation of the term-specific scores is shown in Figure 10.4.

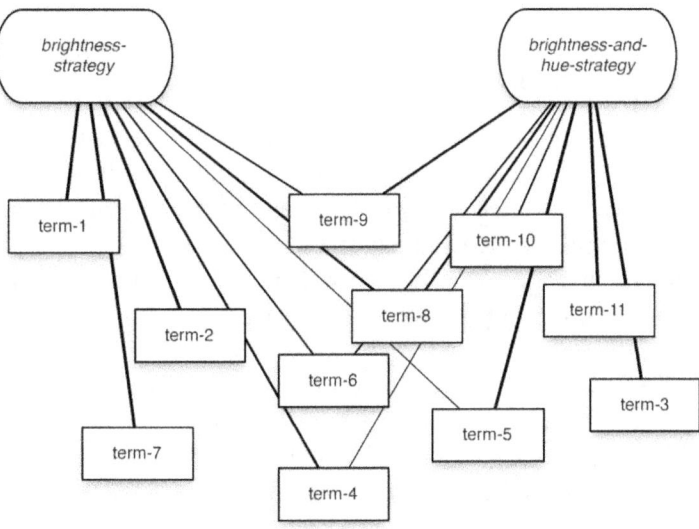

Figure 10.4: Strategies and their item-specific success scores. Each term can be used by both language strategies. Depending on the communicative context and the term this can lead to communicative success which is stored in the item-specific success scores. The thickness of the lines represent these scores: the thicker the line, the higher the score.

The term-specific success ensures the language system can sustain enough variation to allow the shift from one strategy to another. The overall success increases the expected level of systematicity in the language system when it needs to be extended as the agent will do so by using the most conventional and successful language strategy.

10 Linguistic selection of language strategies

Implementation of language strategies

The agents keep track of the OVERALL STRATEGY SUCCESS of each language strategy, which reflects its success in previous language games, regardless of the particular term it was used with. It is the average communicative success of the last 50 interactions in which the strategy was used.

At the same time, the agents keep track of the TERM-SPECIFIC STRATEGY SUCCESS of language strategies. This success will be considered to be the default strategy to produce or interpret this term. More formally, it is the average communicative success of the last 50 interactions in which a strategy is used with this specific term.

Production and interpretation

The general procedure to produce an utterance is implemented as follows. First the speaker tries to use each colour term using the strategy with the highest term-specific success. When none of these default interpretations is successful in the current communicative context, the terms will be reinterpreted using the strategy with the highest overall success. If this fails as well, the speaker will reinterpret the terms using the other strategies ordered by decreasing overall success.

The hearer deploys a similar approach to interpretation, but in most situations knows which term it needs to interpret. It will do so first using the strategy with the highest term-specific success. If this fails, it will reinterpret the term with the strategy with the highest overall success. If this fails as well, it resorts to the other strategies ordered by decreasing overall success.

Alignment

The agents store the strategy they deployed to produce or interpret a particular term to update both the overall and the term-specific strategy success. They also use this strategy to determine which alignment operators to apply: when the brightness strategy was deployed only the L^* value of the used category is updated. When the brightness and hue strategy was deployed, the values of each dimension are updated (see §7.2).

Invention and adoption

Whenever an agent feels the communicative pressure to invent a new colour category, it will use the strategy with the highest overall success. If this strategy does not work, it will try the other strategies sorted by decreasing overall success. The hearer will follow a similar procedure when adopting an unknown form: first it will try the strategy with the highest overall success and when this fails, it will try the other strategies ordered by decreasing overall success.

10.3 Experiment on linguistic selection

In order to focus entirely on the dynamics of the language strategies, I run an experiment in which the set of basic colour categories is fixed. This set is equal to the basic focal colours reported for the Spanish language (Lillo et al. 2007). Which language strategies the agents should use, is left open. They can choose between either the brightness or the brightness and hue strategy using the procedures outlined above. Some terms can be interpreted using both strategies. The term *amarillo* ('yellow') for example, can be used both to indicate a light colour or a light colour with a yellow hue. The contexts consist of three randomly chosen Munsell chips that have a minimal interstimulus distance of 50 distance units in the CIE $L^*a^*b^*$ colour space and that should be faithfully reproducible in the Adobe 1998 RGB colour model.

10.3.1 Measures

10.3.1.1 Strategy success

The strategy success is measured at the population level and is defined as the average overall strategy success of a particular strategy in a population of agents.

10.3.1.2 Strategy usage

The strategy usage is averaged over all agents in the population. The strategy usage for an agent is the ratio of the interactions in which this strategy has been used in the last 50 interactions the agent was involved in.

10.3.1.3 Strategy coherence

The strategy coherence ($SC(P)$) is measured at the population level and is equal to the average scaled strategy coherence of each unique term ($SC_s(f)$) in the population.

$$SC(P) = \frac{\sum_{f \in F} SC_s(f)}{|F|} \tag{10.1}$$

The actual strategy coherence ($SC(f)$) is scaled using the worst-case coherence (SC_{wc}). This ensures the resulting strategy coherence will result in a value between 1 (full coherence) and 0 (no coherence).

$$SC_s(f) = \frac{SC(f) - SC_{wc}}{1 - SC_{wc}} \tag{10.2}$$

The actual strategy coherence ($SC(f)$) of a term reflects the chances that two agents will prefer the same strategy for that term in an interaction. It is based on the distribution of agents over the different strategies ($[s_i...s_n]$). The same function is used to determine the worst-case coherence (SC_{wc}), but then using the worst-case distribution in which the number of agents preferring a certain strategy is evenly distributed over all available strategies. For example, in a population of 10 agents and 2 available strategies, 5 agents will prefer one strategy and the 5 other agents will prefer the other.

$$SC(f) = \sum_{s=s_i}^{s_n} \frac{s}{|P|} \frac{s-1}{|P|-1} \tag{10.3}$$

10.3.2 Results

The resulting dynamics are shown in Figure 10.5 and are rich and complex. In all runs, the communicative success is as high as the baseline communicative success (see Figure 3.4 for comparison) and the agents reach a high coherence on the default strategies to use for each term in their repertoire, as indicated by the strategy coherence measure.

Broadly speaking, two situations arise. In one situation, a single strategy becomes clearly dominant in the population. This could either be the brightness or the brightness and hue colour strategy, depending on small fluctuations in the early choices of the population (Figure 10.5(a)). But I have also observed situations where one strategy becomes dominant first (for example, the brightness strategy) to be overtaken later by the other strategy (in this case the brightness and hue strategy, as seen in the history of English (Figure 10.5(b)). In this case, the two strategies continue to coexist. Brightness is still used in circumstances when there is a word for which the default strategy is still the brightness strategy.

10.3 Experiment on linguistic selection

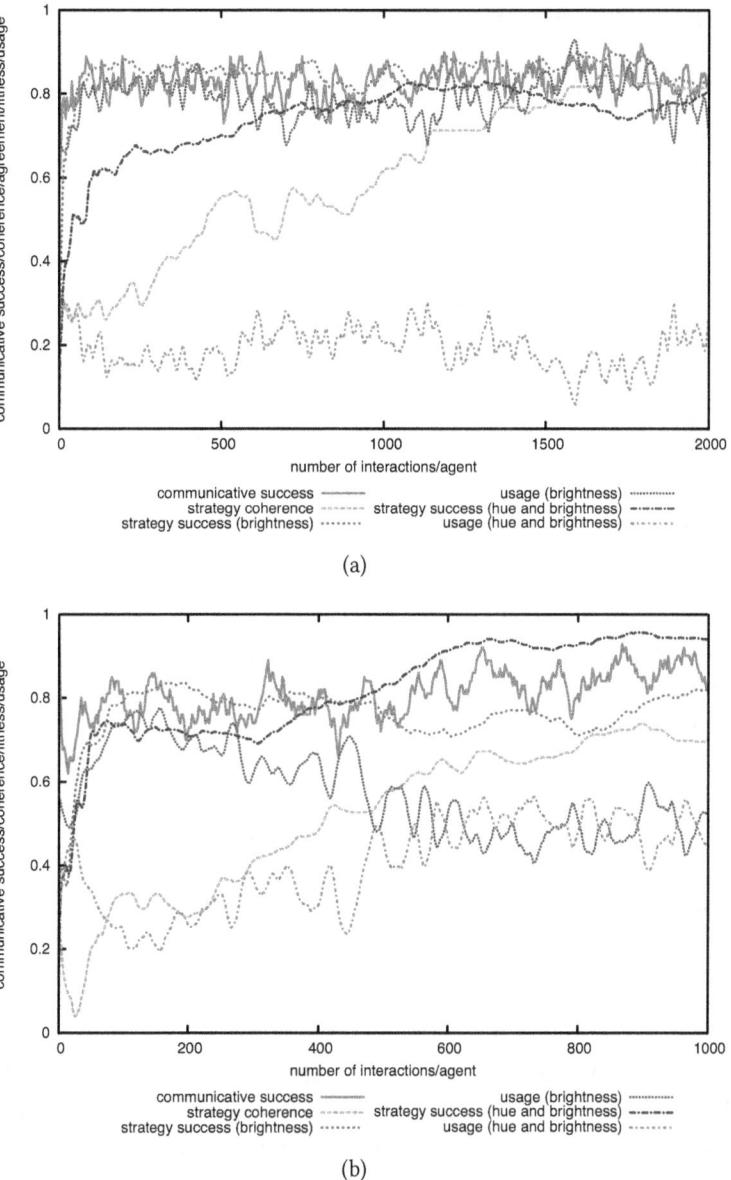

Figure 10.5: The resulting dynamics of the linguistic selection of strategies. In (a) the brightness strategy becomes entirely dominant and is used significantly more, whereas in (b) one strategy overtakes the dominant one which is reflected in the respective use of each strategy.

10 Linguistic selection of language strategies

10.4 Selective advantage

The expected communicative success for a particular language strategy is highly dependent on the linguistic challenges in which it is deployed. By manipulating these challenges, one can try to determine the expected communicative success and to find in which type of contexts one strategy has a selective advantage over the others.

To study the impact of the linguistic challenges on the expected communicative success, I have designed two types of artificially constrained linguistic contexts. In the first type, the CONSTANT BRIGHTNESS CONTEXTS, all samples in the contexts share the same lightness value, so they only differ in hue. In the second type, the CONSTANT HUE CONTEXTS, the samples are all different shades of grey, so they only differ in lightness. By exploring different mixtures of these two types of contexts, I can establish environmental constraints in which one strategy would become more successful than the other.

10.4.1 Experiment

In this experiment I will compare three BASIC LANGUAGE STRATEGIES. In addition to the brightness and the brightness and hue strategy, I will also study the hue strategy in which only the two hue dimensions (a^* and b^* in the CIE $L^*a^*b^*$ colour space) are taken into account. The agents start from a predefined lexicon based on Spanish (Lillo et al. 2007), the contexts consist of 4 Munsell chips with a minimal interstimulus distance of 10 distance units in the CIE $L^*a^*b^*$ colour space. The chips are limited to the ones that are reproducible in the Adobe 1998 RGB colour model. The ratio of constant hue to constant brightness contexts is controlled through the hue difference parameter.

10.4.2 Results

The results are shown in Figure 10.6 and indicate the resulting strategy success after 10k interactions. The communicative success of brightness strategy is optimal when there are no contexts in which the hue is constant, but the success drops when more contexts of constant brightness are present in the challenges. The opposite is true for the hue strategy which has its optimal success when the contexts are variable in hue. This success decreases as the ratio of contexts which are of constant hue increases. The brightness and hue strategy becomes more successful than the brightness strategy when 3 out of 10 contexts are of constant brightness. This shows the selective advantage of one strategy over the other.

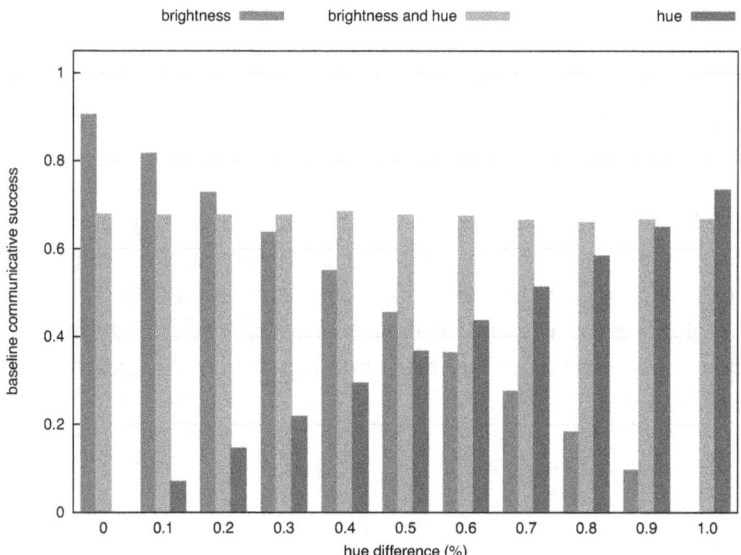

Figure 10.6: Selective advantage of the brightness, hue and brightness and hue strategies. The baseline communicative is compared in mixtures of two types of contexts. The hue difference reflects the ratio of constant hue to constant brightness contexts.

It might seem surprising that brightness strategy is more successful than the brightness and hue strategy in black-and-white contexts as the latter uses more information. This is due to the semantics in production which considers only the category that is the most similar one to the topic. When all dimensions are relevant, only the three achromatic colour categories (black, grey and white) can be used as these are most similar to the black and white samples. When only one dimension is deemed relevant, each category will cover a small part of the axis between white and black, resulting in higher communicative success.

10.5 Conclusion

I have explored how agents can align their choice of which language strategy to use through linguistic interaction. I have hypothesised that there should be a

10 Linguistic selection of language strategies

second level of selection in which agents keep track of the overall success of the language strategies they are using. This level of selection can be used to increase the level of systematicity when the language system needs to be expanded and to minimise potential misunderstandings when certain terms are used in an unconventional way. At the same time language systems should be able to sustain enough variation to allow for shifts in dominance from one strategy to another. This is why agents should also keep track of which strategy is most commonly used with a particular item. I have shown how these principles can lead to a model in which agents reach high coherence in what strategies to use, but that is further open as to which strategy becomes dominant. The same model is also capable of replicating the observed phenomenon presented in the introduction of this chapter. I have also shown that the selective advantage of one strategy can be systematically studied by manipulating the communicative contexts in which it is deployed.

11 Origins of language strategies

In Part II, I have explored the semantic and syntactic templates behind some of the language strategies for colour. In this chapter I will explore the origins of these templates. The semantic templates are considered to be the result of a combinatorial search process of basic cognitive operators. On the syntactic side, the templates are implicitly represented in repair strategies which can be used to express these newly generated semantic templates. These repair strategies have been implemented and tested in an experiment.

11.1 Generation of semantic templates

In Part II the semantic templates were predefined. These templates can also be generated based on a combinatorial search process in which the cognitive primitives are combined to form a semantic constraint network. When such a network turns out to be successful, it can be stored by the agent and act as a semantic template.

An illustration of such a combinatorial search process is shown in Figure 11.1. This search process is based on four primitives: Equal-to-Context, Filter-by-Colour, Filter-by-Membership and Select-Most-Activated which have been introduced in Part II. Initially (node 1), the constraint network is empty and contains only an open variable for the topic entity which is of type colour-entity. Next, the search process traverses the library of primitives to find a primitive of which the first variable is compatible to the open variable. In this example, the library contains only one such primitive (Select-Most-Activated). The network is extended with this primitive by making its first argument equal to the open variable. The open variable is now removed from the list of open variables. All but the first argument of the primitive are added to the list of open variables. The network is evaluated, but returns no evaluation results (node 2). The second node does have an open variable (for the second argument of Select-Most-Activated), so the search process can continue. This time the library is traversed to find a primitive that has a first argument of type entity-set. Three such primitives seem to be found: Equal-to-Context (node 3), Filter-by-Colour (node 4)

11 Origins of language strategies

and FILTER-BY-MEMBERSHIP (node 5). Node 3 can be evaluated, but does not return any satisfactory results. Moreover this node also does not have any open variables any more, so this branch can not be expanded any further. Nodes 4 and 5 also do not return the right binding, but as they still have open variables they can still be further explored.

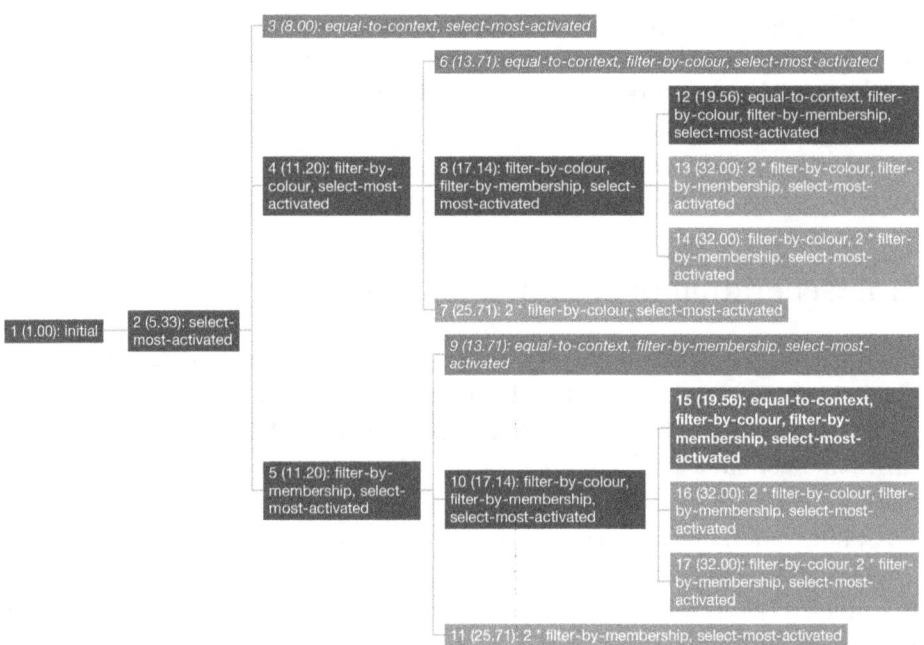

Figure 11.1: Example of a combinatorial search process to construct a new semantic template. Each node represents one step in the search process in which additional primitives are added to the network that is being built up. When more than one expansion is possible the search tree splits. The green node (number 15) contains the solution of the current communicative problem. Grey nodes (for example 3 and 6) show nodes that have been evaluated but didn't return the correct binding for the topic variable. These nodes could also not be expanded any further. Light blue nodes (for example 7 and 11) are nodes that could still be explored. Blue nodes (like 4 or 5) have been evaluated but did not return any evaluation results.

11.2 Repair strategies

The search process continues and finds some other interesting networks, such as node 6, in which the network involves a single categorisation process based on colour. This network however seems to be insufficient to reach the current communicative goal. Finally, the search process finds a solution for the current goal in node 15. This network consists of two categorisation processes: one based on colour and another based on membership. The resulting semantic network is shown in Figure 11.2.

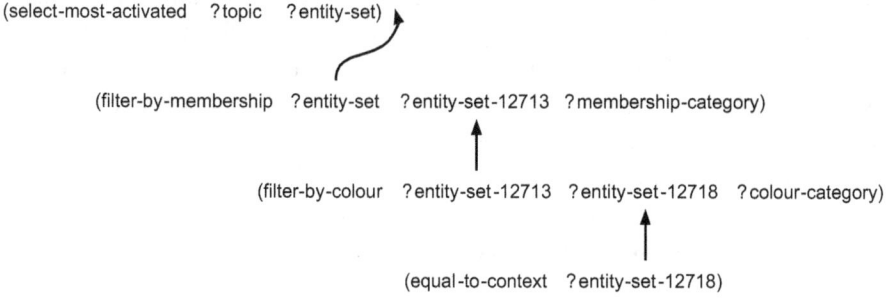

Figure 11.2: Example of a semantic template generated by the combinatorial search process. It involves two categorisation processes. The first is based on colour and the second is based on membership.

In order to generate the most complicated semantic templates of Part II, the search process outlined above needs to be extended. Additional variable equalities are required that do not involve the first argument of a primitive, like for example between the category used in the first categorisation process and the transformation operation of the category sets in for example the category combination strategy. In order to account for these networks, I have introduced another expansion operator which makes two open variables of compatible type equal.

11.2 Repair strategies

In this section I will introduce the repair strategies that allow an agent to learn the constructions that are needed to express semantic templates in language. Currently the main approach adopted to express semantic constraint networks in language is identical to the one introduced in Chapter 3. The semantic network

11 Origins of language strategies

is divided in three layers of units: (a) entity units containing the semantic entities, (b) functional units which make direct use of such a semantic entity and (c) contextual units which contain any remaining operations of the semantic constraint network that do not make direct use of any semantic entity. This division is illustrated in Figure 11.4 for the semantic networks shown in Figure 11.3(b).

11.2.1 Construction of a syntactic category system

The construction of the system of syntactic categories is organized as follows: the repair strategies try to re-use any syntactic category which would allow the re-use of a previously learned rule. If no such syntactic category is found, the repair strategy constructs a new syntactic category. This basic mechanism results in a one-on-one mapping between syntactic and semantic categories at the lexical level, but at all other levels syntactic categories are only invented when needed and one cannot easily reconstruct a similar mapping unless one takes into account the linguistic development of each agent.

11.2.1.1 Starting from scratch

The first time an agent has to express/interpret a semantic network (similar to the one shown in Figure 11.3(a)), which could represent the semantics of a sentence like *block*) it has no syntactic categories and hence it needs to invent two new syntactic categories. One specifies the syntactic association between the entity unit and the functional unit (e.g. Noun), and the other one specifies the association between the functional unit and the contextual unit (e.g. Noun-constituent). This kind of process is schematically shown on the left hand side of Figure 11.5.

I suppose that the agent now has to express/interpret a variation of this semantic constraint network in which the semantic entity is a prototype of a pyramid instead of one of a block. This provides a first opportunity for the agents to re-use a syntactic category, because if the syntactic category of the entity unit for the pyramid would be identical to the one of the entity unit of the block (e.g. Noun), it would allow re-use of all the other syntactic categories (and rules) it constructed for the previous semantic constraint network. This process is schematised on the right hand side of Figure 11.5 and typically occurs at the level of syntactic categories linking entity units and functional units.

11.2 Repair strategies

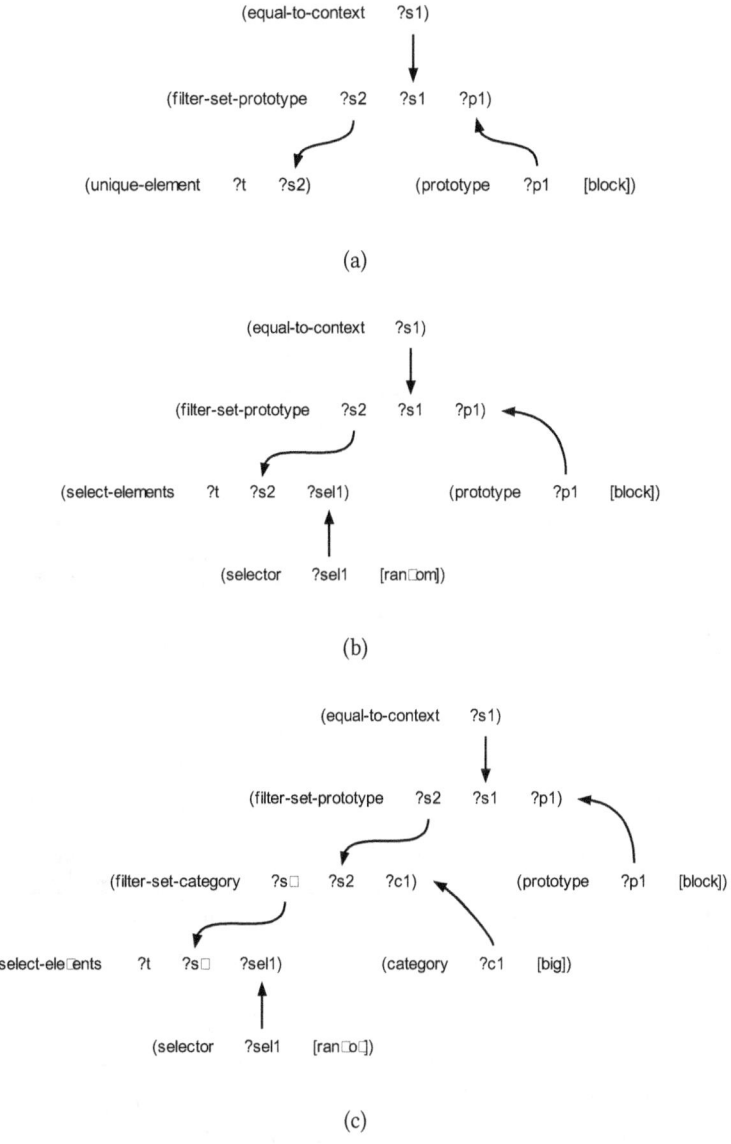

Figure 11.3: Three example semantic constraint networks. (a) is the most basic network, (b) is a similar network in which the selection process is now based on random selection and (c) is a further extension of this network by adding another categorisation process between the first categorisation process and the selection process.

167

11 Origins of language strategies

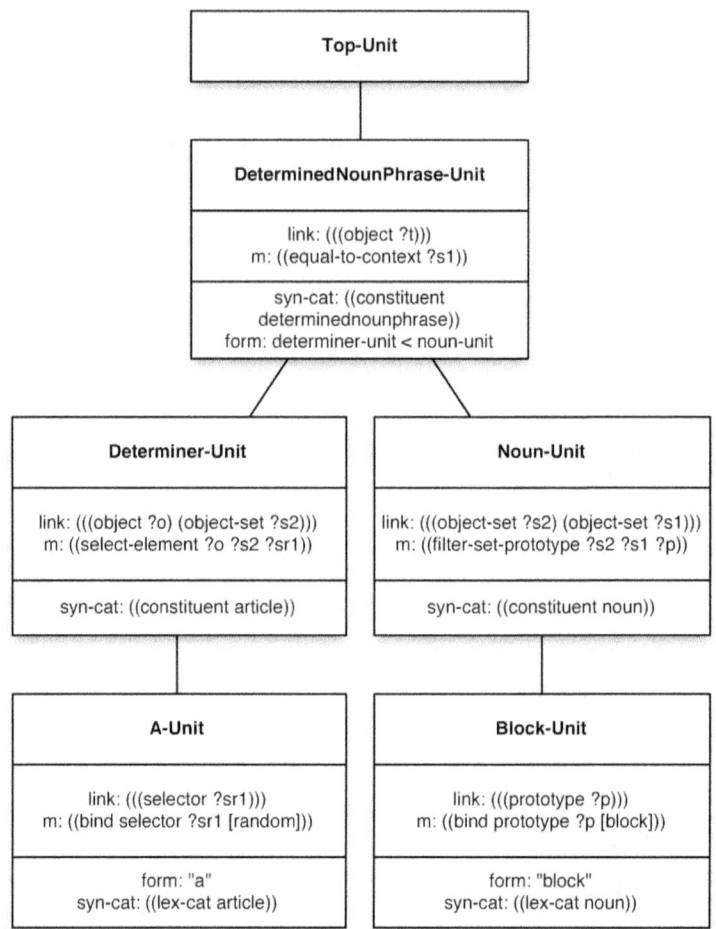

Figure 11.4: Linguistic structure to express the semantic constraint network shown in Figure 11.3(b), divided over three layers of units: entity units (Block-Unit and A-Unit) for the semantic entities, functional units (Determiner-Unit and Noun-Unit) for the primitives that directly use these entities and a contextual unit (DeterminedNounPhrase-Unit) that encapsulates all other primitives. Both syntactic and semantic features are shown in the same structure.

11.2 Repair strategies

Figure 11.5: First set of categories in the syntactic category system. On the left: invention of new syntactic categories A, B and C. On the right: re-use of a syntactic category (A) as expected by the rule (B → A).

11.2.1.2 Substituting a primitive constraint

Now I will consider a semantic constraint network in which a primitive constraint that does not take a semantic entity as direct argument (e.g. UNIQUE-ELEMENT) is substituted by one that does so (e.g. SELECT-ELEMENTS) (an example of such a network is shown in Figure 11.3(b)). I suppose that this network corresponds to the semantics of a sentence like *a block*. The contextual rule of the previous example is now useless as it contains a primitive constraint, namely UNIQUE-ELEMENT, that is not even part of the semantic constraint network at hand. The agents have to invent a new contextual rule, but not all hope is lost, because they can re-use every other previously introduced category (and rule) if they incorporate the syntactic category they previously used to associate the functional unit with the contextual unit (e.g Noun- constituent). This process is shown in Figure 11.6, and typically occurs at the level of syntactic categories linking functional units and contextual units.

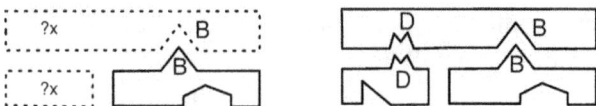

Figure 11.6: Second set of categories in the syntactic category system. Invention of a new syntactic category (D) while reusing a previously learned syntactic category (B).

11 Origins of language strategies

11.2.1.3 Adding a primitive constraint

The final semantic constraint network needing consideration is achieved by starting from the previous one and adding an extra primitive constraint, FILTER-SET-CATEGORY, in between two existing ones, namely FILTER-SET-PROTOTYPE and SELECT-ELEMENTS, which could represent the semantics of a sentence like *a big block*. An example of such a network is shown in Figure 11.3(c). Using the same repair strategy as used in the previous section, the agents could learn a new contextual rule which combines three subunits into one new unit as shown in the middle of Figure 11.7.

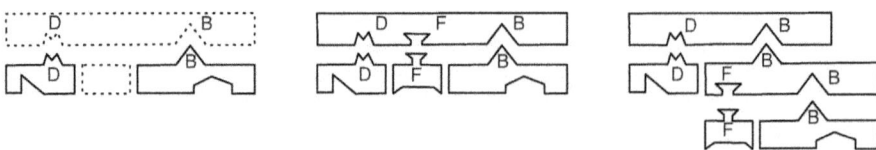

Figure 11.7: Third set of categories in the syntactic category system. To the left and middle: re-use of two previously known syntactic categories (B and D) and invention of a new one (F) in a similar fashion as in the previous section. To the right: another solution which additionally is capable of reusing the contextual rule introduced in the previous §4.2 by adding a truly recursive rule (B → FB).

But an agent can do better by exploiting another repair strategy which allows agents to combine any number of units into one unit. In the example shown on the right of Figure 11.7, the agents are able to come up with a rule that allows them to re-use the contextual rule introduced in the previous section. This particular rule combines two units, one belonging to syntactic category F (e.g. Adjective-constituent) and the other to B (e.g. Noun-constituent). As any other category would block the re-use of the contextual rule, the syntactic category to which this new combination unit should belong, is syntactic category B (e.g. Noun-constituent). This is determined by the deduction mechanism introduced at the beginning of the current section. As this syntactic category is equal to one of the rule's constituents, this new rule is truly recursive.

This recursion becomes clear when considering a semantic network in which another FILTER-SET-CATEGORY is added. To express this network no additional construction needs to be added to the rule-set of the agent. The rules introduced above are sufficient to allow for a complete processing of the semantic network.

11.2 Repair strategies

11.2.2 Implementaton of repair strategies

I have implemented repair strategies allowing both speaker and hearer to learn the grammatical rules. I will now discuss each step in more detail. The first three repair strategies (1.1 to 1.3) take care of learning the rules that ensure the default division in three layers of units: (a) entity units containing the semantic entities, (b) functional units which contain primitives that make direct use of such a semantic entity and (c) contextual units which contain any other primitives that do not make direct use of semantic entities.

Repair strategy 2.1 tries to optimise this process by trying to invent rules that re-use as many previously learned rules as possible. As described in §11.2.1, any of these repair strategies try to re-use the syntactic category system that has been built up so far as much as possible.

I start again with the semantic network shown in Figure 11.3(a). Following the general division in three layers of units, the target linguistic structure is shown in Figure 11.8. Each unit is introduced by another rule. The repair strategies that create these rules are described below.

11.2.3 Repair strategy 1.1: Semantic entities

The diagnostic that is used to trigger this repair strategy, is that a semantic entity is left unexpressed in the case of the speaker, or when a unknown string is encountered by the hearer. The repair strategy computes the required information that is used to instantiate the template. An example of a resulting rule is shown below.

──────────────── Lexical rule for a block ────────────────
```
((?top-unit
   (tag ?meaning
        (meaning (== (bind prototype ?x [block])))))
 ((J ?block-unit ?top-unit)
   (link (((prototype ?x))))
   ?meaning))
<-->
((?top-unit
   (tag ?form
        (form (== (string ?block-unit "block")))))
 ((J ?block-unit ?top-unit)
   (syn-cat (==1 (lex-cat noun)))
   ?form))
```
──

First the repair strategy determines which semantic entity needs to be filled in in the meaning feature. For the speaker this is relatively easy, as it conceptualised

11 Origins of language strategies

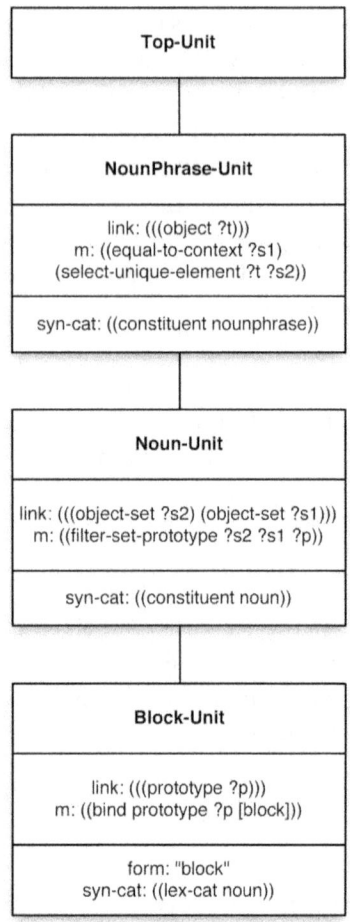

Figure 11.8: Target linguistic structure to express the semantic network shown in Figure 11.3(a), divided over three units: an entity unit (Block-Unit) for the semantic entity, a functional unit (Noun-Unit) for the primitive that directly uses that entity and a contextual unit (NounPhrase-Unit) that encapsulates all other primitives. Both syntactic and semantic features are shown in the same structure.

11.2 Repair strategies

a meaning that it wanted to express. The hearer has to call its conceptualisation mechanism in order to reconstruct the semantic entity that the speaker might have introduced. The link feature of the unit that will be introduced by this rule is easily determined as it repeats the type and the variable of the bind statement for the semantic entity. The repair strategy possibly copies the syntactic category of the functional rule for the functional primitive that will use this entity. Otherwise it introduces a new syntactic category.

11.2.4 Repair strategy 1.2: Functional primitives

Whenever a functional primitive (a semantic primitive that directly uses a semantic entity) is uncovered, the repair strategy for functional primitives is triggered. It creates a functional rule that introduces the semantic entity to the rest of the semantic network. An example of such a rule is shown below.

```
———————————— Functional rule for FILTER-SET-PROTOTYPE ————————————
((?top-unit
  (sem-subunits (== ?prototype-unit))
  (tag
    ?meaning
    (meaning (== (filter-set-prototype ?s1 ?s2 ?p)))))
 (?prototype-unit
  (link (((prototype ?p))))
  (meaning (== (bind prototype ?p ?val))))
 ((J ?filter-set-prototype-unit ?top-unit (?prototype-unit))
  ?meaning
  (link (((object-set ?s1) (object-set ?s2))))))
 <-->
((?top-unit
  (syn-subunits (== ?prototype-unit)))
 (?prototype-unit
  (syn-cat (==1 (lex-cat noun))))
 ((J ?filter-set-prototype-unit ?top-unit (?prototype-unit))
  (syn-cat (==1 (constituent noun)))))
```

The rule is constructed as follows. The meaning feature contains the functional primitive that needs to be covered. For each of the semantic entities the primitive uses a different subunit is created. At the semantic side the links of these units are used to introduce variable equalities between the semantic entities and the arguments of the functional primitive. At the syntactic side these units are specified through the syntactic categories of these subunits. On the semantic side, the new unit that is introduced by this rule will have have a link feature that contains the variables of arguments of the functional rule that are not provided

11 Origins of language strategies

by any of the subunits. At the syntactic side, the new unit might introduce a new syntactic category, unless a contextual rule could be triggered that would impose a specific syntactic category on the new unit.

11.2.5 Repair strategy 1.3: Contextual primitives

The primitives that do not make direct use of semantic entities are grouped together in a contextual unit. This unit is introduced by the application of a contextual rule.

An example of such a rule for the contextual primitives of the semantic network shown in Figure 11.3(a) is given below. It encapsulates two primitives, EQUAL-TO-CONTEXT and SELECT-UNIQUE-ELEMENT. It requires one subunit to be present in the structure which is of syntactic category NounConstituent and which has as link feature two object sets. In parsing, it will ensure the variables in these links are made equal to the variables of the semantic primitives it contains. The newly introduced unit will be of a newly invented syntactic category, Constituent NounPhrase, and will have as link feature the first argument of the EQUAL-TO-CONTEXT primitive.

———————————————— Contextual NounPhrase rule ————————————————
```
((?top-unit
  (sem-subunits (== ?subunit-1))
  (tag ?meaning
       (meaning (== (equal-to-context ?s2)
                    (select-unique-element ?o ?s1)))))
 (?subunit-1
  (link (((object-set ?s1) (object-set ?s2)))))
 ((J ?nounphrase-unit ?top-unit (?subunit-1))
  ?meaning
  (link (((object ?o))))))
<-->
((?top-unit
  (syn-subunits (== ?subunit-1)))
 (?subunit-1
  (syn-cat (==1 (constituent noun))))
 ((J ?nounphrase-unit ?top-unit (?subunit-1))
  (syn-cat (==1 (constituent nounphrase)))))
```
——

The repair strategy constructs these rules as follows. The meaning consists of all the contextual primitives. For each of the functional primitives, a subunit is created. At the semantic side, these subunits specify the links of the units. On the syntactic side, the syntactic categories of the units are specified. The introduced unit will have as link feature the target entity of the semantic network it captures.

11.2 Repair strategies

11.2.6 Re-use of syntactic categories

As outlined above, syntactic categories are re-used as much as possible to keep the resulting grammar as small as necessary. One such example of re-use can be illustrated by considering a semantic network similar to the one shown in Figure 11.3(a). The only difference to this network would be that, instead of a prototype of a block, the prototype of a ball is used.

Repair strategy 1.1 will be triggered to invent a new rule for this new prototype. Before it introduces a new syntactic category, it will first try to underspecify this category by specifying it as a variable. It will then try to apply other rules it already knows, which happen to be the ones that have been described above for repair strategies 1.2 and 1.3. After application of these rules, the repair strategy checks which category got bound to the variable that it specified for the syntactic category. In this case the variable will be bound to the lexical category Noun, as this is the category expected by the functional rule for FILTER-SET-PROTOTYPE. The repair strategy will then re-use this category for the newly invented rule for the ball prototype.

This type of re-use is used by each of the repair strategies, so syntactic categories are also re-used at the level of functional and contextual units. This becomes apparent when studying the second semantic network shown in Figure 11.3(b). Following the proposed division in three layers of units, the target linguistic structure looks like Figure 11.4. Repair strategy 1.1 created a new rule for the semantic entity [random] and, as there is no lexical category it can re-use, invented a new one (for example Article). Repair strategy 1.2 took care of the SELECT-ELEMENT primitive by inventing a new functional rule for it and will also introduce a new constituent category. Learning operator 1.3 invented a new contextual rule for the contextual primitives. It was able to re-use the Constituent Noun category as it was already present in the functional rule for FILTER-SET-PROTOTYPE. The resulting ArticleNoun rule invented by repair strategy 1.3 is shown below.

─────────────────── Contextual ArticleNoun rule ───────────────────
```
((?top-unit
   (sem-subunits (== ?article-unit ?noun-unit))
   (tag ?meaning
        (meaning (== (set-to-context ?s1)))))
 (?noun-unit
   (link (((object-set ?s2) (object-set ?s1)))))
 (?article-unit
   (link (((object ?o) (object-set ?s2)))))
 ((J ?articlenoun-unit ?top-unit (?article-unit ?noun-unit))
```

11 Origins of language strategies

```
?meaning
(link (((object o))))))
<-->
((?top-unit
  (syn-subunits (== ?article-unit ?noun-unit))
  (tag ?form
       (form (== (meets ?article-unit ?noun-unit)))))
 (?noun-unit
  (syn-cat (==1 (constituent noun))))
 (?article-unit
  (syn-cat (==1 (constituent article))))
 ((J ?articlenoun-unit ?top-unit (?noun-unit ?article-unit))
  ?form
  (syn-cat (==1 (constituent articlenounphrase)))))
```

11.2.7 Repair strategy 2.1: Re-use of constructions

Re-use also occurs when the agent already knows a construction which covers part of the conveyed meaning. The operator that handles re-use starts from the best matching construction and tries to detect what prevented it from being applicable. Next, it tries to construct a rule which removes these obstructions. This could be achieved by adding an extra unit which combines two units into one and also by taking care of the variable equalities between the units that are glued together.

The link of this additional unit is calculated as outlined above, but as the links of the units might share some variables, they should also be excluded from the link. This rule also contains word-order constraints, which are either invented (in case of the speaker) or deducted from the utterance (in case of the hearer). The syntactical category is derived from the best matching construction. If this operator would fail, the same problem would be passed on to learning operator 1.3, which will invent a new rule for the contextual primitives.

This repair strategy will trigger for example when the semantic network in Figure 11.3(c) needs to be expressed in language. I suppose repair strategy 1.1 took care of inventing a new entity rule for the category [big] and repair strategy 1.2 invented a functional rule for the FILTER-SET-CATEGORY primitive. The ArticleNoun rule described above now almost triggers and actually covers all the meaning the producing agent needs to express. The main issue is that this rule expects two subunits instead of three, and that the variable equalities are also wrong. Learning operator 2.1 now invents a rule that combines two subunits into one and also takes care of the link features. The resulting AdjectiveNoun rule is shown below. All other rules remain as they were, but the resulting linguistic structure shown in Figure 11.9 is now hierarchical.

───────────────────────── AdjectiveNoun rule ─────────────────────────
```
((?top-unit
  (sem-subunits (== ?noun-unit ?adjective-unit)))
 (?noun-unit
  (link (((object-set ?s2) (object-set ?s1)))))
 (?adjective-unit
  (link (((object-set ?s3) (object-set ?s2)))))
 ((J ?adjectivenoun-unit ?top-unit (?noun-unit ?adjective-unit))
  (link (((object-set ?s3) (object-set ?s1))))))
<-->
((?top-unit
  (syn-subunits (== ?noun-unit ?adjective-unit))
  (tag ?form
       (form (== (meets ?adjective-unit ?noun-unit)))))
 (?noun-unit
  (syn-cat (==1 (constituent noun))))
 (?adjective-unit
  (syn-cat (==1 (constituent adjective))))
 ((J ?adjectivenoun-unit ?top-unit (?noun-unit ?adjective-unit))
  ?form
  (syn-cat (==1 (constituent noun)))))
```
───

The resulting rule is recursive due to the re-use principle of syntactic categories. The syntactic categories of the subunits are the constituents of the functional rules for the FILTER-SET-CATEGORY and the FILTER-SET-PROTOTYPE primitive. The syntactic category of the unit it introduces during application is imposed by the ArticleNoun rule. This category is equal to the subunit for the FILTER-SET-PROTOTYPE (in this case Constituent Noun). As one of the syntactic categories of the subunit is equal to the syntactic category of the new unit, this rule is truly recursive.

11.2.8 Experimental results

The repair strategies discussed in §11.2.2 have been implemented and explored in multi-agent simulations. This experiment is scaffolded in the sense that the world and the conceptualisation component are bypassed. This way, I am able to focus on the development of the repair strategies in an ideal setting.

In the experiment, the complexity of the semantic networks offered to the language component is controlled by the experimenter and is divided into learning stages. Each learning stage extends the previous learning stage by a new challenging constraint network. The first four learning stages are similar to the dif-

11 Origins of language strategies

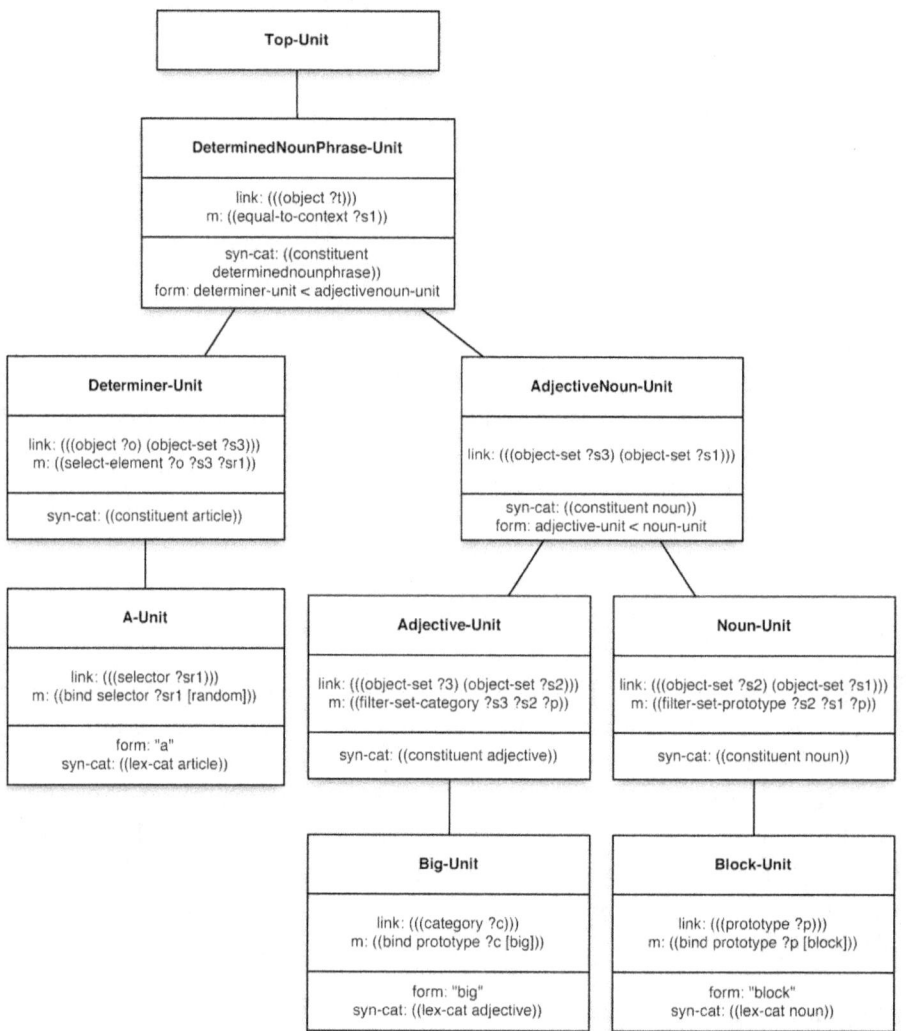

Figure 11.9: Resulting hierarchical structure to express the semantic network shown in Figure 11.3(b). Repair strategy 2.1 invented an Adjective-Noun rule that combines the Adjective-Unit and the Noun-unit into one unit by introducing the AdjectiveNoun-Unit. Throughout the re-use of the syntactic categories, this rule is also truly recursive.

ferent examples discussed before. The fifth one incorporates a different filtering operation which modifies the category it uses (similar to an Adverb as in *a very big ball*) and the sixth one extends this by another filtering operation. The next stage introduces another primitive constraint which constrains objects based on a relation between them (for instance *a ball in a box*). The final learning stage extends this by incorporating another filtering operation.

The graph depicting the dynamics of the experiment is shown in Figure 11.10. The population size is 10. Each time the learning stage is increased, the language of the agents experiences a period of turbulence after which the communicative success of the agents stabilises on perfect communicative success. At each stage in which new semantic entities are used by the semantic constraint networks the lexicon sizes of the agents overshoot before settling down on a one-on-one mapping between semantic entities and lexical entries. On the level of grammatical rules one can observe a similar pattern but this should be interpreted as the agents trying to reach a consensus on which word-order they will use to express a certain combination of syntactic categories (for example putting the Article before or after the Noun). One can also observe the agents are not inventing new grammatical rules for each level of complexity which points to the fact that the agents are truly re-using their grammatical knowledge.

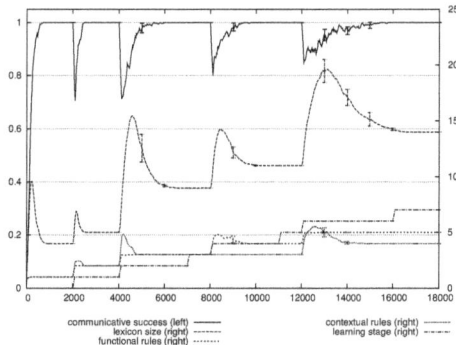

Figure 11.10: Dynamics of a multi-agent simulation in which the agents deploy the repair strategies introduced in §11.2.2. The semantic networks they need to express increase in complexity over time (as shown by the learning stage). At each increase of the learning stage, the communicative success of the agents drops because they have to align new constructions. Once the agents have aligned their constructions, the communicative success becomes maximal again.

11.3 Conclusion

In this chapter I have introduced the general combinatorial search process that can construct semantic templates and repair strategies to express semantic templates in a compositional manner. These strategies try to maximise the re-use of previously learnt grammatical rules and to construct a system of syntactic categories that is as economical as possible. These principles lead to interesting phenomena, such as the emergence of recursive grammatical rules. The resulting rules are compositional, which allow the agents to express more complex meaning without inventing additional linguistic rules.

Part V

Conclusion

12 Discussion and conclusion

Although languages around the world exhibit a high variation in how they describe colours, most of the research on colour categorisation and colour naming has focussed on the use of single colour terms. In a cross-cultural study, Alvarado & Jameson (2002) study how modifiers are used in English and Vietnamese. Their results show that both languages use different naming strategies. English speakers employ a greater variety of basic colour terms whereas Vietnamese speakers prefer to use modifiers over single-word basic terms. These observations reflect that different languages use different strategies to describe colours, which reflect the general strategy used in a language. This, in turn, casts serious doubts on the results obtained by the research paradigm which focusses solely on the use of basic colour terms, which has been the mainstream paradigm in anthropological research up until today (Kay et al. 2010).

The main goal of this book is to propose a similar shift in the computational models for colour in the domain of artificial language evolution, which so far have always been limited to single colour terms. This shift requires richer semantics to model the meaning of more complex colour descriptions and richer syntax to express these meanings in language. Although these models are more complex, great care should be taken to ensure they are still computationally tractable.

12.1 Contributions

12.1.1 Identification of language strategies

The first contribution of this book is the identification of different language strategies based on the way colours are described in unconstrained colour naming studies, anthropological research and psychology. This identification allows to establish clear goals and defines a clear scope for this book. I have chosen to focus on four different language strategies: the basic colour strategy, the graded membership strategy, the category combination strategy and the basic modification strategy.

The basic colour strategy limits language users to use a single term to describe a colour sensation. This strategy has received by far the most attention in colour

12 Discussion and conclusion

research. Examples in English are *green* and *blue*. In the graded membership strategy language users are able to specify the degree of membership of a particular colour sample to a basic colour category, as for example in *very green* or *greenish*. The category combination strategy allows language users to combine more than one category to describe a colour in more detail, like in *blue-green*. This strategy can be extended with the graded membership strategy, which would allow to specify how well the colour sample represents one of the constituent categories, as in *reddish brown*. The final language strategy I consider in this book is the basic modification strategy which allows a language user to modulate particular subdimensions of a colour, such as the lightness modifiers *light* and *dark* and the chromaticity modifiers *pale* and *bright*.

12.1.2 Operationalisation of language strategies

The operationalisation of the basic colour strategy draws on the previous models proposed in the field of artificial language evolution for the domain of colour (Steels & Belpaeme 2005). These models make use of perceptual colour spaces in which each colour sensation is represented by a unique point. In one of these models (Belpaeme & Bleys 2005b), colour categories are represented by a single point or prototype, in the same space which is the best representative of that colour category (Rosch 1973). Colour samples are categorised as the colour category of which the prototype is most similar to the perceived colour sample. Naming these samples is achieved through an associative network that assigns symbols to these categories.

The graded membership strategy is implemented using the categorisation principles of the basic colour strategy, but additionally the agents can express the distance to the prototype of that category. This ability is operationalised through a categorisation process based on the similarity between the prototype of the colour category and the colour sample that needs to be described. This second categorisation process is based on a nearest neighbour classification algorithm which uses prototypical similarity values as categories. These categories are named using symbols which are stored in an associative network.

The category combination strategy also builds on the categorisation process of the basic colour strategy. Before applying a second categorisation process based on colour, the set of colour categories needs to be transformed. The transformation I have implemented is moving each of the categories in the set in the direction of the category that was used during the first categorisation process. This allows the language users to re-use the same set of colour categories to further specify the subregions of the basic colour category. This strategy can be extended with a third categorisation process based on similarity, similar to the one introduced for the previous strategy.

Finally, the basic modification strategy is operationalised similar to the category combination strategy. The main difference is that basic modifiers are only specified in some dimensions of the colour domain, so a different transformation method is required. I proposed a scaling method which places each of the modifiers on the borders of the original colour category.

I have also proposed naming benchmarks to determine the performance of each of the operationalised strategies. These benchmarks are based on psychological studies which identified the colour samples that represent a certain category or colour description best. Some of these studies also reported a set of consensus samples, which is defined as the subset of all samples that are named consistently by all participants in one experiment. The naming benchmark consists of naming all these reported samples and verifying whether the resulting descriptions correspond to those reported in literature. All operationalisations reached more than satisfactory results on these benchmarks, indicating the validity of the proposed operationalisations.

12.1.3 Self-organisation of language systems

I have introduced the learning operators for the basic colour strategy and the graded membership strategy. The adoption and alignment operators allow agents to acquire colour categories and membership categories from other agents. The performance of these operators have been evaluated in an acquisition experiment in which a learning agent needs to acquire the language system of a teaching agent. Additionally, the invention operator allows agents to establish their own language system based on these strategies, which has been evaluated in a formation experiment.

Furthermore, I have used the basic colour strategy to study the impact of statistical distributions of colour in the environment, the use of language, and embodiment on the resulting colour category systems.

Some researchers claim the statistical distribution of colour has a significant impact on the colour category systems that are formed within them (Yendrikhovskij 2001). To verify this hypothesis, I have compared three artificial environments: one based on natural scenes, one based on urban scenes and one in which the chance of encountering a colour was uniform. I used an individual learning algorithm in which agents need to learn to categorise these worlds and compared the resulting category systems to English colour categories. Although most of the previously reported correlations were also present in the uniform

12 Discussion and conclusion

data set, a small yet positive impact of the statistical distribution of colour on this correlation was present in the natural and urban data sets.

In a second experiment I have compared individual learning to social learning in a population of agents using language as mediator. I compared the resulting colour category systems to similar data of 110 natural pre-industrial languages around the world (Kay et al. 2010). The study of these natural languages revealed some universal tendencies in the position of colour categories. The impact of language on the similarity to these tendencies was found to be positive but rather low.

In a third experiment, I have studied the impact of embodiment on the formation of colour category systems. In most of the previous experiments in the domain of colour, the contexts that were presented to the agents were generated from a uniform set of colour samples. In an embodied setting, colourful objects are presented to the vision system of robots. In this setting, the perceived colours are highly structured and are all situated around the actual colour of these objects. This structure helps the agents to align their colour category systems. But embodiment also introduces an additional factor that hinders communication: as each robot perceives a scene from its own perspective, the colour sensations will never be identical. I have shown that the proposed algorithms are robust enough to overcome this problem.

12.1.4 Evolution of language strategies

Language strategies evolve over time. If one looks at the history of the basic colour strategy for English, an interesting meaning shift of the basic colour categories occurred: they simultaneously shifted from a brightness sense to a hue sense. I have presented a model to study this phenomenon in which linguistic selection occurs at two levels: at the level of linguistic items that are used by the agents in the interactions and at the level of language strategies. This additional level can be used when the language system needs to be expanded without endangering the systematicity of the system, but it can also be used to lower the risk of misunderstandings in more creative language use. The presented model exhibits similar dynamics to the ones observed in the history of English.

12.1.5 Compositional semantics and language

Throughout the book, great care was taken to ensure a high level of compositionality, both at the level of semantics and at the level of language. This compositionality increases the level of potential re-use of certain parts of knowledge, which results in a higher level of expressivity without the cost of establishing new agreements in the population. I have introduced repair strategies that allow agents to invent and coordinate a compositional language for the compositional semantics they are using. I have shown experimental results in which a population of agents invents and aligns its compositional language.

12.2 Discussion

12.2.1 Tractability

Tractability of the semantic templates is mainly an issue during the conceptualisation process in which the speaker has to find the appropriate semantic template and categories to discriminate a colour in a specific context. During interpretation tractability is less of an issue as the hearer should be able to understand which categories and semantic template are used.

The semantic templates can be implemented in many different ways. It is for example possible to implement the category combination strategy by generating all possible combinations of two basic colour categories and choosing the combination that describes the target entity (or set) best. This would however be inefficient as the combinatorial process would generate a huge number of colour categories. The number of categories can be restricted by incorporating the context of the current interaction. In the semantics I propose in this book, the first filtering operation limits the number of base categories that are relevant in the current context. If the context, for example, consists of two shades of green and one purple colour, it ensures only the green and the purple category would be considered as base categories, and would for example exclude yellow as relevant base category. Incorporating the context at each possible step in the semantic template increases its tractability during conceptualisation.

12.2.2 Compositionality

In order to allow a population of agents to bootstrap a complex language, it is crucial to ensure it can reach this level by starting from simpler languages that can be made more complex in a stepwise fashion. In the proposed semantic templates, this is achieved by implementing semantic primitives in such a way that they can be re-used in a wide range of semantic templates. For example, the FILTER-BY-COLOUR primitive can be used both in the basic colour strategy and in the category combination strategy in which it is used twice. This re-use in turn ensures that more complex templates can be conceived as minor extensions of simpler ones.

As these semantic templates are used in linguistic interactions, the linguistic rules that are used to express these templates should reflect the same compositionality. This allows an agent to re-use much of the previously established language when they need to express a more complex semantic template and it also allows agents to establish only small parts of the language system at the time. By implementing the semantic and syntactic templates in a compositional way, the agents can gradually build up a complex language system.

12.2.3 Flexiblity

Although compositionality allows agents to bootstrap a complex language from simpler languages, the actual expressive power depends on the number of ways the semantic primitives can be combined in new semantic templates. The proposed semantic primitives are designed to reflect a high level of flexibility and re-use. In the basic modification strategy case I propose a transformation of the set of modifiers. But depending on the contexts the agents have to communicate about, this transformation might not be needed. Another example would be the use of the modifiers in the different language strategies. The proposed templates for the graded membership strategy could also be used with the set of lightness modifiers by replacing the primitive that retrieves the set of categories from the ontology of the agent.

12.2.4 Generality

Although the proposed semantic and syntactic templates are limited to the domain of colour, they are considered to be general and therefore can be applied to examples from other domains. For example, the FILTER-BY-MEMBERSHIP primitive can be used to represent the graded membership in any domain, such as time (e.g. *very soon*) or space (e.g. *very near*). The proposed transformation SCALE-CATEGORY-SET-TO-CATEGORY of the set of categories can also be used to represent the transformation required to describe the colour of a more specific concept, such as *wine*. The colour categories used to describe wine are different from the their original meaning as the colour of *white wine* for example, is in fact more yellowish than white, indicating that a transformation might be required.

The main principles behind the proposed syntactic templates and the repair strategies for learning these templates are also considered to be general and applicable to any kind of semantic constraint network. The link feature will always be required to ensure the different semantic primitives are combined in the right order and the re-use of syntactic categories can be used to restrict the number of applicable grammatical rules during the parsing of utterances.

12.2.5 Related models and approaches

12.2.5.1 Models of colour naming

Most other computational models for the domain of colour focus on the naming of certain colour samples. Some of them store the names and related foci based on predefined colour dictionaries (Mojsilovic 2005), others use the colour information of images found on the web (van de Weijer, Schmid & Verbeek 2007), while a third approach uses data from psychological experiments (Menegaz et al. 2007). Naming a colour sample boils down to finding the focus that is most similar to a particular colour sample.

The method proposed in this book is more general, as it fully embraces the idea of the living nature of spoken languages. By using richer semantics, the proposed model is also capable of predicting certain compound colour terms that are not part of the predefined lexicon. By enabling the adoption and alignment operators, the proposed model could also acquire the meaning of new colour descriptions and store them for later use.

12.2.5.2 Fuzzy sets

Fuzzy set theory is an often pursued approach to the semantics of the domain of colour. It stipulates that colour samples are rarely a complete member of a single category, but are better approached by fuzzy members that are part of several categories. This approach might lead to the unsatisfactory treatment of some of the basic colour categories (Kay & McDaniel 1978). It is also unclear how to scale it to conceptual spaces with a dimensionality higher than one. One solution to this problem might be to artificially divide some dimensions in planes (Benavente, Vanrell & Baldrich 2008).

This approach seems particularly promising for the category combination approach, but it is less clear how it could be extended to suit the graded membership approach. Some suggestions have been made on how to deal with adverbs (Hersh & Caramazza 1976), but these seem unsatisfactory in explaining why the use adverbs should be preferred in language.

12 Discussion and conclusion

12.2.5.3 Conceptual spaces

The theory of conceptual spaces probably provides the most similar approach to the semantics proposed in this book. The approach for the basic colour strategy is based on this theory (Gärdenfors 2004). How concepts should be combined however is only loosely defined. The work in this book tries to formalise some possible transformations that could fit this bill.

12.2.5.4 Vantage theory

Another approach to semantics that resonates with the proposed semantics is the vantage theory. In this theory, the set of colour primaries are some reference points that can be used to construct more complex colour categories. Each colour category is defined as a series of processes based on similarity and distinctiveness. These processes can be either based on hue or on brightness. The colour categories can be compositional in the sense that they incorporate more than one hue. Overall, it allows for a wide variety on how colour categorisation could take place. Although this theory focusses on the organisation of a single category, it is clear that it shares some ideas with the proposed semantics (MacLaury 1992; 2002).

12.3 Possible applications

One of the possible applications of the proposed methodology is the development of interactive tutoring systems. These systems can be used to tutor colour systems, e.g. the Russian colour system, to human students. In each interaction, a set of colour samples is presented to the student. The system describes one of the samples to the student and the student has to guess which colour sample the tutor intended. In the background, the system constructs a model of the student by applying the adoption and alignment operators. This will allow the system to predict how the student will describe each sample and, if this mismatches with the target description the system has in mind, to draw the attention of the student on that particular sample.

But the roles in the tutoring system can also be reversed. The human now becomes the tutor and the system learns the language of the human tutor using the adoption and alignment operators. In each interaction the system generates a set of colour samples and the tutor types in a description of one of the colours. The goal of the system is now to guess which colour sample is intended by the human tutor. When the human tutor is satisfied by the performance of the system, the system stores all linguistic and conceptual knowledge it has built up. This knowledge can later be used to tutor the stored language system to another human student.

A prototype of such a tutoring system based on the basic colour strategy has been implemented and could be extended to more complex strategies. This prototype can be used as the starting point for other tutoring systems which focus on aspects of languages that are hard to learn, such as aspect in Russian or the use of posture verbs (*staan, zitten* and *liggen*) in Dutch.

12.4 Future work

The most direct and exciting way to extend the current work is to implement an experiment that focusses on the origins of language strategies. This work could start from the repair strategies presented in this book. The corresponding experiment has to be extended in order to allow agents to generate their own semantic templates. It would be interesting to see what kind of templates arise and what mechanisms might enable agents to align the templates they are using.

Although the scope of this book is limited to the domain of colour, it would be interesting to apply the proposed semantic to other domains, such as space or time. This could also include naming the colour of more general concepts (such as *wine*) or to use the typical colour of a concept to describe a colour (as in *blood red*).

A Colour spaces and systems

The colour information used in this book is reported in a wide variety of colour spaces. The main colour space used in my own experiments is CIE 1967 $L^*a^*b^*$, but data reported in incorporated studies are often reported in other colour systems. Some studies (e.g. Lillo et al. 2007) used the CIE 1967 $L^*u^*v^*$ colour space whereas others (e.g. Sturges & Whitfield 1995) used the Munsell colour system to report their results. The vision system of the Sony humanoid robots uses the YCbCr colour model to encode the colour information of the objects they perceive.

This chapter introduces the different colour spaces and systems and the functions that are used to convert this data from one colour system into another, as shown in Figure A.1. Some conversions are impossible to compute in one step and hence require some intermediary steps. Most of these functions are based on Bruce Lindblooms's website.[1]

A.1 CIE 1931 XYZ colour space

Central to the conversion diagram (Figure A.1) is the XYZ colour space. The XYZ colour space was established by the Commission Internationale de l'Eclairage (CIE) in 1931. It standardised the colour-matching functions which describe how to combine the different amounts of primaries into unique colours and how to establish the primaries themselves. It was based on two experiments (Wright 1928; Guild 1931) which independently estimated the colour-matching functions for humans with normal colour vision, based on the principles of trichromacy and Grassmann's laws of additive colour mixture. The experiments matched to such a level of degree that the CIE decided to put them forward as the standard set of colour-matching functions.

Although the XYZ primaries are based on studies of human subjects, they are imaginary and do not map directly on the primaries established by the studies. This is mainly done to eliminate some mathematical properties of the original

---
[1] http://www.brucelindbloom.com

Appendix: Colour spaces and systems

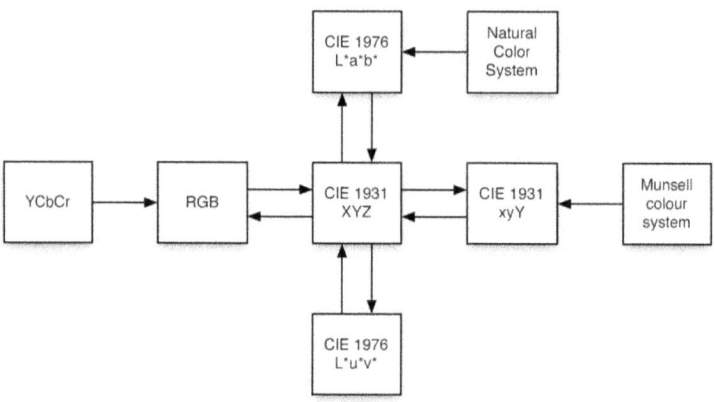

Figure A.1: A diagram representing the conversions between the different colour models and spaces. To convert colour information from the YCbCr colour model to the CIE 1967 $L^*a^*b^*$ colour space for example, it first needs to be converted to RGB which can be converted to CIE 1931 XYZ which can finally be converted to CIE 1967 $L^*a^*b^*$.

colour-matching functions and to incorporate the results into the previously established system of photometry. More exactly, the primaries for X and Z are imaginary as they do not produce any luminance response, whereas the primary for Y is the luminance response (Fairchild 1998).

A.1.1 Illuminants and chromatic adaptation

As the appearances of colours change under different light sources, these sources are also incorporated in the model as idealised illuminants which reflect their spectral power distribution. These distributions determine how much each wavelength contributes to the total illumination. Some of them, such as illuminant A, try to model a typical domestic lighting, whereas others, such as illuminants C and D65, try to reconstruct natural daylight conditions. In all reported experiments, D65 is used as standard illuminant. For each illuminant a reference white can be defined which represents the colour white under such illuminant. The reference whites for some illuminants are shown in Table A.1.

To adapt *XYZ* values from one illuminant to another, several chromatic adaptation algorithms have been proposed. All these algorithms first transform the *XYZ* values into the cone response domain before scaling the actual values de-

Table A.1: Reference white tristimulus values for illuminants A, C and D65

Illuminant	X	Y	Z
A	1.09850	1.00000	0.35585
C	0.98074	1.00000	1.18232
D65	0.95047	1.00000	1.08883

pending on the source and target illuminant. The algorithms differ in how they do the transformation to the cone response domain. The Bradford method is considered to be the best one.

All steps of this transformation can be compiled into one matrix multiplication. To convert from illuminant C to illuminant D65, Equation A.1 was used.[2]

$$\begin{bmatrix} X_{D65} \\ Y_{D65} \\ Z_{D65} \end{bmatrix} = \begin{bmatrix} 0.9904476 & -0.0071683 & -0.0116156 \\ -0.0123712 & 1.0155950 & -0.0029282 \\ -0.0035635 & 0.0067697 & 0.9181569 \end{bmatrix} \begin{bmatrix} X_C \\ Y_C \\ Z_C \end{bmatrix} \quad (A.1)$$

A.1.2 Chromaticity diagrams and CIE xyY colour space

Chromaticity diagrams were developed to provide a convenient two-dimensional representation of colour which removes the luminance information. This is achieved by means of a one-point perspective projection onto the unit plane of the XYZ colour space. The transformation from the XYZ coordinates to the xy plane can be computed using Equations in A.2.

$$x = \frac{X}{X+Y+Z} \quad y = \frac{Y}{X+Y+Z} \quad z = \frac{Z}{X+Y+Z} \quad (A.2)$$

Given the nature of the projection the third chromaticity coordinate z can always be computed from the other two because the three sum to unity. z can also be computed using Equation A.3.

$$z = 1.0 - x - y \quad (A.3)$$

The inverse transformation from chromaticy coordinates x and y can only be computed when one of the original tristimulus values is given. In most cases

---

[2] More chromatic transformations can be found on Bruce Lindbloom's website: http://www.brucelindbloom.com/Eqn_ChromAdapt.html.

Appendix: Colour spaces and systems

this is the luminance value Y. The inverse transformation from xyY to XYZ is computed using Equations A.4

$$X = \frac{xY}{y} \qquad Z = \frac{zY}{y} = \frac{(1.0 - x - y)Y}{y} \qquad (A.4)$$

A.2 CIE 1976 $L^*a^*b^*$

The CIE 1976 $L^*u^*v^*$ and $L^*a^*b^*$ (CIELUV and CIELAB for short) colour spaces were designed to provide uniform practices for the measurement of colour differences. To determine the colour difference (ΔE^*_{ab} or ΔE^*_{uv}) it suffices to use the Euclidean distances between two colours represented in these spaces. To achieve this goal, the colour spaces are extended with dimensions that correlate to lightness, chroma and hue. These spaces also incorporate features to account for chromatic adaptation and nonlinear visual responses.

In the CIELAB space, the L^* dimension represents lightness, the a^* dimension approximately redness-greenness and the b^* dimension approximately yellowness-blueness. Chroma (C^*_{ab}) and hue (h_{ab}) can be computed by the Equations in A.5. The value for L^* ranges from 0 (black) to 100 (white). The values for a^* and b^* can be both positive and negative and are only limited by the physical properties of materials. h_{ab} is expressed as an angle in degrees. The L^*, C^*_{ab} and h_{ab} form a cylindrical representation of the same space.

$$C^*_{ab} = \sqrt{(a^{*2} + b^{*2})} \qquad h_{ab} = \tan^{-1} \frac{b^*}{a^*} \qquad (A.5)$$

Conversion

The equations to convert CIE 1931 XYZ coordinates to CIE 1976 $L^*a^*b^*$ coordinates are shown in Equations A.6-A.14, where ε and κ have identical values as defined in Equations A.25 and A.26. This conversion requires a reference white $[X_r \; Y_r \; Z_r]$ which for my experiments is chosen based on illuminant D65 (see Table A.1).

Appendix: Colour spaces and systems

$$L^* = 116 f_y - 16 \tag{A.6}$$
$$a^* = 500(f_x - f_y) \tag{A.7}$$
$$b^* = 200(f_x - f_y) \tag{A.8}$$

$$f_x = \begin{cases} \sqrt[3]{x_r} & x_r > \varepsilon \\ \dfrac{\kappa x_r + 16}{116} & x_r \leq \varepsilon \end{cases} \tag{A.9}$$

$$f_y = \begin{cases} \sqrt[3]{y_r} & y_r > \varepsilon \\ \dfrac{\kappa y_r + 16}{116} & y_r \leq \varepsilon \end{cases} \tag{A.10}$$

$$f_z = \begin{cases} \sqrt[3]{z_r} & z_r > \varepsilon \\ \dfrac{\kappa z_r + 16}{116} & z_r \leq \varepsilon \end{cases} \tag{A.11}$$

$$x_r = \dfrac{X}{X_r} \tag{A.12}$$
$$y_r = \dfrac{Y}{Y_r} \tag{A.13}$$
$$z_r = \dfrac{Z}{Z_r} \tag{A.14}$$

A.3 CIE 1976 L*u*v*

The CIELUV space is very similar to the CIELAB space: L^* represents lightness, u^* redness-greenness, v^* yellowness-blueness. Chroma C^*_{uv} and hue h_{uv} values can be computed using the Equations in A.15.

$$C^*_{uv} = \sqrt{(u^{*2} + v^{*2})} \qquad h_{uv} = \tan^{-1} \dfrac{v^*}{u^*} \tag{A.15}$$

Conversion

The equations to convert CIELUV coordinates to CIE 1931 XYZ coordinates are shown in Equations A.16-A.26. This conversion requires a reference white based on an illuminant $\begin{bmatrix} X_r & Y_r & Z_r \end{bmatrix}$ which for my experiments is chosen to be illuminant D65 (see Table A.1).

Appendix: Colour spaces and systems

$$X = \frac{d-b}{a-c} \tag{A.16}$$

$$Y = \begin{cases} \left(\frac{(L+16)}{116}\right)^3 & L > \kappa\varepsilon \\ \frac{L}{\kappa} & L \leq \kappa\varepsilon \end{cases} \tag{A.17}$$

$$Z = Xa + b \tag{A.18}$$

$$a = \frac{1}{3}\left(\frac{52L^*}{u^*13Lu_0} - 1\right) \tag{A.19}$$

$$b = -5Y \tag{A.20}$$

$$c = -\frac{1}{3} \tag{A.21}$$

$$d = Y\left(\frac{39L^*}{v^* + 13Lv_0} - 5\right) \tag{A.22}$$

$$u_0 = \frac{4X_r}{X_r + 15Y_r + 3Z_r} \tag{A.23}$$

$$v_0 = \frac{9Y_r}{X_r + 15Y_r + 3Z_r} \tag{A.24}$$

$$\varepsilon = \frac{216}{24389} \tag{A.25}$$

$$\kappa = \frac{24389}{27} \tag{A.26}$$

A.4 Munsell colour system

In the Munsell colour system, a colour is defined based on three dimensions: hue, value (or lightness) and chroma (or purity). The hue dimension is divided in 5 principal colours: red, yellow, green, blue and purple, and a number of intermediate hues as shown in Figure A.2(a). Value, or lightness, is divided in 10 steps ranging from black (value 0) to white (value 10). Chroma represents the purity of a colour and the maximal possible chroma is dependent on the values of the hue-value pair. The three dimensions are shown in a diagram in Figure A.2(b).

Appendix: Colour spaces and systems

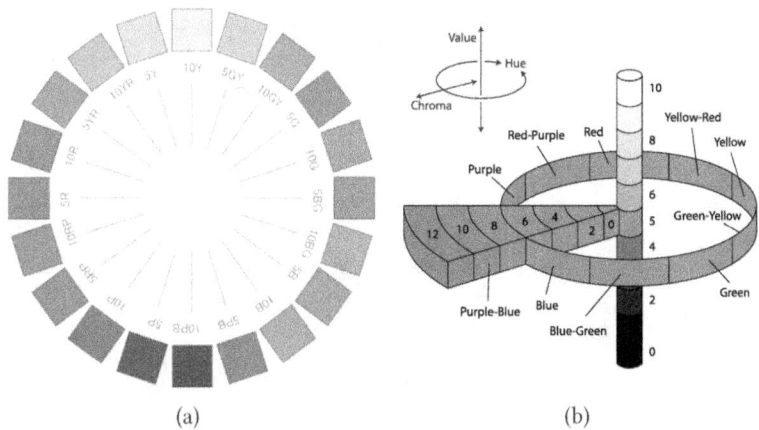

Figure A.2: (a): a colour wheel representing different hue values in the Munsell colour system; (b): a diagram representing the three dimensions of the Munsell colour system: hue, value and chroma. (CC-BY-SA Jacob Rus)

A.4.1 Development

The original goals of Albert H. Munsell were to develop a system that is both psychophysically equidistant, meaning that it faithfully represents the differences between different colours as experienced by human subjects, and precisely applicable.

The development of the Munsell hue and chroma scales, which lead to publication of the first *Book of Color* in 1929, is poorly documented (Berns & Billmeyer 1985). Only the research leading to the scale for value has been properly documented but was based on the judgment of a low number of human subjects (six to fourteen). A projection of the colour samples in the Book of Color of 1929 on the a^*b^* plane of the CIE $L^*a^*b^*$ colour space is shown in Figure A.3.

Most of the shortcomings have been addressed in a follow-up study (Newhall, Nickerson & Judd 1942), which critically reviewed and extensively revised all three dimensions based on the judgment of fourty participants and on more recent psychophysical findings. This study also enlarged the Munsell solid to incorporate all colours within the MacAdam limits, which is the theoretical maximum visual reflectance factor for specified chromaticities (MacAdam 1935). A projection of the resulting colour samples on the a^*b^* plane of the CIE $L^*a^*b^*$ colour space is shown in Figure A.4. These colour samples clearly cover a wider range of possible colours when compared to those of the Book of Color in Figure A.3.

199

Appendix: Colour spaces and systems

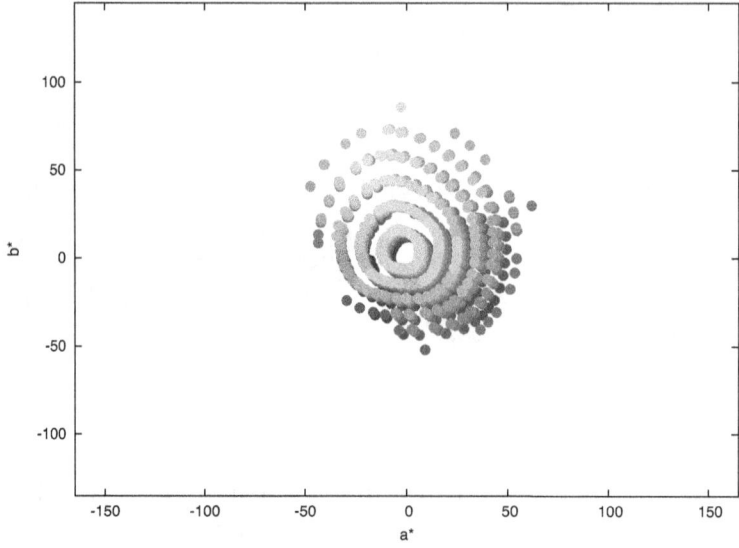

Figure A.3: A projection of the colour samples that appear in the Munsell *Book of Color* of 1929 on the a^*b^* plane of the CIE $L^*a^*b^*$ colour space.

A.4.2 Conversion

The Munsell Color Science Laboratory, a research laboratory supported by the Munsell Color Foundation at the Rochester Institute of Technology, released three datafiles[3] which map colour chips from the Munsell colour system to corresponding CIE xyY coordinates. One of these datafiles lists all Munsell colour chips within the MacAdam limits as reported by Newhall, Nickerson & Judd (1942). The coordinates of most of these colours chips are only approximations which are extrapolated or interpolated from a set of measurements of a small subset of chips.

All coordinates stored in these datafiles use illuminant C. Care has been taken to convert them to illuminant D65, using Equation A.1, as this is the illuminant assumed in all experiments reported in this book.

---

[3] Publicly available at http://www.cis.rit.edu/mcsl/online/munsell.php.

Appendix: Colour spaces and systems

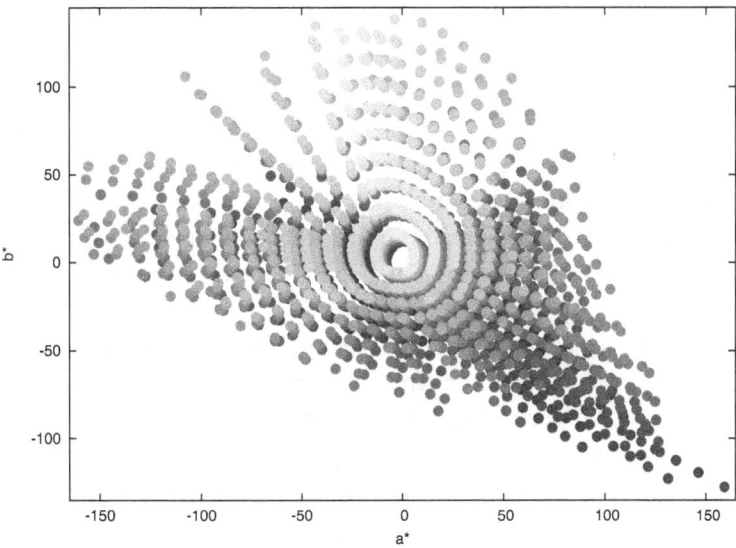

Figure A.4: A projection of the colour samples resulting from the study by Newhall, Nickerson & Judd on the a^*b^* plane of the CIE $L^*a^*b^*$ colour space.

A.5 Natural Color System

The Natural Color System (NCS) is a proprietary colour system is based on Hering's opponent-colour theory. A colour is defined by three attributes: *blackness* (s), *chromaticness* (c) and *hue* (ϕ). A yellow colour for example can be described as 0580-Y10R, where 05 corresponds to 5% blackness, 80 to 80% chromaticness and Y10R to a hue of 90% yellow and 10% red.

Converting colours reported in the Natural Color System can be done most precisely using a lookup table (SIS SS 19104), which describes tristimulus values for NCS coordinates and can be obtained from national standardization offices. Derefeldt & Sahlin (1986) report on an approximative method to transform NCS coordinates to the CIE $L^*a^*b^*$ colour space. In this book, I use the NCS navigator software[4] to compute the same conversion. This software is more precise than the method suggested by Derefeldt & Sahlin (1986), but returns only integer values in the CIE $L^*a^*b^*$ colour space. Moreover, not all colour samples are present in the software. Whenever a colour sample was missing in the software, it was approximated using the nearest colour sample that was available in the software.

---

[4] Available online at http://www.ncscolour.com.

Appendix: Colour spaces and systems

A.6 RGB

RGB is a technical colour model that is used in a wide range of devices, such as in television sets and computer screens, to reproduce colours. It is highly device-dependent as each RGB device comes with its own colour profile and needs to be approached with considerable care when used in colour research. Efforts have been made to define a common colour profile that could be supported by any RGB device, but these can at best be simulated on RGB devices that are commonly used as they are not natively supported.

Another important aspect of the RGB colour model is the gamma correction, which is used to counter the non-linearity between the voltage applied to electrons and the resulting brightness on a screen. This correction can be approximated by raising the values by a power of gamma, which for most devices has a value of 2.2. Before RGB values are transmitted to a screen, they can be gamma compressed by raising to the power of the inverse of gamma.

On a final note, RGB devices are not capable of reproducing all colours of the complete colour gamut, but of reproducing rather a (small) subset of it. For example, both the Adobe RGB (1998) and PAL/SECAM colour profile encode only half of the complete gamut. This is the reason why some of the colour chips that are known to be foci of basic colour categories, such as orange, can not be reproduced on an everyday colour device.

The equations to convert any XYZ value using the D65 reference white, to an RGB value for a device that is using the Adobe RGB (1998) colour profile and a gamma correction of y is shown in Equations A.27 and A.28. When the values for R_t, G_t or B_t are not within the range between 0 and 1, they are not reproducable using this colour profile.

$$\begin{bmatrix} R_t \\ G_t \\ B_t \end{bmatrix} = \begin{bmatrix} 2.04148 & -0.0564977 & -0.344713 \\ -0.969258 & 1.87599 & 0.0415557 \\ 0.0134455 & -0.118373 & 1.01527 \end{bmatrix} \begin{bmatrix} X \\ Y \\ Z \end{bmatrix} \quad (A.27)$$

$$R = R_t^{1/y} \quad G = G_t^{1/y} \quad B = B_t^{1/y} \quad (A.28)$$

A.7 YCbCr

Robotic vision data is typically delivered by one of the cameras in the head or body of the robot. The colour information that is recorded by these cameras can be stored in a wide variety of encodings. The robots that have been used in my

Appendix: Colour spaces and systems

experiments deploy the YCbCr colour model. In order to utilise this information, it needs to be converted to the XYZ colour space, which happens in two steps. First it needs to be converted to a RGB colour model using the Equations A.29–A.31. Finally, these coordinates can be converted to the XYZ using Equations A.32 and A.33 which assumes the SECAM/PAL colour profile.

$$R = (Y + 1.402(C_r - 128))/255 \tag{A.29}$$
$$G = (Y - 0.34414(C_b - 128) - 0.71414(C_r - 128))/255 \tag{A.30}$$
$$B = (Y + 1.772(C_b - 128))/255 \tag{A.31}$$

$$R_t = R^Y \quad G_t = G^Y \quad B_t = B^Y \tag{A.32}$$

$$\begin{bmatrix} X \\ Y \\ Z \end{bmatrix} = \begin{bmatrix} 0.4306190 & 0.3415419 & 0.1783091 \\ 0.2220379 & 0.7066384 & 0.0713236 \\ 0.201853 & 0.1295504 & 0.9390944 \end{bmatrix} \begin{bmatrix} R_t \\ G_t \\ B_t \end{bmatrix} \tag{A.33}$$

References

Alvarado, Nancy & Kimberly A. Jameson. 2002. The use of modifying terms in the naming and categorization of color appearances in Vietnamese and English. *Journal of Cognition and Culture* 2(1). 53–80.

Baronchelli, Andrea, Tao Gong, Andrea Puglisi & Vitorrio Loreto. 2010. Modeling the emergence of universality in color naming patterns. *Proceedings of the National Academy of Sciences* 107(2403).

Barstow, David R. 1979. *Knowledge-based program construction*. New York: Elsevier.

Batali, John. 2002. The negotiation and acquisition of recursive grammars as a result of competition among exemplars. In Ted Briscoe (ed.), *Linguistic evolution through language acquisition: formal and computational models*, chap. 5. Cambridge University Press. http://www.isrl.uiuc.edu/~amag/langev/paper/batali02theNegotiation.html.

Belpaeme, Tony. 2002. *Factors influencing the origins of colour categories*. Vrije Universiteit Brussel PhD thesis.

Belpaeme, Tony & Joris Bleys. 2005a. Colourful language and colour categories. In *Proceedings of the second international symposium on the emergence and evolution of linguistic communication*, 1–7.

Belpaeme, Tony & Joris Bleys. 2005b. Explaining universal color categories through a constrained acquisition process. *Adaptive Behavior* 13(4). 293–310.

Belpaeme, Tony & Joris Bleys. 2007. Language, perceptual categories and their interaction: insights from computational modelling. In Caroline Lyon, Chrystopher Nehaniv & Angelo Cangelosi (eds.), *Emergence of communication and language*, chap. 18, 339–353. Springer-Verlag, London: Springer-Verlag.

Belpaeme, Tony & Joris Bleys. 2009. The impact of statistical distributions of colours on colour category acquisition. *Journal of Cognitive Science* 10(1). 1–20.

Belpaeme, Tony, Luc Steels & Joris van Looveren. 1998. The construction and acquisition of visual categories. In A. Birk & Y. Demiris (eds.), *Proceedings of the sixth European conference on learning robots* (Lecture Notes in Artificial Intelligence 1545), 1–12. Berlin: Springer.

References

Benavente, Robert, Maria Vanrell & Ramon Baldrich. 2008. Parametric fuzzy sets for automatic color naming. *Journal of the Optical Society of America A* 25(10). 2582–2593.

Bergen, Benjamin K. & Nancy C. Chang. 2005. Embodied construction grammar in simulation-based language understanding. In J.-O. Östman & M. Fried (eds.), *Construction grammar(s): cognitive and cross-language dimensions*. John Benjamins.

Berlin, Brent & Paul Kay. 1969. *Basic color terms: their universality and evolution*. Berkeley, California: University of California Press.

Berns, Roy S. & Fred W. Billmeyer. 1985. Development of the 1929 Munsell Book of Color: a historical review. *COLOR research and application* 10. 246–250.

Bleys, Joris. 2006. Next-generation language-games: the guessing game revisited. In Pierre-Yves Schobbens, Wim Vanhoof & Gabriel Schwanen (eds.), *Proceedings of the 18th Belgium-Netherlands conference of artificial intelligence*.

Bleys, Joris. 2008. Expressing second order semantics and the emergence of recursion. In Andrew D. M. Smith, Kenny Smith & Ramon Ferrer i Cancho (eds.), *The evolution of language: evolang 7*, 34–41. World Scientific.

Bleys, Joris & Luc Steels. 2009. Linguistic selection of language strategies: A case study for color. In George Kampis, István Karsai & Eörs Szathmáry (eds.), *Advances in artificial life: Proceedings of the ECAL 2009 conference* (Lecture Notes in Artificial Intelligence 5778). Berlin & Heidelberg: Springer.

Bleys, Joris, Martin Loetzsch, Michael Spranger & Luc Steels. 2009. The grounded colour naming game. In *IEEE Ro-Man 2009 workshops and tutorial proceedings*. IEEE.

Boynton, Robert M. 1997. Insights gained from naming the OSA colors. In C. Hardin & Luisa Maffi (eds.), *Color categories in thought and language*, 133–150. Cambridge University Press.

Boynton, Robert M. & Conrad X. Olson. 1987. Locating basic colors in the OSA space. *COLOR Research and application* 12(2). 94–105.

Bradley, Paul & Usama M. Fayyad. 1998. Refining initial points for k-means clustering. In *Proceedings of the 15th international conference on machine learning*, 91–99. San Franciso, CA: Morgan Kaufmann.

Burgress, Don, Willett Kempton & Robert E. MacLaury. 1983. Tarahumara color modifiers: Category structure presaging evolutionary change. *American Ethnologist* 10(1). 133–149.

Casson, Ronald W. 1997. Color shift: evolution of English color terms from brightness to hue. In C. Hardin & Luisa Maffi (eds.), *Color categories in thought and language*, 224–239. Cambridge: Cambridge University Press.

Chomsky, Noam. 1957. *Syntactic structures*. The Hague: Mouton.

Conklin, Harold C. 1995. Hanunóo color categories. *Southwestern Journal of Anthropology* 11(4). 339–344.

Conover, W.J. 1999. *Practical nonparametric statistics*. New York: John Wiley & Sons.

Coradeschi, Silvia & Alessandro Saffiotti. 2003. An introduction to the anchoring problem. *Robotics and Autonomous Systems* 43(2-3). 85–96.

Croft, William A. 2001. *Radical construction grammar: syntactic theory in typological perspective*. Oxford: Oxford University Press.

De Beule, Joachim. 2008. The emergence of compositionality, hierarchy and recursion in peer-to-peer interactions. In Andrew D. M. Smith, Kenny Smith & Ramon Ferrer i Cancho (eds.), *The evolution of language: evolang 7*. World Scientific.

De Beule, Joachim & Luc Steels. 2005. Hierarchy in Fluid Construction Grammar. In Ulrich Furbach (ed.), *Proceedings of the 28th annual German conference on AI, KI 2005* (Lecture Notes in Artificial Intelligence 3698), 1–15. Berlin & Heidelberg: Springer Verlag.

Derefeldt, Gunilla & Christer Sahlin. 1986. Transformation of NCS data into CIE-LAB colour space. *COLOR research and application* 11. 146–152.

Dowman, Mike. 2007. Explaining color term typology with an evolutionary model. *Cognitive Science* 31. 99–132.

Dowty, David R., Robert Wall & Stanley Peters. 1981. *Introduction to Montague semantics*. D. Reidel Publishing Company.

Fairchild, Mark D. 1998. *Color appearance models*. Reading, MA: Addison-Wesley.

Fujita, Masahiro, Yoshihiro Kuroki, Tatsuzo Ishida & Toshi T. Doi. 2003. Autonomous behavior control architecture of entertainment humanoid robot SDR-4X. In *Proceedings of the IEEE/RSJ international conference on intelligent robots and systems (IROS '03)*, 960–967, vol. 1. Las Vegas, Nevada.

Gärdenfors, Peter. 2004. *Conceptual spaces: The geometry of thought*. MIT Press.

Garrod, Simon & Gwyneth Doherty. 1994. Conversation, co-ordination and convention: An empirical investigation of how groups establish linguistic conventions. *Cognition* 53. 181–251.

Goldberg, A. E. 1995. *Constructions: a construction grammar approach to argument structure*. University of Chicago Press.

Goldberg, Adele E. 2003. Constructions: A new theoretical approach to language. *Trends in Cognitive Sciences* 7(5). 219–224.

Guild, J. 1931. The colorimetric properties of the spectrum. *Philosophical Transactions of the Royal Society of America* 230. 149–187.

References

Hersh, Harry M. & Alfonso Caramazza. 1976. A fuzzy set approach to modifiers and vagueness in natural language. *Journal of Experimental Psychology: General* 105(3). 254–276.

Howard, Celeste M. & Johannah A. Burnidge. 1994. Colors in natural landscapes. *Journal of the Society of Information Display* 2(1). 47–55.

Kalman, Rudolf E. 1960. A new approach to linear filtering and prediction problems. *Transactions of the ASME-Journal of Basic Engineering* 82(1). 35–45.

Kay, Paul & Luisa Maffi. 2008. Number of basic colour categories. In Martin Haspelmath, Matthew Dryer, David Gil & Comrie Bernard (eds.), *The world atlas of language structures online*, chap. 133. Munich: Max Planck Digital Library.

Kay, Paul & Chad K. McDaniel. 1978. The linguistic significance of the meanings of basic color terms. *Language* 54(3). 610–646.

Kay, Paul, Brent Berlin, Luisa Maffi, William R. Merrifield & Richard S. Cook. 2010. *World color survey* (CSLI Lecture Notes). University of Chicago Press.

Kelly, K. L. & Deane B. Judd. 1955. The ISCC-NBS method of designating colors and a dictionary of color names. *National Bureau of Standards (USA)* 553.

Komarova, Natalia L. & Kimberly A. Jameson. 2008. Population heterogeneity and color stimulus heterogeneity in agent-based color categorization. *Journal of Theoretical Biology* 253(4). 680–700.

Lammens, Johan. 1994. *A computational model of color perception and color naming*. Graduate School of State University of New York at Buffalo PhD thesis.

Lillo, J., H. Moreira, I. Vitini & J. Martín. 2007. Locating basic Spanish colour categories in CIE L*u*v* space: identification, lightness segregation and correspondence with English equivalents. *Psicológica* 28. 21–54.

Lin, H., M. R. Luo, L. W. MacDonald & Arthur W.S. Tarrant. 2001. A cross-cultural colour-naming study. Part I: Using an unconstrained method. *COLOR research and application* 26. 40–60.

Lloyd, Stuart P. 1982. Least squares quantization in PCM. *IEEE Transactions on Information Theory* 28(2).

Loetzsch, Martin, Joris Bleys & Pieter Wellens. 2009. Understanding the dynamics of complex lisp programs. In *Proceedings of the 2nd European lisp symposium*, 59–69. Milano, Italy.

Loetzsch, Martin, Michael Spranger & Luc Steels. 2010. The grounding of object naming and identity. submitted.

Loetzsch, Martin, Remi van Trijp & Luc Steels. 2008. Typological and computational investigations of spatial perspective. In *Modeling communication with robots and virtual humans* (Lecture Notes in Computer Science 4930), 125–142. Berlin: Springer.

MacAdam, David L. 1935. Maximum visual efficiency of colored materials. *Journal of the Optical Society of America* 25. 249–252.

MacLaury, Robert E. 1992. From brightness to hue: An explanatory model of color-category evolution. *Current Anthropology* 33(2). 137–186.

MacLaury, Robert E. 1997. *Color and cognition in Mesoamerica.* Austin: University of Texas Press.

MacLaury, Robert E. 2002. Introducing vantage theory. *Language Sciences* 24(493-536).

Marriott, Kim & Peter J. Stuckey. 1998. *Programming with constraints: an introduction.* The MIT Press.

Menegaz, G., A. Le Troter, J. Sequeira & J. M. Boi. 2007. A discrete model for color naming. *EURASIP J. Appl. Signal Process.* 2007(1). 113–113. http://dx.doi.org/10.1155/2007/29125.

Mojsilovic, Aleksandra. 2002. A method for color naming and description of color composition of images. In *Proceedings of internal coference on image processing, ICIP 2002.*

Mojsilovic, Aleksandra. 2005. A computational model for color naming and describing color composition of images. *IEEE Transactions on Image Processing* 14(5). 690–699.

Newhall, Sidney M., Dorothy Nickerson & Deane B. Judd. 1942. Final report of the O.S.A. subcommittee on the spacing of the Munsell colors. *Journal of the Optical Society of America* 33(7). 385–418.

Paramei, Galina V. 2005. Singing the Russian blues: an argument for culturally basic color terms. *Cross-Cultural Research* 39(1). 10–38.

Pollard, Carl & Ivan Sag. 1995. *Head-driven phrase structure grammar.* Chicago: University of Chicago Press.

Puglisi, Andrea, Andrea Baronchelli & Vittorio Loreto. 2008. Cultural route to the emergence of linguistic categories. *Proceedings of the National Academy of Sciences* 105(23). 7936–7940.

Regier, Terry, Paul Kay & Richard S. Cook. 2005. Focal colors are universal after all. *Proceedings of the National Academy of Sciences* 102(23). 8386–8391.

Roberson, D. 2005. Color categories are culturally diverse in cognition as well as in language. *Cross-Cultural Research* 39. 56–71.

Roberson, Debi, Ian Davies & Jules Davidoff. 2002. Color categories are not universal: replications and new evidence. In B. Saunders & J. van Brakel (eds.),

References

Theories, technologies, instrumentalities of color, 22–35. Lanham, MD: University Press of America.

Rosch, Eleanor H. 1973. Natural categories. *Cognitive Psychology* 4. 328–350.

Rucklidge, W. J. 1997. Efficiently locating objects using the Hausdorff distance. *International Journal of Computer Vision* 24(3). 251–270.

Safuanova, Olga V. & Nina N. Korzh. 2007. Russian color names: Mapping into a perceptual color space. In Robert E. MacLaury, Galina V. Paramei & Don Dedrick (eds.), *Anthropology of color*, 75–106. Amsterdam: John Benjamins.

Shepard, Roger N. 1987. Toward a universal law of generalization for psychological science. *Science* 237. 1317–1323.

Shepard, Roger N. 1992. The perceptual organization of colors: an adaptation to regularities of the terrestrial world? In J. Barkow, L. Cosmides & J. Tooby (eds.), *Adapted mind*, 495–532. Oxford: Oxford University Press.

Simpson, Jean & Arthur W.S. Tarrant. 1991. Sex- and age-related differences in colour vocabulary. *Language and Speech* 34(1). 57–62.

Siskind, Jeffrey M. 2001. Grounding the lexical semantics of verbs in visual perception using force dynamics and event logic. *Journal of Artificial Intelligence Research* 15. 31–90.

Smith, Kenny, Simon Kirby & Henry Brighton. 2003. Iterated learning: A framework for the emergence of language. *Artificial Life* 9(4). 371–386.

Spranger, Michael. 2008. *World models for grounded language games*. Humboldt-Universität zu Berlin MA thesis.

Steels, Luc. 1996a. A self-organizing spatial vocabulary. *Artificial Life* 2(3). 318–332.

Steels, Luc. 1996b. Perceptually grounded meaning creation. In M. Tokoro (ed.), *Proceedings of the second international conference on multi-agent systems*, 338–344. Menlo Park, CA: AAAI Press.

Steels, Luc. 1997. Construction and sharing perceptual distinctions. In M. van Someren & G. Widmer (eds.), *Proceedings of the European conference on machine learning*. Berlin: Springer.

Steels, Luc. 1998. The origins of syntax in visually grounded robotic agents. *Artificial Intelligence* 103(1-2). 133–156.

Steels, Luc. 1999. *The Talking Heads experiment. Volume 1. Words and meanings*. Antwerpen: Laboratorium.

Steels, Luc. 2000a. Language as a complex adaptive system. In M. Schoenauer (ed.), *Proceedings of PPSN VI* (Lecture Notes in Computer Science), 17–26. Berlin: Springer-Verlag.

Steels, Luc. 2000b. The emergence of grammar in communicating autonomous robotic agents. In W. Horn (ed.), *ECAI 2000: proceedings of the 14th European conference on artificial life*, 764–769. Amsterdam: IOS Publishing.

Steels, Luc. 2003. Language-reentrance and the "inner voice". *Journal of Consciousness Studies* 10(4–5). 173–185.

Steels, Luc. 2007. The recruitment theory of language origins. In C. Lyon, C. L. Nehaniv & A. Cangelosi (eds.), *Emergence of language and communication*, 129–151. Berlin: Springer.

Steels, Luc & Tony Belpaeme. 2005. Coordinating perceptually grounded categories through language: a case study for colour. *Behavioral and Brain Sciences* 28. 469–529.

Steels, Luc & Joris Bleys. 2005. Planning what to say: second order semantics for Fluid Construction Grammars. In A. Bugarin Diz & J. Santos Reyes (eds.), *Proceedings of CAEPIA '05. Lecture notes in AI*. Berlin: Springer Verlag.

Steels, Luc & Joris Bleys. 2007. Emergence of hierarchy in Fluid Construction Grammar. In *Proceedings of the SLEA workshop at the 9th European conference on artificial life*.

Steels, Luc & Joachim De Beule. 2006. Unify and merge in Fluid Construction Grammar. In P. Vogt, Y. Sugita, E. Tuci & C. Nehaniv (eds.), *Symbol grounding and beyond: proceedings of the third international workshop on the emergence and evolution of linguistic communication* (LNAI 4211), 197–223. Berlin: Springer-Verlag.

Steels, Luc, Joachim De Beule & N. Neubauer. 2005. Linking in Fluid Construction Grammars. In *Proceedings of BNAIC. Transactions of the Belgian Royal Society of Arts and Sciences*. 11–18. Brussels.

Steels, Luc & Martin Loetzsch. 2008. Perspective alignment in spatial language. In Kenny R. Coventry, Thora Tenbrink & John. A Bateman (eds.), *Spatial language and dialogue*. Oxford University Press.

Steels, Luc & Pieter Wellens. 2006. How grammar emerges to dampen combinatorial search in parsing. In Paul Vogt (ed.), *EELC 2: Symbol grounding and beyond* (LNAI 4211), 76–88. Berlin & Heidelberg: Springer Verlag.

Sturges, Julia & T. W. Allan Whitfield. 1995. Locating basic colours in the Munsell Space. *Color Research and Application* 20. 364–376.

Tomasello, Michael. 1995. Joint attention as social cognition. In Chris Moore & Philip J. Dunham (eds.), *Joint attention: its origins and role in development*. Hillsdale, NJ: Lawrence Erlbaum Associates.

References

Tribushinina, Elena. 2008. *Cognitive reference points: semantics beyond the prototypes in adjectives of space and colour* (LOT Dissertation Series 192). Utrecht, The Netherlands: LOT publications.

van de Weijer, Joost, Cordelia Schmid & Jakob Verbeek. 2007. Learning color names from real-world images. *IEEE Conference on Computer Vision and Pattern Recognition*. 1–8.

Van den Broeck, Wouter. 2007. A constraint-based model of grounded compositional semantics. In Stephen J. Cowley Luís Seabra Lopes Tony Belpaeme (ed.), *Language and robots: proceedings of the symposium. 10-12 December 2007, Aveiro, Portugal*, 93–98. Universidade de Aveiro.

Van den Broeck, Wouter. 2008. Constraint-based compositional semantics. In Andrew D. M. Smith, Kenny Smith & Ramon Ferrer i Cancho (eds.), *The evolution of language* (Evolang 7). World Scientific.

Van Wijk, H.A.C.W. 1959. A cross-cultural theory of colour and brightness nomenclature. *Bijdragen tot de taal-, land- en volkenkunde* 115. 113–137.

Vogt, Paul. 2003. Anchoring of semiotic symbols. *Robotics and Autonomous Systems* 43(2-3). 109–120.

Wang, Emily & Luc Steels. 2008. Self-interested agents can bootstrap symbolic communication if they punish cheaters. In A. D. M. Smith, K. Smith & R. Ferrer i Cancho (eds.), *The evolution of language. Proceedings of the 7th international conference on the evolution of language*, 362–369. Singapore: World Scientific.

Wellens, Pieter, Martin Loetzsch & Luc Steels. 2008. Flexible word meaning in embodied agents. *Connection Science* 20(2). 173–191.

Winograd, Terry. 1972. *Understanding natural language.* Academic Press.

Wright, W. D. 1928. A re-determination of the trichromatic coefficients of the spectral colours. *Transactions of the Optical Society* 30. 141–161.

Xu, Fei. 2002. The role of language in acquiring object concepts in infancy. *Cognition* 85. 223–250.

Yendrikhovskij, Sergej N. 2001. A computational model of colour categorization. *Color Research and Application* 26(1). 235–238.

Name index

Alvarado, Nancy, 8, 71, 183

Baldrich, Ramon, 62, 78, 189
Baronchelli, Andrea, 3, 11, 44, 45, 103
Barstow, David R., 25
Batali, John, 3, 18, 19
Belpaeme, Tony, 3, 11, 18, 19, 44, 45, 60, 62, 103, 106, 109, 123, 129, 130, 184
Benavente, Robert, 62, 78, 189
Bergen, Benjamin K., 27
Berlin, Brent, 3, 5, 12, 123, 130
Berns, Roy S., 199
Billmeyer, Fred W., 199
Bleys, Joris, 3, 11, 17–19, 24, 41, 44, 45, 60, 103, 109, 123, 151, 184
Boynton, Robert M., 43, 124, 154
Bradley, Paul, 126
Brighton, Henry, 3, 18, 19, 103
Burgess, Don, 6, 7, 57, 58, 66
Burnidge, Johannah A., 125

Caramazza, Alfonso, 63, 189
Casson, Ronald W., 14, 153
Chang, Nancy C., 27
Chomsky, Noam, 27
Conklin, Harold C., 5
Conover, W.J., 127
Cook, Richard S., 5, 131
Coradeschi, Silvia, 137
Croft, William A., 27

Davidoff, Jules, 5, 131

Davies, Ian, 5, 131
Derefeldt, Gunilla, 201
De Beule, Joachim, 4, 18, 30–32
Doherty, Gwyneth, 13, 147
Dowman, Mike, 103
Dowty, David R., 18

Fairchild, Mark D., 194
Fayyad, Usama M., 126
Fujita, Masahiro, 136

Gärdenfors, Peter, 46, 73, 190
Garrod, Simon, 13, 147
Goldberg, A. E., 27
Goldberg, Adele E., 27
Guild, J., 193

Hersh, Harry M., 63, 189
Howard, Celeste M., 125

Jameson, Kimberly A., 8, 71, 103, 183
Judd, Deane B., 57, 104, 109, 116, 119, 199–201

Kalman, Rudolf E., 137
Kay, Paul, 3, 5, 6, 12, 62, 67, 123, 130, 131, 140, 183, 186, 189
Kelly, K. L., 57
Kempton, Willett, 6, 7, 57, 58, 66
Kirby, Simon, 3, 18, 19, 103
Komarova, Natalia L., 103
Korzh, Nina N., 5, 7–9, 43, 57, 71, 72, 75, 82, 83, 87, 88, 90, 94, 95

Name index

Lammens, Johan, 46, 62, 73
Lillo, J., 43, 55, 154, 157, 160, 193
Lin, H., 3, 4, 8, 9, 87
Lloyd, Stuart P., 125
Loetzsch, Martin, 3, 17–19, 136, 139, 142
Looveren, Joris van, 129
Loreto, Vittorio, 3, 11, 44, 45, 103

MacAdam, David L., 199
MacLaury, Robert E., 6, 7, 14, 57, 58, 66, 140, 153, 190
Maffi, Luisa, 5, 6, 67
Marriott, Kim, 18
McDaniel, Chad K., 62, 189
Menegaz, G., 189
Mojsilovic, Aleksandra, 57, 73, 189

Neubauer, N., 32
Newhall, Sidney M., 104, 109, 116, 119, 199–201
Nickerson, Dorothy, 104, 109, 116, 119, 199–201

Olson, Conrad X., 43, 124

Paramei, Galina V., 9, 87
Peters, Stanley, 18
Pollard, Carl, 27
Puglisi, Andrea, 3, 11, 44, 45, 103

Regier, Terry, 5, 131
Roberson, D., 131
Roberson, Debi, 5, 131
Rosch, Eleanor H., 3, 43, 46, 57, 184
Rucklidge, W. J., 132

Saffiotti, Alessandro, 137
Safuanova, Olga V., 5, 7–9, 43, 57, 71, 72, 75, 82, 83, 87, 88, 90, 94, 95

Sag, Ivan, 27
Sahlin, Christer, 201
Schmid, Cordelia, 189
Shepard, Roger N., 46, 123
Simpson, Jean, 3, 87
Siskind, Jeffrey M., 19
Smith, Kenny, 3, 18, 19, 103
Spranger, Michael, 139
Steels, Luc, 3, 10–13, 18, 19, 24, 27, 30–32, 41, 44, 45, 59, 62, 101, 103, 109, 129, 130, 136, 139, 142, 151, 184
Stuckey, Peter J., 18
Sturges, Julia, 43, 44, 54, 55, 66, 104, 107, 127, 128, 140, 142, 144, 154, 193

Tarrant, Arthur W.S., 3, 87
Tomasello, Michael, 12, 139
Tribushinina, Elena, 72

van de Weijer, Joost, 189
Van den Broeck, Wouter, 18
van Trijp, Remi, 136
Vanrell, Maria, 62, 78, 189
Van Wijk, H.A.C.W., 123
Verbeek, Jakob, 189
Vogt, Paul, 136

Wall, Robert, 18
Wang, Emily, 12
Wellens, Pieter, 3, 17–19, 27, 101, 136, 142
Whitfield, T. W. Allan, 43, 44, 54, 55, 66, 104, 107, 127, 128, 140, 142, 144, 154, 193
Winograd, Terry, 18
Wright, W. D., 193

Xu, Fei, 104

Yendrikhovskij, Sergej N., 123, 124, 127, 185

Subject index

acquisition experiment, 13, 101
    for basic colours strategy, 104
    for graded membership strategy, 116
adoption operator, *see* learning operators
agent, 10
alignment operator, *see* learning operators
alignment rate
    colour category, 104
    membership category, 115

baseline experiment, 10, 41
    for basic colour strategy, 54
    for basic modification strategy, 94
    for category combination strategy, 82
    for graded membership strategy, 66
basic colour strategy, *see* language strategy
basic colour term, 5
basic modification strategy, *see* language strategy

category combination strategy, *see* language strategy
chunking, *see* IRL
CIE 1931 XYZ, *see* colour space
CIE 1976 $L^*a^*b^*$, *see* colour space
CIE 1976 $L^*u^*v^*$, *see* colour space
CIE xyY, *see* colour space
colour category, 43
colour category alignment rate, *see* alignment rate
colour category invention rate, *see* invention rate
Colour Description Game, *see* language game
colour model
    RGB, 202
    YCbCr, 202
Colour Naming Game, *see* language game
colour space
    CIE 1931 XYZ, 193
    CIE 1976 $L^*a^*b^*$, 196
    CIE 1976 $L^*u^*v^*$, 197
    CIE xyY, 195
colour system
    Munsell, 198
    Natural, 201
communicative goal, 10
communicative success, *see* measures
conceptualisation, 24
consensus samples, *see* colour category
context, 10
contextual primitive, *see* primitive constraint
coupled feature structure, 28

Subject index

embodiment
    impact of, *see* impact

FCG, 27
    linking, 32
    structure building, 30
Fluid Construction Grammar, *see* FCG
focal colour, 5
formation experiment, 13, 101
    for basic colour strategy, 109
    for graded membership strategy, 119
functional primitive, *see* primitive constraint

graded membership strategy, *see* language strategy
Grounded Colour Naming Game, *see* language game

impact
    of embodiment on basic colour strategy, 135
    of environment on basic colour systems, 123
    of language on basic colour systems, 129
Incremental Recruitment Language, *see* IRL
interpretation variance, *see* measures
invention operator, *see* learning operators
invention rate
    colour category, 109
    membership category, 118
IRL, 18
    chunking, 25

language game, 10
    Colour Description Game, 12
    Colour Naming Game, 11
    Grounded Colour Naming Game, 12
language strategy, 4
    evolution, 13
    for colour
        basic colour strategy, 43
        basic modification strategy, 87
        category combination strategy, 71
        graded membership strategy, 57
    linguistic selection of, 153
    modelling, 9
    origins of, 163
    selective advantage of, 160
language system, 4
    self-organisation of, 12
learning operators, 101
    adoption operator, 12
        for basic colour strategy, 104
        for graded membership strategy, 115
    alignment operator, 13
        for basic colour strategy, 104
        for graded membership strategy, 115
    invention operator, 13
        for basic colour strategy, 108
        for graded membership strategy, 118
linguistic structure, 28
linking, *see* FCG

measures
    communicative success, 54
    interpretation variance, 105
    membership category variance, 116

Subject index

number of categories, 105
number of membership categories, 119
strategy coherence, 157
strategy success, 157
strategy usage, 157
membership category alignment rate, *see* alignment rate
membership category invention rate, *see* invention rate
membership category variance, *see* measures
Munsell colour system, *see* colour system

naming benchmark, 41
    for basic colour strategy, 54
    for basic modification strategy, 95
    for category combination strategy, 83
    for graded membership strategy, 67
Natural Color System, *see* colour system
NCS, *see* Natural Color System
number of categories, *see* measures
number of membership categories, *see* measures

primitive constraint, 19
    contextual primitive, 53
    functional primitive, 52
    implementation, 26
profiling, 46
prototype, *see* colour category

repair strategies, 165
repair strategy
    for contextual primitives, 174
    for functional primitives, 173
    for semantic entities, 171
    re-use of constructions, 176
RGB, *see* colour model

semantic constraint network, 19
    evaluation, 21
    generation, 24
semantic entity, 19
semantic network, *see* semantic constraint network
semantic template, 41
    for basic colour strategy, 45
    for basic modification strategy, 88
    for category combination strategy, 73
    for graded membership strategy, 58
    generation, 163
semiotic cycle, 10
strategy coherence, *see* measures
strategy success, *see* measures
strategy usage, *see* measures
structure building, *see* FCG
syntactic template, 41
    for contextual primitives, 53, 79
    for functional primitives, 52, 65, 79
    for semantic entities, 50, 63
    re-use of constructions, 65, 81, 94

YCbCr, *see* colour model

www.ingramcontent.com/pod-product-compliance
Lightning Source LLC
Chambersburg PA
CBHW080803300426
44114CB00020B/2814